PRAISE FOR AWARD WINNING CULTURE

"Hans Appel is the real deal. His message has the kind of depth and truth that can only come from someone who has walked the talk---both as a student and as an educator. This book is a must read for anyone ready to take their school from doing well on paper to actually doing right by their students. Appel's message is the one we should all be tuning in to and shouting from the rooftops right now as it carries the promise of profoundly transforming our schools and, in turn, meaningfully transforming our communities."

~ **Amy Fast**,
High School Principal, Author,
and Education Commentator

"Award Winning Culture, by Hans Appel, gives educators the opportunity to stop and reflect on their practices in the hopes of improving culture and relationships throughout their schools. Hans gives us an insight of how to recharge our belief in all kids and inspires us to see that when we focus on Character, Excellence and Community, great things can happen for an entire school community!"

~ Jimmy Casas,
Educator, Author, Speaker,
Leadership Coach

"Creating a culture that encompasses high academic expectations while attending to the needs of the whole child is no easy task. Hans has developed a roadmap to do just that! Award Winning Culture is a book study that will transform the learning environment of your school."

~ **Marlena Gross-Taylor**,
Social Commerce Entrepreneur,
Founder of EduGladiators, Author, Speaker

"This book is so much more than a breakdown of how to build *Award Winning Culture* into your school building. It's a must-read book full of tactical takeaways on how to change students' lives - and we all want to change students' lives - right? Hans Appel outdid himself with this book! Wow! Read this book - and learn from one of the best!"

~ Rae Hughart,
Director of Training and
Development of the Teach Better Team

"Title does not infer influence. Appel reminds us as he drives home the most essential need for life; to lead with character. His compelling argument that we are each responsible for shaping the character of each student will leave you questioning and redefining your WHY, not because you aren't driven to reach every child, but because Appel will seek out the part of you that needs to be redirected and redefined for the growth of every child as a whole. Be prepared for life-altering change, as you yourself will heal through the learning that each chapter has created for you. This book reminds each of us just how important educational work is to the world. A true masterpiece for the heart!"

~ Kristen Nan,
Teacher, Speaker and Author of
All In: Taking a Gamble in Education

"Award Winning Culture is a timely, essential, and fabulous read that I could NOT put down. From the opening story and throughout this social emotional learning gift, Hans Appel's WHOLE CHILD focus is simply profound! I don't know of another book that is so filled with concrete, simple yet impactful ways to connect with kids to amplify school culture and climate. This book MUST BE in the hands of every educator. BRAVO!"

~ Dr. Michele Borba,
Globally-Recognized Educational Psychologist,
and Author of *UnSelfie: Why Empathetic Kids
Succeed in Our All-About-Me World.*

"I had the pleasure of meeting Hans on several occasions and was instantly impressed with his humble confidence, his quick smile, and the way he makes everyone feel special. It is hard to articulate how powerful it is to now know the story behind his humility and his smile. Hans' huge heart, his leadership, and his, "Let's make it happen!" approach are on full display in *Award Winning Culture*. Hans not only shares his own journey but he also shares valuable resources that have shaped him as an educator. He details how his school transformed from a story of fist-fights to an award-winning story of JOY and student empowerment. I highly recommend *Award Winning Culture* to every educator because there are valuable takeaways for us all."

~ Allyson Apsey,
Elementary Principal and
Author of *The Path to Serendipity*

"I'm convinced, more than ever, that schools should be just as intentional about the whole child and character and leadership development as they are about the academic outcomes they seek. In his book, *Award Winning Culture*, Hans Appel brings incredible energy, excitement, and enthusiasm for creating an irresistible culture of connection, growth, and excellence. You'll be inspired by the stories he shares. You'll be challenged by the ideas he unpacks. Most of all, you'll want to take action to make your own classroom and school a stronger, healthier place for kids and learning."

~ David Geurin,
Award Winning Principal,
Keynote Speaker, and Author of *Future Driven:
Will Your Students Thrive in an Unpredictable World?*

"Intertwined with powerful stories, *Award Winning Culture* reminds us all that culture matters. Hans Appel incorporates best practices and relevant strategies for school and classroom that remind all of us the need and benefits of positive supports for our students. Through vivid details to reinforce each concept, Appel creates "hooks" that seem to anchor the point and make it stick. I can't wait to share this book with other educators and continue our work in focusing on culture!"

~ Neil Gupta, Ed.D.,
Director of Secondary Education
of Worthington Schools, Ohio Speaker Series Network,
and Teach Better Team

"We hear about a place like Enterprise Middle School, see that it's won some awards, listen to the student-led podcasts, visit the campus... and everything seems to be roses. We have a tendency to dismiss it as an anomaly, a mythical land sitting at the end of a faraway rainbow, something unattainable for mortals like us. And then...Hans writes this book, explaining with meticulous detail not just the WHAT of it, but the WHY, and perhaps most importantly for those chasing the white rabbit, the HOW. This work is do-able, it's within our grasp, it's not a unicorn after all. With a powerful and compelling vision, a clearly articulated set of action steps and conditions, and unbridled enthusiasm and love for human beings, Hans gives us a bazillion options and ideas for how to create such a culture. Early on, this question is posed: *'Why isn't every school doing these things?'* We no longer have a rational explanation. We just have to roll up our sleeves and get to it."

~ Pete Hall,
Executive Director,
EducationHall, Twitter:
@EducationHall

"Award Winning Culture beautifully lays out how our real-life lessons have more to do with emotional regulation, relationships, and character. Hans Appel defines his WHY through his story of childhood trauma that gave him the tools to prepare him for life as an educator and counselor. Appel shares through stories, activities, questions, and examples of how schools can change their focus from traditional teaching models that are missing a WHY to a student-centered leadership model that fosters incredible joy based on kindness, empathy, and service. If you want to create a culture of positivity that amplifies awesomeness for learners and everyone in your school community, this is the book for you. *Award Winning Culture* is a must-read for educators who want to create a culture of JOY and deep purpose."

~ Barbara Bray,
Speaker, Podcast Host,
and Author of *Define Your WHY*

"Great school culture is never accidental. As Hans Appel writes, it's "an intentional mindset." *Award Winning Culture* is not just the story of how one school transformed their own culture, it is a call for every educator to embrace the challenge. Appel writes with the credibility of a guy who is on the front lines, making a difference for his students and colleagues on a daily basis. But more than that, he brings to this project the energy and passion that inspires all of us to make a difference in our own school community."

~ Danny Steele,
Educator, Author, and Speaker

"Hans Appel educates and leads with profound empathy and inspiring vulnerability. His book, *Award Winning Culture*, is a motivational, practical, and impactful roadmap to creating a learning environment in which students genuinely feel seen, cared for, empowered, heard, supported, and loved. While staff are critically important in creating a positive and powerful school culture, Hans has additionally embraced the idea that sustained progress is made when students are leveraged as the agents and advocates through intentionally building their capacity, expanding their perspective, and allowing them to truly lead."

~ Dr. Bradford Hubbard,
Superintendent

"Learn how to bring an *Award-Winning Culture* to your school! Hans Appel shares his journey and the journey of his school, a voyage of challenges, reflections, acceptance, and action. When schools are authentically doing the right things for staff and students, culture reinforces students and staff to reach for excellence. Let Hans serve as your guide as you and your team take your school on a journey towards an award-winning culture."

~ Evan Robb,
Principal, Speaker,
Author of *The Ten-Minute Principal*

"This book is a must for educators who want to make a difference for students by creating a positive environment in their classroom or school. One of the most difficult questions educators face today is how to improve school culture. *Award Winning Culture* addresses that challenge by expertly offering a blueprint for making school a place where students and staff want to come each and every day. Filled with stories of success, Hans Appel demonstrates the power of positivity, hard work, and the magic that can happen when we empower our students. This is one of the best books on education I have read in a long time. You will want to make *Award Winning Culture* a part of your educational library. You will not be disappointed!"

~ Kris Felicello,
Superintendent of North Rockland Central Schools,
Co-Author of *The Teacher and The Admin:*
*Making Schools Better for Kid*s and TEDx Speaker

"The foundation of any successful school is relationships and school culture. In *Award Winning Culture*, Hans Appel breaks down how we can develop dynamic school wide approaches to character development, impacting the health and well-being of our communities by sharing tried and true practical strategies. Appel illustrates what it takes to establish and maintain an Award Winning Culture by sharing stories that will inspire you to redesign current approaches; fostering a sense of belonging for all and taking ideas and setting them into motion. Your school culture is the heartbeat of your school, use this book as a handbook that will help you create a profound impact on the lives you serve–– creating a lasting legacy on lives."

~ Elisabeth Bostwick,
Author of *Take the L.E.A.P.: Ignite a Culture of Innovation*,
Multi-Award-Winning Educator, and Speaker

"In *Award Winning Culture*, Hans Appel shares real stories of how he and his school used a common language and a belief in student empowerment and leadership to create a school culture of character, excellence, and community. The examples used in this book along with real life situations and stories can help turn any school culture into an *Award Winning Culture*. This book is not only good for administrators and counselors but offers ideas for all who serve students and their families."

~ **Jay Billy**,
Principal of Ben Franklin Elementary School,
and Author of *Lead With Culture:*
What Really Matters In Our Schools

"Hans has constructed a detailed blueprint for healthy school culture and whole child investment. *Award Winning Culture* provides the reader a systematic process of developing a vision and mission that focuses on community and empowerment of the people within it, while ensuring autonomy of individuals is honored. I see this book as a way to streamline character, discipline, and learning as a means to honoring the full purpose of education. I was reminded of my WHY as I read through this MUST HAVE tool for success!"

~ **Bethany Hill**,
Assistant Principal

"Creating school cultures marked by joy, kindness, caring, and compassion are critical to student, staff, and school success. In *Award Winning Culture*, Hans Appel shows us specific and practical steps we can take to create such school cultures. This excellent book is so inspiring and uplifting that you will find yourself wanting to visit Appel's school after reading it to see first-hand the amazing work being done there."

~ **Jeffrey Zoul, Ed.D.**,
Author, Speaker, Leadership Coach,
and President of ConnectEDD

AWARD WINNING *Culture*

Building School-Wide Intentionality and Action Through
CHARACTER, EXCELLENCE, AND COMMUNITY

HANS APPEL

Award Winning Culture: Building School-Wide Intentionality and Action Through CHARACTER, EXCELLENCE, AND COMMUNITY

Copyright © 2020 by Hans Appel

All rights reserved. This book, or parts thereof, may not be reproduced in any form or by any electronic or mechanical means, including information storage and retrieval systems, without written permission from the publisher except for the use of brief quotations in a book review. For information regarding permission please contact the publisher at info@edugladiators.com

This book is available at discount pricing when purchased in bulk for educational purposes. For inquiries and further details, please contact the publisher at info@edugladiators.com

Published by EduGladiators LLC

Nashville, TN

www.edugladiators.com

Book Design & Production: EduGladiators LLC

Paperback ISBN: 978-1-7340514-6-9

eBook ISBN: 978-1-7340514-7-6

DEDICATION

To my wife Jennifer for encouraging me to use my influence to impact students' lives and for inspiring me to pursue a better version of myself-- EVERYDAY!

Preface 17

Section 1: Character 23

Chapter 1: Tears of Joy 24
Chapter 2: Curriculum 28
Chapter 3: HIGHLIGHTS 46
Chapter 4: Activity 50
Chapter 5: Rewards-Reinforcers 57
Chapter 6: Accountability 62
Chapter 7: Common Language 68
Chapter 8: Training 71
Chapter 9: Experiential 76
Chapter 10: Reminders 90
Chapter 11: Whole Child 98

Section 2: Excellence 102

Chapter 12: Carmichael Hill 103
Chapter 13: Engagement 106
Chapter 14: Empowerment 126
Chapter 15: Experiential 145
Chapter 16: EPIC 160
Chapter 17: Pete 173

Section 3: Community **180**

Chapter 18: Social Media. 181

Chapter 19: House Rules. 189

Chapter 20: Authentic Branding. 192

Chapter 21: Personal Outreach 199

Chapter 22: Experience 222

Section 4: Cultural Maximizers **235**

Chapter 23: The Y of School Culture 236

Chapter 24: Any Questions?. 238

Chapter 25: Educational Cross Training 245

Chapter 26: Gratitude 257

Chapter 27: Welcome Back 265

Chapter 28: Budgeting 269

Chapter 29: Be Present 272

Chapter 30: Vulnerability. 275

Chapter 31: Signs of Success 279

Chapter 32: Culture vs. Climate 282

Chapter 33: Now What? 285

Chapter 34: Conclusion 289

References. 294

Acknowledgements. 301

About the Author 303

More From Edugladiators 305

PREFACE

Are you acutely aware of the subtle sounds of the back door?

During amazing days, we seemed like the poster family for happiness. We were solidly middle class, had a nice home, and as an only child, I was quite literally the center of my parent's universe. From the outside, we looked the part of a perfect family that had it all together. There were wonderful vacations, elaborate holidays, and spectacular arrays of fun. But there were also dark days. And in comparison, these gloomy experiences were somehow traumatically burned into cognitive dissonance in ways that were arduous to put into words.

As a child, growing up in an abusive home, I found myself highly attuned to my surroundings. Frequently, my house resembled the verbal equivalent of a war zone. In a home filled with anger, tears, and unease, I became talented at navigating pain and suffering in reluctantly skillful ways. For years, I mediated heated arguments before I was old enough to even enjoy a PG movie. During particularly bad evenings, I'd cry myself to sleep clutching an oversized stuffed bunny rabbit named "Jumbo"; wondering if this would finally be the last straw that would end in divorce.

Children growing up with adverse childhood experiences (ACE's) become experts in taking the temperature of the room. They're often able to predict others' behavior from subtle indiscriminate signs, words, and feelings that most people might completely overlook.

I knew with almost certainty, what type of evening or weekend it was going to be, based on how the back door slammed. Typically, my dad would arrive home from work Monday-Friday, between 5-6 pm. On good days, the door would quietly latch, closing behind my dad, as he breezed through the door with an air of enchantment. Dad would invariably be in a festive mood and the house somehow felt lighter and full of energy. On average days, the door would creek closed as he grudgingly made his way into the house with exhaustion, irritation, and annoyance. But there was a different sound that I sometimes heard. This sound is challenging to articulate to those who were fortunate enough to grow up in happy, healthy homes. However, having talked to numerous survivors, it's a sound that far too many of our students at school have memorized...

On the bad days, I would hear the door well before my dad as he aggressively attacked the doorknob, gripping it with force as he ripped open the door. Oftentimes the back of the door would slam into the garage wall before he would charge through. As the door gained intense energy from the wall, it would wildly pick up speed as it returned to its frame with a loud careening: BANG!!! It was such a loud SLAM, that I often wondered if the entire frame might just fall off the wall. The hypervigilance that I experienced listening for this terrifyingly specific sound foreshadowing an evening of sadness...was exhausting.

On these days, I would immediately scatter and demonstrate my best disappearing act.

Through the years, school became my safe haven. It was a welcomed respite from the chaotic tornado that would blow through my existence at home. For those who wonder where my passion for kindness, empathy, and school culture came from...the roots can be directly traced back to these early moments in education. Not to say that school was easy for me, as I could fill books on my own personal challenges, from the middle school learning environment. Still, education was a place I could be assured of safety, peace, and perhaps most importantly, the opportunity to be age appropriate. At school, no one expected me to solve complicated adult emotional problems. I could just be a kid. It was glorious! As I got older, sports became my vehicle to avoid home while subsequently pouring anger, resentment, and fear into a healthy endeavor. Additionally, friends, video games, and reading books on the magical arts were a wonderful distraction in between sporting opportunities. My teachers, coaches, and friends really became like family to me.

As a highly introspective, reflective kid, I was attuned to how these distractions coupled with exceptional school educators aided my own mental health and in college, I shifted from aspirations of a career in magic into a counseling/educational/helping profession. I self-identified how these unhealthy moments of emotional hand holding with my parents; ironically, prepared me for a life of serving others. I was always that kid whose friends confided in him, picked for programs like natural helpers and just seemed to be an empathic listener. As an adult now, I'm able to look back at my childhood as a gift; to better understand abuse, trauma, and divorce in ways that I certainly wouldn't wish on anyone.

Truthfully, there are students who experience far more horrific childhoods. As you know, our students overcome trauma, social unrest, and daily tribulations that would bring the strongest of us to our knees. But alas, it's not a competition. As educators we have a moral imperative to create spaces for healing, growth, and safety. There are students in your offices, classrooms, and schools who are watching EVERYTHING you and their peers do. They want to see how you handle frustrations, disappointments, and challenges. Exceptional educators provide a safe and predictable physical, emotional, and verbal space for all students to heal through learning.

Some educators get stuck on a tunnel vision for their own content and forget that the REAL life lessons being taught may have much more to do with emotional regulation, relationships, and character. Imagine the grownup child of trauma who's never given the tools to properly cope with the stress, pain, and loss from their upbringing. I shudder to think, who I might have become, if I hadn't had culture minded educators teaching me FAR MORE than math, science, and history. And isn't preparing students for life, the REAL WORK? Isn't that the good stuff? The real reason that most of us actually went into education. Perhaps, content is just a vehicle to teach students what matters most...Character, Excellence, and Community.

> **Award Winning Culture is best defined as inspiring a mindset of positive intentionality and action through Character, Excellence, and Community within your sphere of influence.**

When reflecting on one's own sphere of influence, three overarching questions help drive intentional positive effort:

Will you do the right thing? (Character)

Will you do your very best? (Excellence)

What will you do for others TODAY? (Community)

These questions serve as a school-wide umbrella of visionary leadership and a personal mantra for all stakeholders to wrestle with on a daily basis. With a micro and macro focus on Character, Excellence, and Community, schools enjoy the byproduct of a healthy learning environment. This does not infer that schools (even schools that win global kindness awards) are somehow capable of reaching cultural perfection. However, this sustained commitment to chasing greatness EVERYDAY cultivates a thinking that provides an opportunity for exceptional learning, living, and flourishing with JOY.

> **I believe education at its highest level, is about inspiring others to discover and develop their JOY!**

And isn't that what life is all about—living out your WHY. Understanding your own unique strengths and passions and aligning those with some deeper meaning or purpose. I believe that when we take the time to intentionally craft an Award Winning Culture we provide our students with the OPPORTUNITY to pursue joy.

It's no surprise that my why is to help others to create JOY filled learning environments. When we craft an Award Winning Culture, we initiate an invitation for others to cultivate their JOY despite whatever chaos, ugliness, and challenges they might be facing on a daily basis. And I understand these childhood barriers to joy in a deeply personal way...

As educators we have tremendous leverage over student's cultural experiences. Many of our students DESPERATELY need us to carefully insulate them from toxicity; thereby facilitating windows of time to discover their JOY through learning. As you enthusiastically enter your students' world and invariably open up doors to education and life possibilities, perhaps the biggest question remains...

Will you let the door slam, as you walk in?

This book will provide you strategies, examples and ideas to advance your organizational environment. However, my GREATEST hope in writing this book is to impart an intentional mindset towards school culture. Armed with an award winning mindset, you'll be able to apply this lens of cultural thinking towards your own school, classroom, or educational space. Indeed, I believe the best books inspire us to look deep inside, at our own secret sauce to deliver greatness. Therefore, my intention is that readers will come away with a renewed zest for how their intentional positive actions can create EXCEPTIONAL experiences for others. So, let's dig in...

Share your reflections on social media using the hashtag #AwardWinningCulture

SECTION 1
CHARACTER

Will You Do the Right Thing?

(**C**urriculum, **H**ighlights, **A**ctivity, **R**eward, **A**ccountability, **C**ommon Language, **T**raining, **E**xperiential, **R**eminders)

CHAPTER 1
TEARS OF JOY

Joy is the most vulnerable emotion.

-Brené Brown

Does your school culture have the power to evoke tears of joy?

In October 2017, our local KNDU/NBC news station reached out to me to do a story on our school, Enterprise Middle School (AKA Wildcat Nation), for an anti-bullying piece they were working on. I was told that they'd be there, no longer than 45 minutes, as they had an important story on the other side of town that same morning. While the news manager allowed for ¾ of an hour he fully expected his reporter to be in and out in about 20 minutes.

As the news reporter arrived on campus nearly 30 minutes before school was to start, she was immediately struck by our daily Wildcat Nation greeting. At EMS, we start every day with high fives, fist bumps, music and warm hellos as people walk in the main entrances. It's an intentional move to increase school positivity and school spirit through personal connection.

After taking footage and soaking up our spectacular start to school she was off to do some student interviews. She asked students what it's like to go to EMS, what Wildcat Nation really means, and how our CharacterStrong and PBIS Rewards programs impact our culture. What started off as a 45-minute stop in West Richland, turned into over three hours! Frankly, we couldn't get her to leave. She was having an absolute blast! She interviewed dozens of students, teachers, and even attended a leadership class.

Near the end of her visit, I found myself sitting with the reporter and our principal, in the main office...just kind of debriefing what she had seen, experienced, and felt. If I'm being honest...we both had other meetings and were a little antsy to get the news story wrapped up.

All of a sudden, the news reporter burst out in tears. I mean, full on ugly cry as she uttered through a puddle of tears,

"Why isn't EVERY SCHOOL doing these things?"

The principal and I exchanged a quick surprised glance as if to say...what the heck just happened? This unexpected outburst clearly caught us both off guard.

As she reached for tissues, I began to mumble: "Well...I guess...that's why you're here today...so you can help spread the word about how important this work and these programs are." I'm sure we both muttered something else as well but to be real, I was slightly taken aback by this unlikely turn of events.

A moment later, the news reporter got really still and eerily quiet, as she stopped crying for a moment. Again, my principal and I made eye contact as if to say...ah oh...what's gonna happen now?

Seconds later, the reporter looked up slowly, wiping tears away and made direct eye contact with me as she said in a somewhat angry tone,

"Why wasn't it this way, when I was in school?"

For the next 15 minutes she regaled us with tales of mean girls, disinterested educators, and the trials and tribulations of middle school. She detailed the daily struggles that she and her peers experienced throughout her teenage years.

As we comforted this beautiful soul and began to shift back towards laughter, a couple things struck me on that breezy fall day.

Her tears were not about sadness. In her own words, she was overcome with joy at how incredible our school felt. The welcoming atmosphere. The family like mindset. Having been in school herself and then creating stories on local schools for years, she simply had never come across a feeling of positivity quite like that morning.

Additionally, something special was happening at Wildcat Nation. Something sadly outside the norm for education. Indeed, we were on a path towards award winning.

But more importantly, I was reminded how important our educational work is to people around the world. Folks' experience with school culture sticks with them...for years. We have an obligation to strive for an Award Winning Culture EVERYDAY! This news reporter, nearly 20 years removed from middle school, had absolutely held tightly to the painful, awkward, and embarrassing moments.

In truth, she had previously viewed middle school as a survival test... rather than a rewarding and meaningful learning experience. If one could survive middle school, she believed they could survive ANYTHING! Prior to that morning, she couldn't even fathom a middle school authentically focused on kindness, service, and empathy. The idea that school could be welcoming, engaging, and filled with character focused students and staff was incomprehensible.

In the months since her visit, she's moved on from little old Tri-Cities to a bigger news market in Southern California. But it might not surprise you, she still follows our school's story closely on social media. From time to time, she reaches out to check in on Wildcat Nation.

Afterall, how often does a school's culture evoke tears of joy...

Like every school, at Wildcat Nation we're striving for greatness every day. And while most days we probably come up just short, I've held onto this moment as an example of how powerful culture and climate can truly be.

> **Award Winning Culture has the power to heal old wounds within the safe and welcoming confines of the schoolhouse.**

How will your culture alter the emotional, educational, and behavioral trajectory of a new student?

How might parents feel as they walk into your building?

Does your culture have the power to flip a student's life path?

What images are conjured up about your school, by local community members?

How are rival sports teams treated in your house?

Does your staff LOVE coming to work every day?

What "fingerprints of kindness" are on display?

I guess the real question is....

How might YOU elicit TEARS OF JOY Today?

CHAPTER 2
CURRICULUM

Character is revealed by what you do, when you think no one else is watching...but here's the thing, oftentimes someone is watching...and we're just unaware.

High character schools are crafted through a planned implementation of social emotional and character ed. Indeed, the curriculum used to teach these critical soft skills becomes the backbone to the school's mental health compass.

Years before we were inspiring tears of joy, Enterprise Middle School was a reactive school fraught with a pattern of simply putting out one fire after another. This exhausting and unsustainable approach to school safety and social emotional wellbeing was particularly punctuated by one violent spring.

After several hallway and lunchtime fights within a few weeks, our inadequate school culture was brought to a dangerous crescendo in a 7th grade science classroom. During work time, a boy and a girl began to argue rather loudly about the best way to complete the group project. As frustrations grew and patience deteriorated, the scene quickly turned aggressive. The boy lunged at the girl and began choking her, before ultimately climbing on top of her to gain a better advantage to restrict her airway. It took a teacher and 2 students to restrain and remove the unhinged male perpetrator. The office was immediately called in to support and deal with the aftermath. Upon arrival at the scene, our team of administrators and counselors were struck by the intensity and raw emotion of it all. As you can imagine the fallout was brutal. The boy was expelled. The girl, the entire class, and the teacher were traumatized. It was truly awful. Trying to find words to comfort everyone involved was overwhelming...

Throughout the rest of that spring, I found myself in a litany of anger filled meetings demanding that 'WE' ensure OUR school was safe for ALL students. For all practical purposes, I and many of my colleagues felt as though we had hit rock bottom. As I reflected upon the horror over the last couple months of the school year a couple things stood out that may surprise you. First of all, the science teacher was one of our best teachers. This wasn't some neophyte, first year rookie educator. She had great relationships with students and had highly effective classroom management skills. Secondly, the boy and the girl were friends. This wasn't a case of two students who hated each other for years and finally had enough. By all accounts they were even best friends. Still, the inability to regulate and manage emotions obviously led to a scary assault. Lastly, while I felt a HIGH degree of personal responsibility, shame, and guilt for not working with this young man in a more regular proactive way, I came to a powerful conclusion near the end of that school year:

> **Teaching social emotional wellbeing and character education is EVERYONE'S job.**

The weight and even the fate of our school community's mental health rested with our ENTIRE community. During this one unforgettably frightening exchange, my mission and our school's path toward an Award Winning Culture was officially re-ignited. Indeed, an idea was born...

A friend of mine recently said to me:

"Everyone has those *wouldn't it be nice ideas...wouldn't it be nice to do this... wouldn't it be nice to do that...*She said *the difference at your school Hans-- you take those wouldn't it be nice ideas...and you put them into actions*!"

And those intentions + actions at Enterprise Middle School have garnered critical success. In 2018, we won the **ASCD Whole Child Award** for our commitment to kindness, service, and empathy. Additionally, we won the 2018-2019 **Global Class Act Award** for Kindness. Let me repeat that key word for you: GLOBAL. As in...the world. For your frame of reference, there hasn't been a school in our country that has won this award in several years. Furthermore, we were a 2019 **PBIS Film Festival** Finalist and took top prize in the Community, Staff, and Parents category. But our journey toward an Award Winning Culture began by first establishing a school-wide whole child curriculum.

Picking Content

How often do we handcuff great teachers with mediocre programs or curricula?

When determining content to teach, we were committed to finding something spectacular. Because our teachers and students deserve brilliant content. Picking an SEL and/or Character curriculum might seem like an easy task. But for anyone who's sat on an adoption committee, you know there are a multitude of factors that determine the curriculum's effectiveness. In our early years teaching SEL curriculum, we chose a program that was considered best practice and was already being implemented at the elementary level, in our district. And while we had modest success by transitioning to this proactive way of addressing student's mental health, the curriculum we selected lacked student engagement, staff buy-in, and was missing something that took us years to pinpoint. That program was missing a WHY. As we'd learn several years later, character gives social emotional it's WHY. And as Simon Sinek so eloquently explains, when we understand our why, our work has passion, purpose, and meaning and can eventually foster deep joy.

There are dozens of wonderful researched based character focused curriculum and programs to choose from. I'm not here to convince you that one program is better than another. I'd refer you to the Collaborative for Academic, Social, and Emotional Learning (CASEL) for a complete breakdown on impactful whole child curricula. However, after nearly 2 years of searching for the right fit for Enterprise Middle School, we moved all in on a program called **CharacterStrong**. CharacterStrong abandoned fake role plays and cheesy scenarios that often plague other curriculums. Also, unlike other programs it was not initially designed for elementary students and then later adapted to middle schoolers. Instead, its creators were secondary educators who understood the teenage brain. Rooted in a servant leadership model, it perfectly addressed our desire to focus on kindness, empathy, and service within a hands-on experiential format.

After looking at sample lesson plans and videos, I turned my attention to researching its founders: John Norlin and Houston Kraft. I watched YouTube videos, spoke with educators currently using the curriculum, and even contacted co-workers at the cofounder's former school district. I made every effort to not only find the right content but the right people to partner on our whole child journey. John and Houston were absolutely the real deal and I was thrilled to partner with them.

As I soon realized, picking the program (while important and critical) was the easy part of creating a culture of character. Implementing the program in the MOST IMPACTFUL way would require us to shift from proactive to INTENTIONAL.

> ## How might you ensure that the character content you're teaching is what's best for your school?

Gathering Buy-in

Six months after implementing our current SEL curriculum, 100% of staff said they'd seen acts of kindness increase at EMS. 95% of staff had observed students demonstrating greater empathy towards others. Furthermore, 98% of staff surveyed said they had seen the curriculum positively impact the culture and climate at our school. During the same period of time, our school took on 1:1 devices, established a strong social media presence with our community, established a new PBIS matrix and rewards system, and made a concerted effort to increase school/home connectedness.

Naturally, with so many new initiatives, the most common question we started receiving from educators, schools, and districts...HOW DID YOU GET PEOPLE TO BUY-IN? Universally, this continues to be asked over and over. We've met with educators and schools, blogged and presented about it. Our answers have been, what you might already expect...some combination of vision, planning, training, ongoing PD, etc. But the biggest reason for our successful buy-in to our new SEL/Character curriculum was...TIME.

When rolling out CharacterStrong, we moved very slowly. First, our counseling team met with administration to examine lessons, shared our vision, and hope for this new curriculum. From there, we started chatting with small pockets of our school community: PBIS team, leadership team, ASB officers, and PTSA...before introducing this in an entire staff meeting.

As a staff, we discussed the new program for months and allowed people the opportunity to ask questions, think about changes, and process where we were all heading. Clearly, time had been crucial to the successful launch.

> **"All great achievements require time."**
>
> ~ Maya Angelou

And while our office team openly talked about the importance of TIME, I'm not sure it really sunk in for me completely until we attempted to implement another technology initiative almost a year later. Riding the wave of successful buy-in, our office team suggested our school apply for a tech grant in May. With a unified school, focused on doing what's best for students this grant seemed like a natural fit for a school focused on student experience. It was presented at a staff meeting...staff voted...and ballots were tallied. It was UNEQUIVOCALLY shot down! Staff wanted no part of buying into this new tech journey. There would be more money, professional development, and additional staffing. This felt like a can't lose proposition.

But it failed...spectacularly!

WHY?

Time.

We simply forgot the power of time. Indeed, time influences a person's opportunity to buy-in; because, people support what they help build. And a failure to build will almost always result in a failure to support. Which is why I recommend at least a year to properly gather buy-in for a new school culture initiative, program, or curriculum. The heart of intentionally setting aside time to listen and connect is an essential part of great leadership.

In the end, our teachers were right to reject the new tech initiative as this gave us the great gift of feedback. It also gave us a chance to re-look, re-listen, and remind all of us what's most important with any new movement: How will this benefit our students' experience? (Incidentally, a year later, with a more intentionally patient approach, we passed this same technology/innovation grant process)

- Are you providing silence for your folks to ask the really hard questions? (i.e. *Why now? Why This? What makes you think this will work?*, etc.)

- Are you willing to truly listen to divergent thinking in an effort to allow everyone time to gather excitement for the necessary growth?

- Are you allowing time for people to process and make connections to the "New"?

- Are you willing to demonstrate humility, when students, staff, and community remind us that we didn't allow enough time?

Articulating Vision

Articulating a clear vision inspires students, staff, and community by laying out a blueprint or roadmap to achieve greatness. It's not good enough for school culture leaders to have a vision, it must be eloquently shared in such an authentic, vulnerable and impactful way that it's tenents connect with all stakeholders.

When we initially began formulating and sharing a curriculum vision to positively enhance our school's character, we began by acknowledging our past failures. Our vision included a well-developed timeline of highlights, activities, rewards/reinforcers, accountability, training, student roll-out, and reminders.

During one unforgettable staff meeting, everyone learned how the new character curriculum would be tied into EVERYTHING else at school. No longer a stand alone thing for advisory. We had intentionally created a comprehensive plan toward school and community wide implementation. But perhaps my most important act of leadership was opening up and taking blame for past mistakes on curriculum implementation.

I vividly remember standing up in front of our staff and sharing how I'd let them down on previous curriculum implementation. I owned HOW and WHY the previous program failed. Standing up in front of your peers to take ownership of a public failure can be terrifying. However, by embracing and even modeling risk taking through transparent vision, people understood our WHY, HOW, and WHAT so deeply that they couldn't help but be committed to its success. Brené Brown calls this daring leadership. I chose to "brave the wilderness" with a vulnerable truth, while laying out a detailed plan that our team believed would be game-changing. Probably a dozen people approached me following that staff meeting to share how much they appreciated my candor, the school plan, and knowing exactly why I was so confident this new character curriculum would be a smashing success.

> **Are you transparent with your hopes and dreams for the school?**

> **Are you willing to communicate your goals, vision, and plan to achieve those hopes/dreams?**

Creating a TEAM (The Educators All-in Mindset)

Before trying to implement a character curriculum a TEAM must be formed to help roll out the new program. Picking the team is an essential part of the process. Team members should have a growth mindset, be highly influential educators, and open to new ways of thinking. In short, we're looking for Educators who operate with an ALL-IN mindset. Ideally, these educators are a cross mix of individuals who can infuse their positive energy into the character curriculum.

Sometimes, school leaders make the mistake of simply selecting colleges who are stuck in their ways and may need some fresh ideas or thoughts. The thinking being that the new program or initiative will light a fire within these folks. However, these educators tend to either love or hate whatever the new thing is. Teams with close-minded members tend not to inspire others to jump on board.

Other times, leaders open up team membership to committees of interested people. These committees have all the necessary passion but none of the school influence to lead impactful change. These passionate open-minded but low influence folks have an important seat in the gathering buy-in stage of implementation. Their enthusiasm will be crucial to reaching a critical mass or tipping point on moving forward a new school culture initiative. However, their low school-wide influence dampens the impact of their passion on inspiring others.

Introversion or extroversion also makes no difference in TEAM member selection. Don't get caught up in the common mistake of assuming influential people are only our most outspoken or charismatic folks. As Susan Cain expertly lays out in her book *Quiet,* all types of personality can bring strengths and talents to a team setting.

Lastly, leadership titles mean nothing here. It's a mistake to select department chairs just because they're on a school leadership team. Title does not infer influence. Sometimes your most influential school leaders (positive and/or negative) are NOT educators with current leadership positions.

In 1962, a professor of communication studies, Everrett Rogers popularized a theory in his book, *Diffusion of Innovations*, that explains why our TEAM model was so successful. Rogers explained that there were 5 groups of people who adopt or buy-in to something new: Innovators (2.5%), Early Adopters (13.5%), Early Majority (34%), Late Majority (34%), and Laggards (16%). He believed that leaders often shoot for the wrong groups when introducing new ideas, initiatives, or innovation. Instead, Rogers argued that if leaders successfully sought out the early adopters, the innovators would automatically jump on board as their very nature dictated that they'd want to try something new. Thus, if leaders had 15% buy-in of the total population, they'd achieve a tipping point that would ultimately lead to mass success of the new initiative.

In *Start with Why*, Simon Sinek articulates that all organizations have about 10% that just get it. Administrators will recognize these educators as the ones who seem to understand the power of a new program, idea, or system. Thus, in a school of 50 employees about 5 of them will easily recognize the value of the Whole Child Curriculum. [Most administrators can easily identify who those educators are. These are the ones you try pilots with or suggest some new change to experiment with]. The key to a successful TEAM, is selecting those 5 and THEN determining who the other 3 educators are that will create the necessary tipping point for our whole child work to catch hold with 15% of the school. The difference between the 8 educators needed and the 5 who automatically bought in is a critical key that Geoffrey Moore calls: *Crossing The Chasm*. Thus, finding this small pocket of staff is crucial. When leaders take the time to select the right 15% of staff to form the TEAM, the Whole Child curriculum has the opportunity for a highly successful implementation.

Beyond selecting the TEAM, parents, students, and community must be included throughout the early stages as we show sample lesson plans and curricula materials to a wider group of stakeholders. Again, this isn't just to check some inclusion box, but to gather real input and enthusiasm toward the school's new SEL and character curriculum.

Who might be your key TEAM members?

How will you introduce to them the idea of participating on a Character focused TEAM?

What steps will you take to build capacity by bringing on future interested stakeholders?

Roll Out

Part of the TEAM's job is to plan out the effective roll-out of the school's character curriculum. Much like gathering buy-in, a successful character campaign must be an ongoing process. This is not the time for a one shot, all or nothing launch party. Instead, we planned out an entire year to slowly build toward a character crescendo. Afterall, students need just as much intentional time to buy-in to the new curriculum as educators and parents.

Building anticipation for the new character focus included: creating t-shirts to give away on the first day of school, a character assembly on the first Friday of the school year, a strong social media push to generate excitement, and crafting a year long overarching vision with the leadership students.

We also carefully planned out the entire year's lessons. At EMS, we utilize an advisory system to deliver weekly 30-minute lessons, at the beginning of each Friday. We determined how many, which character lessons and in what order they would be completed in advisory. Additionally, we identified additional lessons that would be implemented within our leadership classes.

We established a monthly character trait (Commitment, Patience, Humility, Selflessness, Kindness, Respect, Honesty, and Forgiveness) to help ignite a school-wide focus that directly linked back to the lessons our students were learning each week. To increase visibility, we put all the character traits on the free t-shirt we gave away to students and staff and encouraged everyone to show their school pride by wearing their t-shirts on Fridays.

Beyond the first week, we planned out additional student/staff training opportunities, recognitions, reinforcers, reminders, and a second kindness assembly in late January. This second assembly was like a booster shot of positivity for our school. While all of our regular assemblies throughout the year embedded character components, paying for two different speakers to come in (essentially at the beginning and middle of the year) helped connect the powerful social emotional and character work that our staff was doing to the minds and hearts of our student body.

Anyone can hire a speaker to come in and deliver a great assembly. But few schools take the time to do all of the following: pick a speaker that amplifies the school-wide focus and aligns to our message, intentionally select the time of year to maximize impact, communicate specific needs ahead of time to tie in school language, and then use subsequent advisory time to reflect and follow-up on highlights from the assembly. Any speaker worth his or her salt will tell you that without regular follow through, the inspiring messages from a wonderful assembly are short lived. We were determined to encourage the powerful takeaways to live on in our school through intentional follow-up.

What are the key elements to your 1-year plan for Character Development?

How might you gather input and ideas to evaluate your plans success, throughout the year?

What concerns or questions do you anticipate throughout the first year?

School-Wide Approach to Delivery

Whose job is a whole child vision to character education? Some schools assign counselors or psychologists to teach character and/or SEL to students. While this may seem like a Tier 1 solution to teaching the Whole Child, oftentimes these systems end up more closely resembling Tier 2 or Tier 3 interventions with students who are deemed to "need" these learnings. When mental health educators are the only staff delivering social emotional and character lessons, teachers and other staff find themselves lacking the tools and knowledge to support struggling learners.

Other schools put the once on teachers to teach regular lessons to a group of students. These stand-alone lessons can be helpful, but lack carry over impact to environments outside of the classroom. We were seeking a more unified way of supporting the whole child. It seemed silly to imagine a teacher using one set of language and then a counselor or admin using different verbiage in their setting.

> **Award Winning Culture manifests a school-wide approach to whole child curriculum education.**

To better illustrate our mindset, I've developed a campfire analogy to deepen one's understanding of these wrap-around systems:

Picture a campfire--complete with logs, forest, etc. [*If you're like me, your mind drifts to roasting gooey marshmallows over a white-hot flame.*] No skipping ahead! But believe me, we'll get there. Before we can break out the sweet goodness of crafting the perfect smore, we must first build a strong fire:

CURRICULUM

There is no fire without an initial **SPARK**. This might be from a match, lighter, or flint stick but regardless, a great fire must be ignited by a spark of energy. In a school setting, this whole child spark might be a **PERSON**, **EVENT**, or **EXPERIENCE** that enters a school and/or community and creates a powerful spark that ignites a movement toward Character, Excellence, and Community. This might be a dynamic leader at the building or district level. Many schools have been recently sparked by political push requiring policy to address Whole Child education. Sometimes a transformational speaker, trainer, or consultant can enter a school setting and ignite such a spark. Additionally, whole child sparks can be born from both positive or negative events or experiences. For instance, some schools have been motivated to implement SEL and/or character curriculum following a tragedy such as: suicide, school shooting, global pandemic, or public bullying altercation. You might recall that our venture into this work was elicited by a traumatic student aggression spark.

After the initial spark a fire requires an important element to catch on: **TINDER**. NO not that Tinder! Tinder is the small foundational wood scraps that support the entire flame. Your Character team or **WHOLE CHILD TEAM** acts as a base for turning the initial whole child tier 1 curriculum spark into a full-fledged flame. They support the work with vision, training, reminders, planning, communication, etc.

KINDLING is a crucial part of elevating a fire to the next level. **ADVISORY TEACHERS** take the curriculum and turn it into magic by making it their own. Our advisory teachers loop with their students. This relationship-driven model allows both teachers and students to dig deeper into authenticity, connection, and vulnerability over a three-year period with their same advisory class. Because of the inherent comfort and openness that can be intentionally bred in this culture, students explore topics that are rich in content and purpose. It's like having an immediate family (Advisory) within a larger extended family (Wildcat Nation).

In order to grow a small fire into an eventual huge bonfire of Award Winning Culture, larger firewood **LOGS** are a welcome addition. As larger logs become ignited, the flames become increasingly robust and ultimately burn at hotter temperatures. **LEADERSHIP TEACHERS** take the solid beginning character movement and take the lessons to a stronger and brighter outcome. At EMS, we have leadership classes at 6th, 7th, and 8th grade and these classes have the advantage of one of the key elements of time. Again, time shows up as a useful component when it's mixed with a passionate educator focused exclusively on teaching kindness, service, and empathy under a servant leadership umbrella of hope. [*Don't have a leadership class at your school? How about a passionate educator who can embed life's soft skill lessons within their class, club, or activity? You're basically looking for a way to take weekly lessons and put the learning into action with a smaller fired up group of students.*]

The natural question is what happens if the fire starts to simmer down. Obviously, adding a little fuel to the fire can help us overcome even the stormiest of days. **LEADERSHIP STUDENTS** are the **FUEL**, oil, or gasoline of the fire. They pour their heart and soul into making school more comfortable for all students and staff. With each planned project, activity, assembly, or event the character flame grows to a robust level for a short period of time and then reduces back down to a more consistent temperature.

CURRICULUM

However, these moments of EPICNESS can catch others on fire as our leadership students have an undeniable ripple of influence around the school. If you are unable to offer a leadership class, think about how you might fuel this work with a student council, kindness club, or health class. Don't let your master schedule limit your creativity to accentuate the positive at your school! Every school has students who desperately want to serve and inspire hope. Our job is to identify and empower them to help drive our culture.

OXYGEN is the lifeblood of fire. The absence of oxygen yields the absence of fire. There is no character fire without the **STUDENT BODY**. Have you ever been at your school, in the middle of summer without students—it's completely dead, life-less...dare I say lonely? Students bring energy to fan the flame of our whole child curriculum. A teacher without a student is not a teacher.

On the flip side, if fire is exposed to too much pure oxygen, combustion speeds up dramatically and there can be an overwhelming and out of control explosion. Ever been in a school that's bursting with more students than capacity? Hallways, lunchrooms, and classrooms feel like they might just explode. Regardless, students are critical to our whole child fire.

How do we stoke the fire? Typically, a **POKER** or stick is used to gently influence all aspects of the fire. Perhaps, a log is not burning like we'd hope. **ADMINISTRATION, COUNSELORS and SUPPORT STAFF** help maintain a strong burning character fire with targeted social media, reminders, rewards, training, personal feedback, and accountability. These educators expertly use influence, love, and service rather than power to positively improve, shape, and enhance our culture.

On the outside of fire, we line up **ROCKS** to help give our fire structure, direction, and capture the heat. Our student's **PARENTS** become the rocks in our culture when we include them in learning about the soft skills and character lessons their children are learning each week. By communicating with parents weekly in an open way, we encourage parents to reinforce the whole child language, mindset, and skills that we're teaching. Even better, we challenge and support parents to actively work on their own social emotional and character skills, when they feel directly involved in magnifying the heat of our school-wide whole child vision.

The **FOREST** is all around the fire. Truthfully, all of the wood is supplied by the forest. Our **SCHOOL DISTRICT** provides the resources to create a magnificent fire. You can certainly start a fire without logs, kindling, and tinder from the forest's trees. However, the support of our local forest helps school communities take their fire to the next level.

When we **BUILD** a huge warm fire, people from around the forest will inevitably show up. These **COMMUNITY** members will warm their hands, cook, tell stories, sing songs, and enjoy the cohesive atmosphere. As we learned from Field of Dreams, *"If you build it, they will come."* We've seen our community dive into supporting our school with events, fundraisers, projects, etc. They feel a part of Wildcat Nation as we're a recognized hotbed for positive school culture. Students transfer to our school because of our bonfire of community reputation.

When our community roasts **MARSHMALLOWS** around our incredible whole child fire, **JOY** is the natural bi-product of creating a culture of deep purpose. Joy is achieved for students and staff when everyone feels a part of something bigger than themselves and a connection to meaningful work. When students, staff, parents, and community are all dialed in with a singular purpose of connection you naturally build Joyful Leaders.

A fire that burns very hot releases small pieces of ash that pop out of the fire and float away. These **FLYING BURNING ASH** can be the necessary

SPARK to ignite a character fire in another part of the forest. We've experienced the power of the flying burning ash at EMS. Since beginning a school wide movement with our whole child curriculum, many other area schools have jumped on in. As schools and districts saw the success we were experiencing, other schools sought out the same curriculum to implement. Currently, all secondary schools in the Richland School District and many neighboring districts are utilizing the same CharacterStrong curriculum. Additionally, other area districts dove into this curriculum, in large part to our success. Over the past few years, schools and districts all over the state of Washington and Oregon have shown up at EMS to do school site visits, just to learn some of the secrets to implementing the CharacterStrong curriculum. When you develop something magical, you ignite something special in others.

> **How would a true school-wide approach to character development impact your community's health and wellbeing?**

CHAPTER 3
HIGHLIGHTS

We may be drawn in by someone's personality, but we stay because of their character.

In *Culture as History*, author Warren Sussman points out that our nation moved from a culture of character to a culture of personality in the early 1900's. Returning to a focus on character has been an instrumental strategy by forward thinking whole child educational institutions. When schools intentionally highlight moments of positive character, we magnify the likelihood that our school community will do the right thing in the future. Shining a light on people of high character allows everyone to reinforce and deepen their own understanding of what character in action looks like. And modeling powerful character continues to be a strong predictor of future behavior.

At EMS, we highlight character moments during staff meetings. Taking the time to reflect and share out moments from the classroom either in small groups or whole group discussion allows everyone to celebrate the goodness at EMS. But waiting around for a monthly staff meeting would not provide the regular dose of positivity that this work deserves. Instead, I started sending out regular email highlights filled with anecdotes, stories, videos, pictures or other character captured opportunities.

When I began sharing these joy-filled experiences with staff it was purely to help keep my colleagues up to speed on all the amazing things happening at EMS. In truth, I was seeing so much incredibleness around the building, I wanted to ensure no one else was missing out.

> **If we begin to shift our lens toward celebration, positivity, and amplifying awesomeness, these character moments can't help but find us.**

I started to realize the impact of these regular highlights when other staff members began sending me ideas, stories, articles, videos, etc that are related to the character work we were doing. It was as if our entire school was using a similar lens to tell our school story. In the early days, I gladly incorporated these staff sharings into highlight emails before eventually empowering and influencing others to send out their own highlights. Experienced school story tellers will recognize the power of multiple points of view highlighting character to a school's sense of pride, community, and spirit. Additional highlight platforms included a brag board (to share staff celebrations), a CharacterStrong highlights board (to post pictures from experiential lessons in the classroom), and a thank-you board (to write publicly posted notes of exceptionalness).

Character highlights are all around us. Here's a couple of my favorites from Wildcat Nation:

A 7th grade student wrote a handwritten note offering support to a 6th grade student who was in her old locker from the previous year. Despite never having met the student she detailed, "this was my old locker from last year...if you need someone to talk to my new locker # is..." She shared some personal info about herself and told the anonymous student that she'd love to get to know one another. The ability for this 7th grade student to imagine how if felt to be an incoming 6th grader: MAGICAL!

The two students (who were in VERY different social circles) later connected throughout the year. As a reference point, when I put this letter out on social media, nearly 100,000 people saw this post. This highlight was impacting more than just our EMS family. Many educators, parents, and even students (all over the country) were replying with how they wanted to do something similar in their own schools. Ironically, this only came to adult attention after the 6th grader reported to her teacher, "I've just experienced the most wonderful thing...look at this note I got in my locker." In turn, the 6th grader wrote back and the beginning of the friendship was being formed. How sad would it be for this beautiful story to never be shared with EMS staff and beyond? I shudder to think about the ripples of kindness that we may have missed out on, if we all weren't focused on highlighting character!

Another strangely exceptional character moment showed up in our school restroom. If you work in a middle school, you know that locker rooms and bathrooms can be a pretty disgusting place. One day, we discovered some bathroom graffiti unlike anything I'd ever seen before. In essence, a student had written on a small piece of toilet paper with a pen and left the toilet paper for another student to find. It read:

"Dear anyone in this stall, for all I know you might be going through the roughest of times or the best of times...just make sure you are being the best you can be. YOU GOT THIS! If someone brings you down DON'T let it alter the respect you give yourself."

--a fellow student

Obviously, the form that this highlight took provided some comedy relief to our middle school staff. But the student's heart really showed through. Upon seeing this highlight on our school's social media page, Dr. Michele Borba, author of the world-renowned book on empathy titled, *UnSelfie*, wrote:

"Just caught your bathroom graffiti, LOVE IT! You're doing amazing stuff in creating an empathetic culture."

Ironically, a year later our students had the honor of interviewing Borba--a tease for a later chapter.

How might your staff amplify incredible examples of character at your school?

How might YOU share these special moments?

What platforms or opportunities can you build for others to highlight your community's commitment to character?

CHAPTER 4
ACTIVITY

Spirit days are a popular event in schools. They provide an opportunity to strengthen our school cohesiveness through dressing up in some predetermined garb. Students wearing pajamas, sport or college themed getups, or just a subtle color, offers a welcome break from the grind of the academic year. But many students will tell you that their favorite part about spirit days is when their teachers dress up in some over the top silly way. These real moments of wackiness can underscore the wonderful human connections in our schools. But what if we infused some intentionality into spirit days? By slightly altering the language and inflection point of the day or week, schools can harness the power of spirit days to relate to a bigger overall school character message:

- *You have the SUPERPOWER for KINDNESS. Dress like your favorite superhero to show real kindness!*

- *Demonstrate your COMMITMENT by dressing for your future CAREER!*

- *You had a bad hair day! Show HUMILITY by wearing CRAZY HAIR!*

- *RESPECT your elders-dress in the 70's, 80's, or 90's outfits!*

- *FORGIVE your peers and choose HIGH SCHOOL colors to wear!*

ACTIVITY

- *Show EMPATHY for those struggling with CANCER and wear pink!*

- *Be HONEST-Who's your favorite SPORTS TEAM?*

- *Show SELFLESSNESS by transforming into your favorite DISNEY hero!*

Obviously, these are just a few examples, but you can see how easy it is to incorporate character trait language into spirit days. And culture building through spirit days isn't limited to the school building. Summer break, distance learning, and COVID-19 all provide opportunities away from school to create virtual spirit days. By posting pictures of themselves in fun character infused outfits, students and staff connect to the school even during closed campuses.

While I've always loved spirit days, I've worried that they lacked an inherent inclusiveness that haunted our community building. What if students can't afford to dress up? Our PTSA helps us create a spirit of inclusion. They regularly come in during spirit days to offer free face painting. Whether it's colors, pictures, or highlights, these quick hand painted creations help everyone to feel connected to Wildcat Nation. Additionally, every student is given a school branded t-shirt to wear on Fridays. These t-shirts provide all students with a small way to feel connected to something bigger than themselves.

> *Intentional Tip:*
>
> *We give away a newly designed wildcat t-shirt each year.*

Assemblies are another popular school staple. These may include music, sports, games, and or celebrations. How might schools dial up intentionality with their regularly planned assemblies? And how could this impact student character?

We've used assemblies to recognize monthly character winners, share touching character examples around the community, show a moving video clip, or a choreographed scene demonstrating a particular character trait, and carved out time to dig into relationships and human connection. Again the choice of language and vision for the assembly scripts can be directly tied back to the school wide character work already happening. Again, virtual assemblies that are live streamed can include students and/ or parents who may not be able to be physically present. Furthermore, student leaders have used the assembly platform to shout-out kindness. Here's an example of a story we shared at an assembly.

One of my favorite sports related kindness stories that were shared during an assembly took place on another school's basketball court. After overwhelming a city rival's basketball team in the first half, our coach was approached by the other team's coach to play "fake defense" for one of their special players to score a basket. The coach explained that their athlete was less athletic and coordinated than the other boys and had not made a single basket all year. After our coach shared the request with our Wildcat team, they unanimously agreed to go ALL IN to do something extraordinary in the world of sports.

After a couple, near misses in the second half, the other team's player finally made a basket near the end of the game. As he remained on the court in the 4th quarter, the team managed to help him score one more time. Naturally, the crowd figured out what was going on and started to cheer and celebrate wildly!

Perhaps, the best part of the story is that the athlete's mom (who rarely attended a sporting event in two years) managed to witness the entire moment from the stands that winter day. In the end, Wildcat Nation won the game pretty big... but not a player on either side was worried about the score. The kindness and selfless moment that was generated that evening will stay with everyone who watched the game, for a long time.

ACTIVITY

My favorite part of the story is that I didn't hear about it from our coach or players. Long before highlighting wildcat character was a regular endeavor, a scorekeeper on the opposing team actually brought this incredible story to my attention. The character revealed in that activity was so genuine, that no one from our school besides the 10 boys and 1 coach would have ever known about it. But the beauty of combining character highlights and assemblies is that our ENTIRE school community could relish in this EPIC moment.

Do school assemblies actually create real change?

Following a character focused assembly one 8th grade "mean girls" wrote a note of forgiveness to another girl, who she had been having a year long conflict with. The next day, the other girl reciprocated and wrote a note back. It was incredible that their healing showed up because of being moved by a character focused assembly. Now I can't say that their moment of truce was the catalyst to a friendship, they were however, able to have a healthy respect for one another as a result of feeling inspired by an intentional character assembly. And, they had no further issues for the remainder of the school year.

Here's a few other activities from our playbook that support character development with our leadership students:

Community Strong: This is a popular character evening event that we created to showcase a yearly theme such as: Connecting Hearts and Saving Lives or Health and Wellness. We invite community vendors in, offer breakout sessions and other keynote speakers. Some years we offer silent auctions, food, t-shirts, etc. There is always a Community Spirit award given to someone who has demonstrated exceptional character within the community. The overarching thread through all community strong events is a focus on improving one's character.

Veterans Day Celebration: Each year we put on an elaborate recognition and assembly to honor local Veterans from our community. We invite them in for a day of love with refreshments, songs, heartfelt speeches, powerful video clips and montages, and intentional appreciation.

Daily Lunchroom cleanup: Each day, we have leadership students help clean in and around the lunchroom. This intentional move takes pressure off of our hard-working custodians AND models character traits such as Selflessness, Humility, Respect, and Commitment to our entire student body.

Campus Cleanup: On Mondays and Wednesdays leadership students clean up the entire campus during 4th period. Years ago, we used campus cleanup as a discipline consequence but modeling high character behavior has become more valuable than modeling what happens to students who make bad choices. When your most influential student leaders are willing to roll up their sleeves and do the dirty work, it demonstrates that the dirty work matters.

This point is perfectly drilled home in Legacy, by James Kerr. His book offers readers an uplifting account on creating an exceptional organizational culture from the world's top rugby franchise and arguably the winningest sports team in history. Kerr talks about everyone being willing to "Sweep the Shed" as a powerful metaphor that illustrates the impact of having your best superstars or in the case of school culture (your most influential leaders) practice doing the dirty work. This metaphor and literature by Kerr have shown up in sports locker rooms around the world as the gold standard in best practice. When your most popular leadership students are willing to model character by cleaning up the school, you send a direct message that at our school it's everyone's job to make it a great day.

Wildcat Pals: We have leadership students who work in a variety of settings with our most impacted student programs. I love watching students help high needs students roll a ball during adaptive PE, read to students in extended resources or enthusiastically sit with life skills students at lunch. And believe me, the rest of the school takes notice when the captain of the football team demonstrates gentleness with a fragile wheelchair bound learner. POWERFUL!

Compliment Selfies: One lunch time activity we enjoy is creating compliment boards and encouraging students to take selfies with carefully chosen compliments to send out on social media. Similar to a mad libs type of exercise, students have fun picking out themed customs and design sweet, funny, or inspiring messages to send to a peer. By then pairing these messages with silly and fun costumes, students can send their friends a wacky boost of positivity.

Birthday Singing: We sing happy birthday to EVERYONE in the school. While it started off as a daily practice by our big-hearted PE teacher, it quickly spread to our admin team. Each lunch, our administrators sing happy birthday to anyone celebrating a birthday on that day. Truth be told, they rally the entire lunchroom to serenade the birthday boy or girl. In the past few years, we've created all kinds of crazy over the top whole class or whole grade level singing moments for students or staff. These moments reinforce that everyone is important at Wildcat Nation.

Birthday Reach Out: Our leadership students create personalized cards to hang on lockers, for any student celebrating a birthday. Furthermore, they create birthday cards for staff members as well and then hand deliver them. Mailing birthday cards or e-cards home is a perfect solution for distance learning. Regardless, recognizing student and staff birthdays ensures everyone feels special.

What activities does your school already use to amplify, model, or practice character?

How might intentionality bring a new level of awesomeness to the work you're already doing?

CHAPTER 5
REWARDS-REINFORCERS

Motivation is at the heartbeat of education. The debate of intrinsic vs. extrinsic has been heavily explored by world renowned researchers like Daniel Pink. His findings have far reaching implications on educational facets like PBIS, MTSS, and grading. While the evidence and support of building intrinsic motivation is the far superior method, Pink along with other researchers support a multifaceted approach to motivation development. This approach seems largely due to the fact that humans all have a specific love language that gets beneath extrinsic motivation.

I believe that one of the inherent mistakes that Positive Behavior Intervention and Supports (PBIS) focused schools make with reward systems is the exclusive focus on stuff. While tangible items are successful temporary reinforcers for some students, staff, and community, [*particularly on a variable short-term basis*] when we isolate our demonstration of affection to only tangible items we align ourselves to the weakest of extrinsic motivators that Pink so eloquently warns against. While much of our work in education must continue to facilitate intrinsic motivation, here is our recipe for rewarding and reinforcing students, staff, and parents who may also need some extrinsic motivation to get them moving toward a positive direction.

PBIS Rewards: At EMS, we use a school-wide system called PBIS Rewards. Andrew Epperson, Vice President and Chief Marketing Officer of Motivating Systems explains that "PBIS Rewards is a digital school wide management solution." By helping schools reward, track, and redeem virtual points for items, events, and privileges, PBIS Rewards has become an industry leader in this positive organizational space. Andrew and his team have been incredible to work with. Anytime we've had a thought, idea, or question, this company has not only been responsive...they've taken it upon themselves to literally create the technology to make the request happen.

PBIS Rewards provides an App for teachers to reward students. Students are rewarded based on our eight character traits and receive essentially virtual cash from any educator in the building. Additionally, this reward system is successful with students operating through distance learning, COVID-19 school bans, or non-school days. Which is why virtual token economy systems being far superior options for distance learning institutions that hope to offer some extrinsic reinforcers.

This "cash" can then be redeemed at our wildcat cash shop on Tuesday or Thursday during lunch, in an individual teacher's online class store, or at an event. Additionally, parents and students can monitor their virtual cash from the App to see how their character actions around the school are resulting in the accumulation of virtual wildcat cash to spend.

Overall, we've found that while 6th graders like 'stuff' the 7th and 8th graders prefer privileges, activities with friends, and specific positive feedback. Things like hat day, school wide hide and seek, Wildcat Cafe, Valentine's Parties, Trick or Treating, VIP lunch tables, etc. are all popular purchases.

Still other students never redeem their cash for anything. They view the online reward system as a video game like experience where they accumulate cash like points or badges. For these students, the amount of cash means more than the tangible, events or privileges, their cash could buy. While some PBIS schools worry about their older students not buying into the token economy, we view this as a really good thing. We believe that if student motivation is shifting from extrinsic to intrinsic, throughout middle school, then we're doing something very right. On the flip side, if the success of 8th grade student behavior hinged on their ability to purchase a jolly rancher, we'd be deeply worried that these short-term motivators were actually hindering real personal growth.

Remember, extrinsic rewards are designed to encourage initial positive behavior but are not a long-term plan to create sustained personalized growth. Schools that focus exclusively on PBIS without developing a student's deeper meaning for education can lead to big problems. In *It's the Mission, Not the Mandates*, **Dr. Amy Fast** lays out an absolutely compelling argument for society to redefine the purpose of public education. When educators help students find the "sweet spot" among academic achievement, soft skills, and internal drive, Dr. Fast says that our entire community benefits as students "leave school empowered by the deep belief that they matter in this world." Schools focus on extrinsic rewards should be inversely related with the increase in student age thus, as learners get older, we should be offering fewer and fewer extrinsic rewards.

Character Winners of the Month: Each month our staff nominates students for the character award, based on the word of the month. We send out a google form asking for nominations (who and why they deserve the award). Our office team poured through the nominations and ultimately selected 5-10 winners. Winners are called down to the office to be celebrated. We share a few heartfelt words, give them a character-related t-shirt, certificate, and take their picture to post on social media. They're even recognized at an all school assembly. Lastly, we call their parents and brag about them. These phone calls mean the world to both students and parents! And, if I'm being honest, their bucket fillers of positive energy for the adult educators who place the calls.

> *Intentional Tip:*
>
> *Do you know an educator that needs a win or a jolt of joy? Invite them to make a few of these positive phone calls, complete with script, info needed, and carved out time to place the calls. It's a next level leadership move!*

Academic Excellence Winners of the Month: We use a similar process, selection, and reward system with students ultimately receiving an academic excellence t-shirt. However, the focus is on growth mindset, grit, and perseverance. Improvement and effort are valued over outcome. Rather than just focusing on a kid who got all A's, we want to be targeted with both our criteria and our specific feedback about what made that student's month such a success. Once again, parents are contacted, and students are recognized in person and over social media.

Wildcat Card: Our wildcat card is another effective way to send specific feedback related to a student or teachers' demonstration of a character trait. Online cards are filled out and emailed to a paraprofessional in the building. Our paraprofessional then mail home a copy to the parents and posts another copy of the wildcat card around the school. As you might expect, these cards show up on refrigerators and social media as family and friends proudly share their son or daughter's accomplishments. I've also sent a few wildcat cards to parents to recognize their tireless work with their own child. The beauty of this being an online format is that once again students can give and receive these messages of positive feedback from anywhere. Regardless of attendance, online schooling or other barriers to the school day, positive information can be infused regularly.

REWARDS-REINFORCERS

> *Intentional Tip:*
>
> *Each year, we set aside intentional time for students to write wildcat cards for staff members. This extra dose of positivity is particularly impactful in late January or Early February when educational energy might be waning. These b-12 shots of awesomeness can reinvigorate a tired staff member.*

Additionally, as I mentioned above our paraprofessional educators input and track all wildcard cards to further add a layer of positive behavior data. Obviously, the goal is to ensure that everyone in Wildcat Nation receives specific annual love in the form of a personal feedback card. [*Side note, all discipline data, wildcat cards, and PBIS cash are tracked in the same PBIS rewards app. Thus, it's extremely easy for our PBIS/Leadership teams to drill down on a specific student or staff member to investigate any of the following: items being purchased with token economy, % of positive vs. consequence earned or given out, where a student is most successful, etc.*]. While the data tends to support many of our initial conclusions, sometimes revealing patterns can emerge that help shine a light on character deficiencies within the reward system.

Additional reward ideas include: a community spirit award (to recognize a community member's character), parent of the month award (to highlight parental character), and an educator of the week (to reinforce their service at school).

How would rewards and reinforcers that emphasize character impact the greater school culture?

What types of systems of reinforcement does your school currently have in place?

What data might you examine to evaluate the success of your school's rewards and reinforcements?

CHAPTER 6
ACCOUNTABILITY

Accountability in an Award Winning Culture refers to the mindset of obligation or willingness to accept responsibility for one's actions. Within the character domain we want to build in intentional opportunities to be accountable to modeling, teaching, and reinforcing character in action. These opportunities may be towards oneself, peers, and/or students.

Observe Me signs are an excellent way to increase accountability for ourselves as educators invite others to provide feedback on their class culture. At EMS, we've had some teachers create QR codes on the outside of their door for observers to quickly scan, as they walk into the classroom. The QR code takes observers to a google form to provide targeted feedback relating to culture. Teachers may seek feedback regarding personalized learning, student voice/choice, learner agency, flexible seating impact, embedded social-emotional elements, infusion of character traits, etc. These observable elements may tie directly to professional growth plans or be simply a catalyst for self-reflection. Lastly, they act as indirect guide to students of what class components their teachers truly value.

Other teachers at EMS, have written large '**Dear Students**' letters with poster paper and sharpie, outlining their hopes, dreams, and mission as a teacher; before hanging this up on their hallway door. I love the visual accountability of students walking into a classroom with educators' transparent visual commitment for all to see! An online educator might offer a similar transparency by displaying this type message on their social media banner, online learning management system or hung up behind them as a makeshift backdrop during teacher instructional videos. Sharing who we are as educators is always a strong move toward character accountability.

> DEAR STUDENTS,
>
> AS YOUR TEACHER IT IS MY JOB TO CREATE A CLASSROOM WHERE WE CAN LAUGH, LEARN, AND CARE FOR ONE ANOTHER, BECAUSE WE ARE A FAMILY.
>
> I WANT EVERYONE TO FEEL WELCOME, UNDERSTOOD, AND SAFE. I WANT YOU TO BE INSPIRED TO PURSUE YOUR DREAMS AND CREATE AMAZING WORK.
>
> YOU ARE THE REASON I AM HERE, AND I WANT TO INSPIRE YOU TO BECOME THE MOST AMAZING HUMANS YOU CAN BE.
>
> COME ON THIS JOURNEY WITH ME AND LET'S LEARN TOGETHER.
>
> SINCERELY,
> YOUR TEACHER

Last year, we taught our ASB officers how to explore their **Why**. Next, the officers taught our entire staff during an August inservice day. This purpose driven work with students and staff was the exact "sweet spot," in education that Dr. Fast wrote about. Moreover, in *Define Your Why*, by Barbara Bray, Barbara reveals that this critical work has been instrumental in Japan. Barbara explains that the Japanese word "ikigai means a reason for being." Similarly, to Dr. Fast's findings, Barbara suggests that the intersection of passion, mission, profession, and vocation leads to ikigai. What better form of accountability to ourselves, for both students and staff, than to truly be in touch with one's own life purpose? [

> *Intentional Tip:*
>
> *Check out Barbara's work on identifying what you LOVE, are GOOD AT, the WORLD NEEDS, and what you're VALUED FOR. Her book gives a number of practical activities to work through with students/staff.*

First of all, anytime you have staff listening to students share, present, or teach...it's a WONDERFUL moment! But more importantly, this type of venue encourages staff members to play, explore, and do the real work. Our staff wrote out their why on giant red hearts for our leadership students to ultimately post around the school. Again, a visual representation that says, *This is who I am and what I'm about.*

Educators must be lead learners who model a life-long love of curiosity. One powerful way we've managed to encourage accountability to character learning is with Mandy Ellis' "What I'm currently Reading" sign. When we take care to write out, talk about and share something we're reading or studying we model that learning is for EVERYONE. Additionally, by posting our current reading, it encourages others to ask questions or follow-up and ultimately hold us accountable as learners.

Obviously, tracking discipline and rewards as previously mentioned is another strong form of accountability. I have been pleasantly surprised by the teachers' reaction to see that they've given out FAR LESS positive feedback, than their peers. The visual nature of lining up rewards next to consequences for a teacher to view can be overwhelmingly powerful to promote self-change.

At EMS, accountability extends to our weekly advisory lessons. Our office staff push out into classrooms every week to take pictures/videos, learn with students, and increase visibility. There are a couple cool points of accountability. First of all, we're communicating to students that these character lessons are important because school leaders come in each week to check it out. Sometimes we're there to interact, participate or just watch. But each week we show up! Secondly, our presence reinforces with teachers that we want to see your A-game because these advisory character lessons are our tier 1 solution to whole child education. They truly impact our culture and climate at Wildcat Nation. This is not the time to phone it in to and retreat back into core content lessons. This is the time to maximize connection and relationship building during these character infused advisory opportunities. Lastly, there's multiple office staff that are committed to going into classrooms each week. Therefore, it's easy to unofficially assign an accountability partner to ensure I show up...even if I'm busy or not feeling up to it that day. Thus, there's built in accountability for the school leaders to be a part of advisory time.

How often do school leaders talk about getting into classrooms more regularly, only to have their job get in the way of making these visits a priority? When I know someone is counting on me or prepared to call me on being lazy during advisory time, I'm more likely to intentionally carve out this time to make it a personal priority. Additionally, we take a couple minutes to debrief what we observed, pictures or videos we captured for social media or students and staff that we may want to intentionally follow up with.

Accountability partners not only help with our to do list. They can also be instrumental to staying committed to our TO-BE list. Some of my accountability partners have kept me focused on my "why" by asking me tough questions like:

- What need is this student's behavior communicating?

- How would you feel if you were in this student's life?

- Are there students who you haven't checked-in with recently, who might need your support?

These are a few of the simple questions posed by peers that have helped me realign my thinking, when I've felt stuck. And we can be accountability partners to others who may feel frustrated or overwhelmed.

I've had the privilege of working with my wife at Wildcat Nation for years. As a fourth-generation educator, Jen comes from a long lineage of talented game-changers. Her family includes superintendents, lunch ladies, paraprofessionals, teachers, principals, and everything in between. Family reunions are like educational conferences. And though her parents are retired, family dinners are similar to an educational staffing. I often feel like I must be up to date on my brain research, ed policy, or have some interesting stories to share over our meal. Quite frankly, Jen and her family have forgotten more about education than I'll ever know. Jen is simply the BEST teacher I've ever worked with. She has a genius mind, huge heart, and servant's work-ethic. And she's been an important accountability partner to me.

One day, I was expressing frustration about an at-risk student who was off task, mouthing off, and generally overactive around the school. Gerry, a blond 6th grade busy body was the poster child for frequent classroom disruptions and teacher heartache. He absolutely led the school in principal visits, referrals, and poor grades. Knowing that he was highly successful in Jen's classroom, I couldn't understand what Jen was seeing in him that I was missing. While using her best listening skills, she managed to both challenge a few of my assumptions and share a little bit of background on what she knew about Gerry.

Gerry was a clear-cut ACES student who had dealt with mental health, poverty, academic struggles, a history of domestic violence, and substance abuse. In no uncertain terms, she explained to me that the only thing I could change about Gerry was how I was interacting and relating with him. She really helped open my eyes to how little I actually knew about him and how I hadn't taken the time and energy to learn his story.

ACCOUNTABILITY

Following our conversation, my focus moved entirely on how to connect with him rather than manage him. Her willingness to hear my frustration but then challenge and inspire me to be a more empathic counselor helped me transform my relationship with Gerry. And regular reminders from our accountability partners can yield life altering results for our students.

My office dream team provides me with consistent accountability partners outside of the school day. For instance, during school closures or off-peak school seasons, these regular conversations, texts, and virtual touch points ensure that we all stay on track to our bigger mission of creating joyful learning for all students.

Successful leaders have multiple accountability partners. In *Daring Greatly* Brené Brown refers to these key accountability partners as her "square squad." And my wife along with the dream team definitely are in my squad!

Who is YOUR accountability partner(s)?

How are they keeping you focused on Character Building?

What if WE evaluated our day based on the number of hearts we touched?

CHAPTER 7
COMMON LANGUAGE

I recently engaged in a discussion with a fellow educator about the need for a canned social-emotional/character curriculum. While they recognized the value in teaching soft skills, within the classroom, they did not understand the need to purchase a set curriculum. Their belief is that teachers can simply embed this work within their content area and render expensive structured whole child programs obsolete. Her essential question is why pay for something I can just create on my own? She's partly right you know. Relationship-driven educators who have a strong understanding of whole child work probably can create amazing material to use with students. Heck, some of the top character or social-emotional programs on the market were actually originally created by exceptional classroom teachers.

Of course, it's naive to assume that all educators are equally equipped and trained to be able to independently create whole child content that is capable of producing Award Winning Culture. Curriculum is critical to a school's unified approach to whole child development. And the discrepancy largely speaks to a successful outcome of those schools who take the time to craft an Award Winning Culture in partnership with a set of lessons: Common Language.

COMMON LANGUAGE

Schools that are willing to collaborate toward a cultural masterpiece with universal character lessons ensure that all students and staff are receiving a similar verbiage. Common language is such a helpful tool in the counseling setting and or discipline setting as conversations can take on more meaning when all parties understand the language on a personal connection level. Discipline conversations naturally lend themselves more closely to resemble coaching rather than consequence based in nature. And the level of personal insight that can be reached for students who are used to exploring purpose, meaning, and relationship connections is a game-changer. For example, a discussion on right and wrong becomes relatively straightforward when students have learned how and where they fit into the greater family of Wildcat Nation. This Award Winning Culture mentality is akin to a successful sports team. The best teams are willing to serve and sacrifice for the betterment of the team. They fear letting down teammates or coaches and tend to bring their best in all interactions. This commitment to character begins with removing any potential language barriers and all being on the same page with expectations, vision, and what it means to do the right thing when no else is looking.

Common language also extends to parents and community. How rich can family conversations about character become when parents know specifics about weekly lessons being taught? Each week we send out information over all social media platforms to parents on the week's character lessons, objectives, and language being taught during advisory. This information is a wonderful conversation starter to parents and allows them to reinforce the same messages, ideals, and character focus that we're striving for each day.

Furthermore, when you lead with character, the words you use become the community wide vernacular. It's so meaningful and rewarding to see coaches, local businesses, and media are sharing Wildcat Nation character language in their settings. I simply love meeting people within our community that already understand what our school stands for.

Lastly, students don't even need to be physically present at school to stay committed to a common set of language. Recently, during a COVID-19 outbreak that required school closures, one benefit of staying focused during times of crisis was in our use of universal words and ideas: Wildcat Nation, Kindness, Character, Excellence, Community, Empathy, etc. When everyone's speaking the same language, we effectively provide everyone with the same compass to navigate their way to doing the right thing at Wildcat Nation.

What is your school's universal definition for constructs like Kindness, Empathy, and Service?

What does your school value and how is that communicated to everyone?

How might having a common language keep a large school community focused in the same direction?

CHAPTER 8
TRAINING

Training was a key character aspect that I overlooked, when we started our whole child journey years ago. Back then, we believed that if lessons were already created and required no extra prep, teachers would make their own success. This short-sided view didn't explore student training, support staff training, nor provide the front-line teachers with the necessary foundational knowledge to turn lessons on a page into character gold.

> **Award Winning Culture seeks out varied and ongoing training opportunities that facilitate an intentional development of one's own character.**

Who's observing our character? And what might they notice? Are you willing to engage someone who can't possibly benefit you? Are you capable of putting your agenda aside for someone else in need? Who are you...when you think no one's paying attention?

I assure you that if you think you're reaching students on a school-wide whole child model but do not have a highly developed plan for ongoing training of all school community members, you simply aren't fostering an Award Winning Culture.

As a point of reference, we provided three staff training opportunities before teachers ever taught a single character lesson. We worked exclusively with the curriculum developers to deliver a chance to live the work on multiple occasions. Those training were the most impactful professional development I've experienced in my 20 years in education. As good as it was, co-founder **John Norlin** reiterated to us that "we need to be reminded more than we need to be taught." The underlying message being that while most educators understand the basic principles of modeling high character, frequent reminders ensure that we stay laser focused on our school mission and personal WHY.

His passionate plea fueled our desire to build out a three-year plan on staff training. Indeed, almost everything we did with staff development during those three years related directly back to whole child work. This included multiple book studies, formal inservice, staff meetings, and PD training. Additionally, we sent nearly every certificated staff member (including new folks) to one and two-day CharacterStrong curriculum workshops. And at EMS all means all! Beyond certificated staff, all of the following educators have received extensive training: paraprofessionals, secretaries, custodians, school resource officer, etc. With each new employee coming into Wildcat Nation we took advantage of the opportunity to send a new wave of staff to be trained in the delivery of our character work.

Beyond specific character training, whole child work requires an examination of other barriers to learning. I worked with some area experts to deliver staff training on all of the following topics: anxiety, LGBTQ, poverty, culture, suicide, sexual abuse, and trauma. We even brought in highly acclaimed author, speaker, and leadership consultant James C Hunter to personally work with our school on character development.

TRAINING

These experts guided staff into a deeper empathy of how to become highly effective with all students.

The impact and personal growth that many of us received was plentiful! Perhaps, no one person exemplified more growth than a long-time beloved EMS secretary. Through the years, this wonderful soul had become jaded and hardened by the tribulations of public education. Her active participation in formal training and ongoing book studies led to an incredible character resurgence. She became such a champion of this whole child work she was recognized for her excellence in education at a district board meeting. Not bad for a woman who contemplated retirement just a year before EMS began focusing on character development. However, my favorite part of her story is that she ended up teaching some of this character work to an adult bible study group. I'm so proud of her!

Additionally, school wide book studies on leadership development, character, and trauma-invested practices helped elevate our training to the next level. Sometimes these extended learning opportunities led to school and/or district partnerships with authors, speakers, and experts. After our staff read, "Fostering Resilient Learners" and "Relationships, Responsibility, and Regulation" by Kristin Van Marter Souers and Pete Hall, our district reached out to Kristin to offer additional district-wide training.

Great training opportunities are all around us. And it doesn't even require a school building. For instance, the Teach Better Team has created a highly impactful online academy for professional development and ongoing learning that educators can do in the comfort of their own home. Nothing like getting better, while you're in your pajamas! Character development on my own time. LOVE IT!

> ## When educators are given the tools, time, and support to dig in on their own character, the work that they can lead, teach, and model is MINDBLOWING!

While we were confident that the character lessons would strongly support our whole child work, we also knew that training and teaching students would require multiple touch points. Thus, we contracted with several local agencies to provide additional school-wide social-emotional training.

We determined that our health classes were a natural spot to interject additional training opportunities. Our local health district provided hands on prevention instruction to students on the following topics: drug, alcohol, and vaping. Additionally, we arranged for our community Support Resource Advocacy Center (SARC) to deliver lessons in internet safety, sexual harassment, and cyber-bullying. Lastly, our regional youth suicide prevention team shared curricula for our health teachers to have rich discussions on depression and suicide.

In my campfire analogy earlier, you learned the cultural weight that leadership students bear in an Award Winning Culture. It won't surprise you that we put a heavy emphasis on training our leadership students as well. Beyond additional CharacterStrong lessons in leadership class, leadership students go through a two-day leadership bootcamp in August and a leadership workshop in late January. A select group of leadership students were also taken to our statewide leadership conference: SERVUS. This six-hour training gives students a chance to work with students, educators, and experts from around our Washington state leadership scene.

TRAINING

The key takeaway on training is that it's never done. We're always looking to strengthen the character of the leaders (both student/staff) who model, teach, and practice this work on a daily basis.

How are you currently teaching character development to staff?

What training do your student leaders need to play a larger role in creating an Award Winning Culture?

What are some creative ways to infuse regular training into educators outside of the classroom?

CHAPTER 9
EXPERIENTIAL

At its most basic level, experiential learning is doing and then reflecting on the doing. I'm a huge fan of experiential learning! I believe that character and social emotional work can't just be something we talk about, but it must be experienced in the real world, in order to truly touch minds and hearts. In this section, I'll share a few of our favorite experiential whole child activities that have impacted our school culture.

The Wildcat Award: We originally heard about an idea from Norlin of CharacterStrong called the "Golden Broom." He spoke about organizing a group of leadership students to help the custodians empty the trash cans. While we loved the thinking, we had a larger community-wide vision for what this could become. And over time, found an intentional model to elevate this to next-level special. Our version of the golden broom which we call the Wildcat Award is:

> **A demonstration of SERVICE to those who SERVE US!**

Anyone in or out of the school community is fair game to receive the wildcat award. Essentially, it's an opportunity to overwhelm someone with LOVE through a heartfelt surprise. But the intention behind all the work is what makes this so spectacular. Here's how it works:

One of our leadership classes discusses a deserving adult or adults to present the award to. Sometimes they ask around, talk with friends or visit with other adults in the building to learn about some amazing demonstrations of character. The class votes on 1-3 people that they want to surprise. Next the leadership class breaks into small teams: recon, presentation, swag, misdirection, and video.

Recon: Research background knowledge necessary to pull off a surprise. This may include discovering favorite snacks, goodies, planning time frame to present the award, details, etc. It could include work schedule, habits, or personality insights. For instance, is the person who's receiving the Wildcat on s gluten free or diabetic diet? How do they feel about public displays of attention? What time of the day is ideal to pull off a surprise? Basically, any information that will be needed to make it happen.

Presentation: This team is in charge of writing and ultimately orally presenting the award to the person(s). This requires draft, rehearsal, and presentation practice. This may be a small intimate presentation in a classroom, hallway, or office, a whole school setting, or a public presentation at an out of school or outdoor event.

SWAG: This team is responsible for helping secure and or create posters, decorations, costumes, goodies, treats, award certificates, etc. They do whatever it takes to help transform the environment into a full-fledged demonstration of love. It might be as elaborate as dressing up like the award recipient, baking treats, or as simple as making a personalized poster, handwritten card or drawing to use during the presentation.

Misdirection: Because of the surprise factor, there's a certain level of misdirection that every successful wildcat award requires. The surprise factor plays heavily on the power of the moment! The misdirection team devises a plan to pull the entire event together. Perhaps, it requires getting someone out of their office, or coordinating with multiple educators. On occasion this may entail a phone call to a local business, family member, or boss. This group of positive magician-like kindness ambassadors turn the Wildcat Award into an elaborate piece of theater! With the goal being to shower the unsuspecting with admiration. Afterall, love is magic!

Video: Our video team might film the Wildcat Award in action, create a personalized thank-you video from friends, family and/or students or just help tease upcoming wildcat award moments. They a so take photos and/or coordinate with yearbook members to get footage of the award presentation.

Examples of award recipients:

- Presenting the PATIENT bus drivers with homemade cookies and hot chocolate.

- Celebrating a COMMITTED staff member becoming an official US Citizen by lining up to shake her hand and then giving her flowers.

- Presenting our HUMILITY fueled secretaries with GIANT thank-you cards and gardening supplies because they love to garden.

- Surprising our SELFLESS night custodian with a collection of hugs and money to support her dream of taking a Vegas vacation.

- Acknowledging a beloved KIND and PATIENT paraprofessional with handwritten letters and treats because she helped students learn how to write.

- Creating a personalized video with family and friends for 3 outstanding educators and watching it, while enjoying a personalized dessert bar.

- Visiting the local grocery store to take goodies and share a heartfelt face-to-face thank-you with every PATIENT store employee for putting up with middle schoolers coming in and out of their store each week.

- Providing coffee, donuts, and personal fellowship to our community veterans before honoring their COMMITMENT and SACRIFICE at a moving assembly.

- A group of band students publicly recognize their band director with speech and personal tribute because his PASSION inspires them.

- Providing lunch to recognize KIND educators.

- Providing flowers and baby gear to a teacher who SELFLESSLY adopts a child.

- Arranging for others to do RESPECTED administration's lunch duty so that they could have some relaxation time to eat some handmade refreshments.

- Cleaning up the cafeteria during the lunch hour for our COMMITTED day custodian so that he can enjoy his gluten free treats on the stage, in front of the entire school.

Intentionality: You'll notice that each award is personal to the individual in set-up, reason, identified character trait, setting, and acknowledgement. Sometimes awards are given because a person is loved. Other folks win awards because students recognize the role they play in creating an Award Winning Culture at Wildcat Nation. Occasionally, students select a Wildcat recipient based on a special event or circumstances.

We've even had award recipients selected because students wanted to CHOOSE LOVE with an adult who they themselves didn't even particularly like. However, they believed that this form of positive recognition was exactly what a difficult person most needed. Oftentimes the hardest people to love are the ones who most need it. This is such a powerful application of student empathy and a lesson that will stick with them for the rest of their lives.

Debriefing the award execution with student leaders afterwards is an important element of crystallizing the character-building learning moments through individual and group reflection. I'm blown away when students talk about how they felt when showering an adult with intentional kindness. We know these lessons are sticking with kids because they refer back to these experiential moments of awesomeness years later.

The wildcat utilizes a concept I refer to as the **Triangle of JOY**. Like a triangle, there are three distinct points that inspire joy in each award. The first part of the triangle is the rush of joy that the **Student Leaders** feel when putting together the award. There is such a powerful sense of pride, accomplishment, and joy in the pre-planning, execution, and reflection after the award. In fact, as a counselor observing and participating in these after event reflections the learning takeaways are priceless. I'll never forget hearing a group of students talk about how tired they were after cleaning up the cafeteria all hour for our custodian. When they made the revelation that it took 25 students, just to do his job...MINDBLOWING! Having deep empathy and understanding of another person's world is an unbelievable gift to provide our students. It ends up being an intense instance of personal joy for them as their learning becomes filled with purpose and meaning.

Naturally, there's a surprising moment of joy for the second leg of the triangle: **Award Recipient**. Essentially, we're communicating to someone all of the following: *I see you, I love you, and thank-you for making our school community special.* These moments are often filled with tears, laughter, smiles, and connection. The award recipient is often overcome with bucket filling joy that fuels their work for some time. I've heard comments like "this will keep me going for a while" or "that just made my year." The joy that these recognized adults experience is pretty long lasting!

The third and often overlooked point on the triangle of joy is from the **Observers** who witness or hear about the award. Because the Wildcat Award is done in a public setting many people (students, educators, parents, community members) may witness the act of kindness. As we know from research, observing kindness fills others with joy and fuels their desire to create a similar experience for people in their lives. These ripples of kindness can cycle through a community like doing the wave at a sporting arena. Additionally, we take videos and photos of pre-planning and execution of each award and post those on social media. These postings effectively magnify the number of wildcat award observers and ultimately the individuals experiencing joy.

AWARD WINNING CULTURE

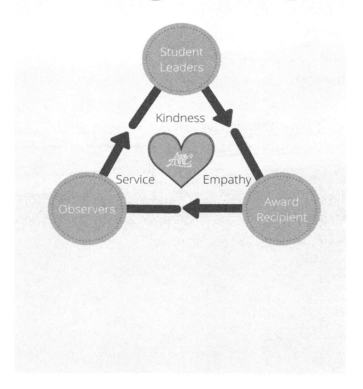

Evidence of the third leg of the triangle is how many students ask about participating in future Wildcat Awards, make suggestions on who should be nominated, or positively interact with live Wildcat Award presentations or on social media posts.

By capitalizing on the Triangle of Joy, we intentionally craft an Award Winning Culture while filling students with a deep connection to brightening the days of others. When a school commits to creating an exceptional learning environment and taking the time to see and recognize individuals as valuable members of the family, learning isn't just a possibility but an all out likely outcome in this joy rooted educational system.

EXPERIENTIAL

Other experiential joy can be generated in combination with PBIS events. One of our most popular PBIS rewards events we've created is called the **Wildcat Cafe**. In essence, we reimagine and repurpose two teachers' classrooms and transform them into a coffee style cafe between 7:25 a.m.-7:50 a.m. (school officially starts at 7:55 a.m.). In its dressed down form, we are essentially providing a place for students to enjoy hot cocoa, apple cider or Italian soda a few times per year. And outside observers less experienced in intentionality may miss all the beauty of what turns this seemingly typical reward into cultural magic. How on earth could a cup of hot chocolate elicit a sense of wonder and enchantment? Let's examine.

Pulling off a Wildcat Cafe requires all of the following teams within our leadership class: Baristas, Servers, Check-in, Hostess, and Set-up. Our wildcat cafe is about recreating the experience of going to a charming cafe complete with amazing service, ambience, and human connection over a cup of joe (ahh...I mean cocoa). In order to create this powerful moment, all 5 leadership teams will work together in conjunction with other school volunteers to make an incredible over the top event.

Set-up: These students stay after school the afternoon before the event to decorate the rooms, in order to create a wonderful cafe setting. There are tablecloths, centerpieces, menus, signs, etc. Oftentimes, they create table games or activities that students can enjoy with their friends. They also work with our music department to either arrange live entertainment OR create a playlist of soothing songs to enchant with background music. Lastly, they help take down the entire event in under 5 minutes.

Check-in: Students within the check-in group, use iPads/iPods to virtually check students in using the PBIS app. It is important to note that prior to using PBIS Rewards app, we simply took Wildcat Paper Cash (token economy) and provided wristbands. These students run our wildcat cash shop using the same technology and become experts at quickly facilitating PBIS purchases.

Hostess: Upon entrance into the cafe, students are warmly greeted by a hostess who asks them how many students are in their party? Yes, students actually practice how to greet, seat, and interact with other student guests. The hostess then seats them, orients them to the cafe and lets the server in that area know that new "customers" are there.

Server: Welcome each new group of customers by sharing the available items (i.e. different flavors of Italian soda), variations within the items (i.e. marshmallow, whipped cream, or candy cane topping), and then take the groups order. Servers wear Wildcat Nation inspired aprons and are prepared with a small notepad and pen to record requests.

Baristas: As you'd expect, our baristas make the drink. They accommodate food allergies, specific requests, and then ensure that the server takes the right order to the correct table. As you can imagine practice making the drink is a highly important job and these students relish the opportunity to taste test their own work!

All leadership students report to the wildcat cafe at 7:00 a.m. sharp to prepare for their 30-minute character performance. We also offer complimentary Starbucks coffee to any educator who wants to come down and check it out which serves as another intentional decision to increase adult participation. There are typically two other adult bouncers (teachers) who help create the ambience of whimsy and a handful of student volunteers who help out between 7:30 a.m.-7:50 a.m. At the conclusion, the entire event is packed up and taken down so that our 1st period class may begin at 7:55 a.m.

So, how successful is the wildcat cafe?

Students typically begin sitting in line for the cafe at 7:00 a.m. By 7:15 am there is a line 30 deep, to get into the cafe. We have even had to purchase cones and rope barriers to help manage the line of students waiting to access the cafe. As a reference point, the first time we put on the cafe, after serving 100+ students, we still turned away 50 students who couldn't even get in. Over time, we've created VIP passes, a to-go line, and expanded the event by as much as 10 minutes. Students have overwhelmingly loved the event!

Why go through all of this trouble? We've tried traditional hot chocolate giveaways, and nothing has reached the same crescendo of positivity and servant leadership practice as the Wildcat Cafe. Students repeatedly share how much they love the experience. Many of our students of poverty rarely go out to eat and never have been to a coffee style cafe. They appreciate being served and shown love and attention in such a uniquely intentional way. Students write unprompted handwritten notes of thanks, post touching pictures and moments on social media, and are EXCEPTIONALLY well behaved in the cafe. Our students realize that other area schools are not creating Award Winning Culture with this level of intentionality and care. And, similar to the Wildcat Award, the Wildcat Cafe offers us the highly coveted triangle of joy for workers, participants, and observers.

Additionally, the Wildcat Cafe capitalizes on something Dan Heath and Chip Heath write about in their bestselling book *The Power of Moments*. In their inspiring work, the Heath brothers explain that moments can be intentionally created that become game-changing culture builders. And very often these profound experiences play out in one of the following elements: moment of elevation, moment of insight, moment of pride or moment of connection. The fact that the Wildcat Cafe touches on several of these defining opportunities speaks volumes to the impact on all students' school experience. And I believe that Dan and Chip would be impressed at how equally both student leaders AND student patrons, at the cafe, are impacted by this form of whole child education.

While The Wildcat Award and Wildcat Cafe require more extensive planning and preparation, some experiential learning can offer relatively spontaneous shots of cultural positivity with much less elbow grease. **Heartfelt Handshakes** is a quick yet powerful character demonstration that's easy to set-up. The only requirement is a group of students and a packet of post-it-notes or notecards. Basically, any group of students write down something they like about the target of their affection. It could be a sentence or just a word. But the more specific and personal the better. Everybody writes a post-it-note or card to the same person. Then the group of students all line-up, in a single file line near the person. One by one each person, makes eye contact, shakes the person's hand, says "thank-you or I appreciate you" and then hands them the sticky note which details WHY they appreciate them. After everyone has presented them their thank-you, the group of students break out in a round of applause and then disappear. The point is not to linger around looking for thank-you and appreciation. It's designed to be a short (less than 3 minutes) high energy moment that leaves the target person feeling AMAZING! Once again, the element of surprise and the triangle of joy show up in tandem as folks are recognized. We've used this form of thank-you for students, staff, and community. It never fails to deliver whimsical positivity.

Our **Wildcat Snack Cart** is a 100% stolen idea from wonderful educators around the world. The dose of intentionality with our snack cart is that it's completely kid run. Students are the ones delivering goodies to teachers and educators and we do an exceptional job planning out the best time of day to hit each adult. For instance, some teachers love to invite the snack cart into their room and make a big thank-you production out of the moment. Other teachers hate to be interrupted while they teach. Students know to return later, when an adult educator is busy or in the middle of something. Thus, students formulate a plan of how to pull off this simple thank-you in the least intrusive way. We also pride ourselves on having a variety of options to meet dietary or allergy needs, healthy vs. indulgent goodies, and still provide ease of transportation. As you'd expect, students must learn a good amount about their teachers likes, dislikes, and preferences. Therefore, the wildcat snack cart provides a built-in relationship development component as students are interested in learning about their teachers. As with all wildcat experiential character learning filled with kindness, service, and empathy, the snack cart shows up all over social media. This ensures students, parents, and even the community can benefit from witnessing moments of intentional joy.

Following any of our experiential character-building moments, leadership students reflect on ways to improve, takeaways, how they felt, and what they observed and learned about spreading kindness through servant leadership. These reflections might take the form of discussions, writing, or video in nature. But the key is to intentionally build in time and expectation to further crystallize character development, and connection to purpose. We want students to openly identify examples of all three parts of the triangle of Joy.

Another element of high impact experiential learning is: **Timing**. As any great comedian will tell you: 'timing is everything.' When trying to be intentional with when to do a Wildcat Award, Snack Cart, etc. and WHO to recognize, try applying some specific thinking around timing. Are there natural dips in energy within the school year? When are the high stress times for specific educators and/or students? Here's a small list of character opportunities that can prove to be a lifesaver in the right moment:

- Tech week for drama kids and/or drama teacher.

- March/April for special education staff dealing with last minute evaluation requests and IEP completion.

- The first week of school for lunch ladies as they deal with student orientation in the lunchroom.

- ALL TEACHERS/STUDENTS during STATE TESTING.

- Administration before Christmas break, spring break and summer break as they attempt to manage elevated student excitement and challenging behavior.

- Counselors before or after winter break as they often amplify student support due to increased family stress of their students.

- ELA teachers right after essays are turned in.

- ALL STUDENTS during finals week.

- Music students or music teachers during concert season.

- Coaches and/or athletes during playoffs/districts/state sporting season.

- Secretaries during open registration before school starts.

- Custodians during lunch time.

- Speech therapist right before consult week.

Obviously, this list is not meant to be exhaustive and is truly the tip of the iceberg, when thinking about timing of increased positivity through experiential learning.

Can experiential learning occur outside of school? YES! Building in experiential character building or SEL moments just requires a bit of creativity: students might rake leaves for a neighbor, cook a meal for their family, or send a handwritten letter to a former impactful teacher. This list of character opportunities in an online or virtual school setting is literally only limited to our own imaginations.

While there are numerous other experiential examples of character building at Wildcat Nation (Podcasting, AWC-TV, Digital Leadership, etc.), I don't share experiential learning with you in hopes that you'll simply replicate our wildcat award or heartfelt handshake. Instead, I believe the real value in this chapter is studying the intentionality that goes into every character-building opportunity.

Sometimes character-building events and academic content mastery are married together to create exceptional whole child teaching. As is the case with **Rae Hughart's**, *Teach Further* model. Rae is an award winning teacher, speaker, and author who also happens to be the Director of Training and Development for the Teach Better Team. *Teach Further* combines core curriculum, creativity, and connections while giving students the opportunity to participate in themed internships, sponsored by local businesses. During these experiential moments, tied to the community, learners directly apply their soft skills in conjunction with the subject area (i.e. math, history, LA, science, etc.) to create meaning around the concepts they are learning within their academic content. Thus, teaching students how to greet, serve, persevere, or brighten someone's day has real meaning within the context of an actual job or career. Teaching learners that kindness, service, and empathy aren't just a good idea but are also actually crucial to their future career success has a deep societal workplace impact that leadership gurus like Simon Sinek seem to be on fire to support. Indeed, building high character future leaders through experiential opportunities as a child creates a positive pipeline to making a better world!

What role does experiential learning play in your school's whole child work?

How will you apply this level of intentionality to your own school's experiential learning opportunities?

How might you capitalize on the Triangle of JOY in your school's next kindness event, activity or moment?

CHAPTER 10
REMINDERS

My principal cautions against the mistake of drinking from the fire hose when creating change. Instead, she preaches the better choice for long term success as in a drip, drip, drip style of a leaky faucet. Her analogy conjures up a visual image of favoring a steady dose of reminders over one flooding of learning. Learning research supports her belief that character learning (much like math, science, or history) is recalled much more effectively if the learning occurs over an extended pericd of time. Thus, a cramming session on character really doesn't do much. It is probably why school's get very little bang for their buck with one shot kindness assemblies by masterful guest speakers. While an inspiring presenter can be a catalyst to create significant cultural change, students and even staff need to hear, see, and experience regular character reminders in order to learn on a deep visceral level.

> **Award Winning Culture provides frequent reminders of character.**

Each month we hang posters, displays, and/or signs to deliver remembrance of the character trait of the month. These quotes, anecdotes, pictures, and people give students and staff subtle reminders as they move about the school. These can show up in hallways or classroom walls, bulletin boards, bathroom stalls, library display cases, college & career center, main office, stairways, etc. They can be student created, content specific, or adult manufactured. These are not just permanent landscapes that ultimately become overlooked and are relegated to background filler because of daily observance. Instead, these items are regularly changed and updated throughout the year to provide novel reminders of the character work happening at school. Ideally all of the above show up in a big way, throughout the year. Here's a few **Visual** specific examples:

Character Trees: In the winter, Wildcat Nation students set-up and decorate multiple trees that focus exclusively on character traits, common language from our whole child curriculum, and our wildcat nation brand. Ornaments are pictures of EMS moments of character, common language, and/or character words. While the trees may offer some specific purpose such as a place to put gifts and/or food for families in need, more importantly, they offer a strong visual reminder of our school-wide focus on character with a thread of connection to childhood gift giving such as Christmas, Hannika, or Festivus (a silly nod to my Seinfeld friends).

Art Projects: Our art teacher frequently infuses whole child themes within a project. One of my favorite themes came after a Houston Kraft assembly on Choosing Love. The teacher created a platform for students to paint a tile mosaic with their connection to Kraft's phrase - "Choose Love." After presenting their artistic takeaway from the assembly, to the class, the students created one giant mural using all of the student work to hang in the main office as a visual reminder of the character lessons learned from Kraft's message.

Significant Leaders: A history teacher organized a project where students identified a great leader (i.e. Walter Payton, Jesus, Martin Luther King Jr, Oprah, Abraham Lincoln, etc.) and created a short write-up with pictures to be presented and then hung on a bulletin board in the hallway.

Library Display: Our amazing librarian creates regular character-themed displays that encourage thinking, reading, and exploring both in the library and in the display case outside of the library. The goal being to always keep these character traits, and other soft skill points of emphasis at the forefront of student, staff, and parents' minds.

Principal Monday Memo: Every Monday our principal sends out a *Monday Memo* to staff with important points to know which include: calendar of events, news and noteworthy information, staff celebrations, etc. However, without fail, our principal embeds an excerpt, video, quote, etc. that is character related. By keeping character a focus point for teachers each Monday, our administration subtly encourages and models this work for teachers.

By intentionally modeling this character reminder, other staff members have developed similar character connections within their classrooms as both entry task and content preset. For example, several teachers start each day with a quote on character. Then teachers connect the quote to that day or week's lesson. For example, a quote on resilience might be used to open class instruction by a math teacher delving into challenging work with fractions. The more we keep character on the minds and hearts of the adults who most impact student character—-THE BETTER.

Obviously, this *Monday Memo* must change in form somewhat during extended absences from school. During an elevated crisis or just normal online learning setting, leaders must default away from only sending long emails and instead create rich videos that allow staff members to personally connect with their leader's message. Seeing a leader's face and voice can be comforting when physical distance prevents in-person contact.

Character Lesson Overview: Providing character lessons to our office team, parents, and community through social media, email, newsletter, etc., we're able to bring a weekly reminder of what it means to do the right thing at Wildcat Nation through character-led leadership. I'm amazed how many schools take the time to teach SEL and/or character and then fail to share those lessons beyond the classrooms. If our goal is teaching learners to apply and generalize these skills, in all parts of their life, we must ensure that all adults are in position to reinforce these soft skill takeaways outside of the classroom.

Yearbook: While most schools create yearbooks, they may forget to infuse Character reminders within the pages. Our yearbook provides another place to infuse character traits, powerful character quotes, and pictures of our character winners of the month. By making character a piece of their lifelong memory etched in their school yearbook, we ensure that our school focus is front and center for anyone who thumbs threw our beautifully designed memory keepsake. Furthermore, having a group of yearbook students with a focus for seeking out meaningful character moments and armed with a camera in hand, ensures that additional reminders of doing the right thing are front and center.

Character reminders also take the form of **Auditory** in nature. These reminders, while not seen, are certainly still absorbed through listening:

Morning Announcement: Each day provides an Award Winning Culture with an opportunity to promote doing the right thing with the intentional selection of a meaningful quote, quick story, or inspiring words from the person on the announcements. Don't just read the pledge and tell students what's for lunch. Make your time and their attention count! Infuse some purpose and character with a few well-planned words. For example, using character specific language to reinforce and remind this work can occur during routine announcements.

"Awesome job by our 7th grade B football team yesterday showing a COMMITMENT to not giving up as they stormed all the way back in the 4th quarter to win the game!"

"Congrats to Connor for leading the 8th grade A basketball team with 8 assists. His SELFLESSNESS on the court really paved the way for an incredible team win!"

Dream Team: Our office staff calls ourselves the dream team because we believe we're fortunate enough to be working with the best of the best. Our gratitude for our office colleagues extends beyond administration and counselors to include secretaries, administrative assistants, school psychologist, speech therapist, and school resource officer.

Each Monday morning, we begin the week with a regular Dream Team meeting. This standing meeting allows us to collaborate and coordinate efforts to best serve and support the school. I'm shocked how infrequently these types of meetings are happening in education as it sets the tone and focus for staff. As we review attendance, academic, discipline, and personal/social data, we are able to design specific interventions, ideas, and help that directly tie to student, staff, and parent character. Additionally, we carve out time for character specific book studies, challenges, reflections, picking student or staff character winners, etc. This intentional time is set aside to stoke our school-wide character fire, review accountability of ourselves and peers, and dig in on taking our character work to the next level.

Staff Meetings: Many top leaders advocate for NOT having staff meetings just for the sake of having a meeting. They make a strong plea to leaders to stop wasting employee time; however, when real purpose, connection, and reflection exist, staff meetings can be invaluable. Meetings provide a platform for staff to share ideas, challenge thinking, and explore character in a community learning format. We have leveraged staff meetings as a way to remind peers and ourselves about our whole child work. For instance, staff may take time to write Wildcat Cards, share moments of gratitude, connect the unconnected, or share their "why" with each other for teaching social-emotional learning and/or character.

In the *Happiness Advantage,* Shawn Achor reminds us that two minutes of gratitude for 21 days can transform our happiness quotient. As mentioned earlier, we have used staff meetings as a successful training ground to explore a variety of topics that impact the whole child which includes modeling gratitude. Gratitude letters, lists, and reminders are highly effective happiness generators during holiday breaks or when learning might be virtual. While breaks and closures might mean time off for some, Award Winning Culture continues to emphasize key elements that students and staff might miss while apart. Furthermore, as you've probably already figured out, video conferencing ensures that staff meetings can continue even when the school building isn't open.

Morning Meetings can be a great classroom strategy to connect, regulate, and address student needs. Whether it's in a circle on the floor, in small group learning pods, or full class discussions from their desks, these meetings can provide a safe check-in time for students and teachers to review what doing the right thing might look like today. For instance, Katelynn Giordano digital content editor for the Teach Better Team and 6th grade ELA rock star teacher, advocates for the power of morning meetings. In a blog post by Katelynn, during the COVID-19 outbreak, Katelynn illustrates how important these regular "family circle times" have become in her Illinois middle level classroom. She explains how she developed a Flipgrid for her homeroom class which allow students to record their responses for their weekly Friday Circle Time. Thanks to creative thinking educators like Katelyn school culture is not sacrificed during distance learning opportunities.

Experiential learning shows up as a powerful tool in creating an Award Winning Culture through character, excellence, and community. Moreover, it can also serve as a helpful character reminder, when schools create exceptional platforms such as a podcast, tv or radio show. These platforms provide a way to deliver regular auditory reminders, examples, and stories of doing the right thing when they're played over the speaker, shown on cafeteria or library televisions, during assemblies, or blasted in classrooms by teachers during class.

Social Media: Obviously, poignant pictures, videos, and posts lend themselves to visual and even auditory character reminders by putting out frequent messages of positivity, community building, and social-emotional practice. However, when we put students in the driver's seat of digital leadership, we establish an experiential character-themed reminder to student leaders. In *Social Leadia*, Jennifer Casa-Todd explains:

"A positive digital presence happens effortlessly when you embrace digital leadership."

For example, at Wildcat Nation, we've created a **Human Wildcats** social media Instagram account. This student run leadership account allows students to share positive student and staff stories. Each post includes a picture or video with the student or staff member answering a character related question. Here's a few examples:

- What character trait is most important to you and why?

- Who do you look up to and why?

- Who at EMS inspires you and why?

- What would you like to do in the future and how will you get there?

- What's your favorite part about Wildcat Nation?

- What does it mean to be a leader?

- What's the kindest thing someone has ever done for you?

- What do you wish people knew about you?

- What advice would you give to future students to find success at EMS?

By keeping our school-wide eye on the character prize and meeting students where they are (on social media), we're able to subtly and consistently remind everyone to do the right thing! Incidentally, students can create this same character reminder through online platforms like Zoom, Google Hangouts, Facetime, Skype, etc. to interview other students. Thus, whether a real brick and mortar school or a virtual learning situation, school-wide reminders of character are absolutely achievable.

CHARACTER can't just be a thing that schools do once a week or when necessary. Character should be on constant display and practice throughout a school community. When schools are authentically doing the right thing, culture reinforces students to reach for excellence.

> **What ways will you remind your community to do the right thing? Share on social media using #AwardWinningCulture**

CHAPTER 11
WHOLE CHILD

"Empathy is the root of humanity and the foundation that helps our children become good, caring people. But the Empathy Advantage gives them a huge edge at happiness and success"

-Dr. Michele Borba

Dr. Tim Elmore, from Growing Leaders says that the average student today has as much anxiety as the average psychiatric patient of the 1950's. In an increasingly anxiety ridden society it's scary to know that Borba's research indicates that as anxiety goes up, empathy goes down. In fact, just since 2012, empathy has dropped 29% in college age students which came on the heels of a 40% drop in empathy among college students between 2000-2010. The frightening inverse relationship between anxiety and empathy makes sense. If students are more stressed, worried, and anxious about their own lives, it's harder to focus on what's going on in other's lives. *If I'm worried about ME, it's almost impossible for me to be thinking about YOU!*

I first met Caleb, underneath his desk in a 6th grade social studies classroom. The room was empty, except for Caleb's teacher who had called for me to come down and visit with him. Upon arrival I learned that Caleb had hid under his desk for most of the class period and stayed put as students transitioned to their next class. Luckily, the teacher had her prep period and was in a perfect position to call for reinforcements.

Caleb was one of the most intense cases of student anxiety I ever had encountered. Over the next few months, I'd learn that Caleb's dad had died, while he was in elementary school and that he had learned of his father's passing after being woken up in the middle of the night by his family. He dealt with depression, anxiety, selective mutism, and PTSD. Over the next several years, Caleb struggled to stay in class as he became comfortable with retreating to the counseling center. While we slowly overcame the need to hide under his desk or disappear in a restroom, he regularly came to me to regulate his emotions.

Some days, we talked about superhero movies, video games, or delved into more sensitive topics like sleeping habits and suicidal ideations. Other times, he slept on our counseling center couch for an hour or so to replenish a little energy he was losing from staying up in fear, for all hours of the night. On rare occasions, I sat with him in silence for nearly 45 minutes as he was unable to utter a single word. Being that present yet not stepping on the moment with my words took extreme patience, selflessness, and kindness.

I regularly heard concerns from a few colleagues that we weren't preparing him for high school. That he was losing all kinds of academics and that we needed to move toward tough love to encourage him to move on from losing his father. Some educators worried about key data points like test scores, grades, and homework completion. They acted as if he was losing at learning and was a complete failure.

In Simon Sinek's new book, *The Infinite Game*, he explains that education and learning are not finite games to be won and lost. And while data can provide information about progress, the goal in an infinite game like education is to stay in the game. Keep learning. My approach with Caleb was that we had to focus on his social emotional skills and character in an effort to help him cope with his own anxieties and mental health challenges so that he could eventually return to a love of learning.

> **Award Winning Culture welcomes ongoing critical examination of a school's current educational practices, and intentionally infuses relevant Whole Child strategies into the school's ecosystem.**

Caleb spent more time learning things like emotional regulation and coping strategies than solving fractions or learning about Washington State History. Looking back at my relationship with Caleb, I realize that just being present, listening, and offering steady encouragement kept him functional long enough to heal. I'd written him wildcat cards, hung out with him in classrooms, and dropped everything when he felt like opening up about his father. And this form of kindness eventually led to real growth. Throughout high school he would come visit with me. I think it was comforting for him to know that when things got too overwhelming, he could make a trip to see Mr. Appel for a little KINDSIGHT.

> **Kindness is the ozone layer of emotional safety which allows students to focus on learning.**

It's so important for schools to focus on the big picture of student development. Academics are important but teaching our students the soft skills, internal motivation, and deep sense of purpose is what eventually allows them to pursue their own strengths and passions. Character gives students the tools to overcome adversity in a pursuit of finding authentic meaning. And developing one's meaning in life leads directly to JOY.

It's amazing how much my conversations with Caleb have changed through the years. Nowadays, he asks me questions, is genuinely interested in my life, and actively listens with an emphatic ear. Such a far cry from the anxious 12 year-old internally focused on survival!

Seeing him now as a well-adjusted young adult and graduated from high school, who's ready to pursue his own hopes and dreams, fills me with such profound satisfaction. Caleb and I both know he's fully capable of success. And I know this is directly related to our whole child work, from his middle school days.

Which elements of CHARACTER are you most successful at in your classroom? School? District?

What unique strengths or passions do you show up with that might enhance school culture?

How will you mobilize students to reach award winning levels of character building?

SECTION 2
EXCELLENCE

Will You Do Your Very Best?

4E's of Excellence: (**E**ngagement, **E**mpowerment, **E**xperiential, **E**PIC)

CHAPTER 12
CARMICHAEL HILL

During winter of my 4th grade year, on a cold snowy day in December, I went sled riding on Carmichael hill. In the Tri-cities, Carmichael hill is well known for providing kids a steep and slippery hill to race down. Like many bundled up 10 year-olds, I was a mix of anticipation and intrepidness as I ventured up and down this legendary wintery spot. After multiple runs on tires and makeshift plastic mats I moved my attention to a red wooden sled. It had the ability to turn with smooth precision to expertly maneuver around the snow. During one unlucky run, I found myself positioned out a little outside my normal target zone. After several quick turns to narrowly avoid kids walking back up the hill, I abruptly ran into a metal fence on the far-right outskirts of the hill. Immediately upon the collision, I knew things were not right. My leg hurt and I couldn't stand up. My friends and family quickly raced down the hill along with other concerned onlookers and then slowly carried me back up the hill, to get in the car to venture to our local hospital.

Upon arrival at the hospital's ER, nurses and doctors quickly cut my pants off to get a look at my injured leg. I had suffered a broken tibia during the sled riding accident and would need a cast and 6 weeks to recover.

This inconvenient accident coincided with my 4th grade year in Mrs. Nussbaum's class. Nussbaum was one of my all-time favorite teachers and had assigned us a research project on a country of our choosing, which I had been working on diligently. We were expected to include, notecards, illustrations, rough draft, final copy, and then present our research in front of the class. I recall feeling a bundle of nerves and nausea, at the thought of presenting this project to the class. Truly, I think every kid in that class was worried about sharing their work in such a visible and vulnerable way. I believe it was our first full oral presentation in elementary school. Despite pain and discomfort from a broken leg, I managed to finish the written portion of the project.

I remember feeling so compelled to get everything finalized to present my project to the class. Nussbaum would have surely given me a grace period on completing my Germany project...she even told my parents not to have me worry about completing it. As I recovered at home, they informed me that I was under no obligation to make it back to present on time and that she'd excuse me from the project, given the timing of my injury. That being said, I was determined to deliver. Ultimately, I presented it without incident to Nussbaum and my class of peers.

Why did this matter so much to me?

I can tell you that since my time in 4th grade, I've had plenty of other due dates that I missed or generally cared less about. What made this project so important to me? Three things stand out from the 30+ years removed from my crutch-filled presentation on essentially one good leg. First of all, I had already spent a lot of time researching, writing, drawing, etc. about Germany. While there were parameters to fulfill, I was given a lot of freedom to pursue a country I was interested in and the time and support to tell that country's story. Sharing your learning can be an incredible catalyst to overcome discomfort. I knew I was the class expert on Germany, and I thought I had some interesting insights, facts, and anecdotes to share.

Secondly, Nussbaum was one of my favorites and I knew she thought very highly of me. I could not bare the thought of possibly letting her down by taking the easy way out. Incidentally, I received a 96% on the research project. She deducted points for sloppy penmanship and uninspired illustrations, two skills I never mastered despite Mrs. Nussbaum and countless other educators' best efforts.

Lastly, I imagined what my peers might have thought if I was simply excused from the assignment. Would they think less of me? Would they be envious that I hadn't had to stand up in front of the class? Would they have failed to learn about Germany since no one else had researched that country. I was the class leader for the country of Germany. In my mind, we were all nervous and I respected them enough to be part of this experience.

Looking back at a challenging elementary injury, I recall less and less about the slippery slope of Carmichael Hill, but instead remember with great pride the completion of my first ever research project and oral presentation.

> **Award Winning Culture inspires students to achieve more than they think they're capable of by relying on the 4 E's of Excellence: Engagement, Empowerment, Experiential, and EPIC.**

My challenge to educators is to create an environment of inspired learning where students feel COMPELLED to complete exceptional work for their peers, adult educators, and most importantly...FOR THEMSELVES!

How might YOU foster relationships, learning, and school community in such a profound way as to create a culture of excellence?

CHAPTER 13
ENGAGEMENT

In order for students to truly do their very best, engagement is critical to foster a high degree of attention, curiosity, interest, optimism, and passion. These important characteristics of engagement support motivation to maximize effort. Within traditional teacher prep programs, classroom management is a key skill that many founding educational experts believed aided a student's opportunity for engagement. The early thinking was if students were forced to be on task, they would somehow be more likely to engage with academic content. Perhaps, the phrase classroom management no longer carries the same effectiveness as we once thought.

> **What if schools reframed classroom management into classroom LEADERSHIP?**

Afterall, we manage things, but we LEAD people. Can you hypothesize what impact building educational and/or student leaders would have on a school community's overall culture?

ENGAGEMENT

"Leadership is the skill of influencing people to action, with character that inspires confidence and excellence."

-James C. Hunter

A couple years ago, I was thrilled to bring in leadership expert James C. Hunter to speak to our district about the incredible influence educators have on the world. Hunter is a bestselling author, world renowned speaker, and leadership consultant. He works with Fortune 500 companies, all the military branches, and countless organizations around the world.

One of the highlights with Hunter included him regaling us with tales from behind the scenes of his critically acclaimed book *The Servant* over dinner. There's something truly special about asking an author specific questions about choice, process, and background that led to such groundbreaking work. It was an exceptional time with a wonderful gentleman!

During Hunter's formal presentation for our district, he differentiated between power and authority explaining how authority is the skill of getting people to willingly do your will because of your personal influence. On the other hand, Hunter also shared,

> *"Power is the ability to force or coerce others to do your will, even if they would choose not to, because of your position or your might."*

He explained that leaders with authority can influence greatness out of their followers by explaining that people will say things like *"I'll do it for her...but not for him."* Hunter challenged our district's administration by simply asking,

> *"Are you the type of leader who creates a culture where teachers want to transfer to?"*

Furthermore, he believes that teachers should be striving for classrooms that students are begging to get into.

As you can imagine, the 2 ½ hour presentation was peppered with Wooden-esk leadership brilliance. It's the type of learning experience we dream our students might have, in our own classrooms - electric and empowering!

To be fair, my 24 hours with Hunter included so many lessons, takeaways and insights, I couldn't possibly do it justice in a single story. But here's one anecdote that ties directly to classroom leadership magnifying engagement.

A couple days prior to Hunter's presentation, our principal mentioned in a staff meeting that she would love Wildcat Nation staff members to sit up close in the High School Auditorium, during the leadership presentation. She explained that this would be a great way to show respect to Hunter and that she did not anticipate the auditorium being filled so it would be nice to all move toward the front. Now, any experienced performer will tell you, that if it's a small crowd, it is always best to squeeze everyone into the front of the performance space, so that it feels more like a community, but teachers generally do not gravitate to the front rows in a staff gathering. Our principal did not make her request to move closer to the stage a mandate or requirement. She certainly made no threat or attempt to force us to sit up front. She simply said, *"I'd really appreciate it, if you guys would help me out and sit near the front,"* and then articulated why this was important to her.

The morning of Hunter's presentation was filled with excitement. Numerous EMS staff members showed up early with anticipation of listening to someone whose work we had studied the previous year. There was a buzz in the room, as our folks were passing out handouts, helping set up technology, and chatting about Hunter's books. As expected, every Wildcat Nation staff member that entered the auditorium, invariably made their way down to sit in the front rows.

ENGAGEMENT

Standing near me was a leader from another building whose staff was also there to hear Hunter speak. It became clear to me that the other school had not been given the expectation to sit up near the front. Additionally, staff from other area schools felt no need to show up early, help set up, or jump in to help create a fantastic presentation experience. There was a lack of engagement felt among other staff that was clearly resulting from a failure to foster mutual respect among staff and their principal.

Indeed, as educators from other buildings entered the auditorium, they were immediately barked at by the leader standing next to me with comments like:

"MOVE TO THE FRONT...YOUR NOT SITTING IN THE BACK...SLIDE DOWN...I DON'T WANT ANYONE SITTING IN THE BACK...I DON'T WANT TO ASK AGAIN... WE NEED EVERYONE TO MOVE TO THE FRONT!"

Most everyone from the other schools eventually obeyed the "order" and moved toward the front of the auditorium; however, it may not surprise you that there were about four educators who sat in the very last possible row of the auditorium. I'm not even sure they could see the stage, as they had a partially obstructed view. From my vantage point, it appeared to be a complete "screw you" to the loud, power-driven leader who was attempting to control or "manage" the environment, as people entered the building.

I could not help but imagine if these four adults were instead students in a class taught by this leader, how might this power struggle play out? Ultimatums? Threats? Calling an administrator? Referral? Worse yet... police?

At the same time, standing near the leader was a counselor, a vice principal and an officer from my school. While the this leader was shouting orders, the three servant leaders greeted, smiled and welcomed people into the auditorium. They shook hands, and along with numerous other staff from Wildcat Nation happily showed up early to support our staff. It was a completely different experience, depending on who greeted you and what building you were from.

I thought back to how different this might have gone, had the other building's administrator and other district leaders taken the time to set clear expectations of sitting in the front and explained the "why" behind the request. It was also a little sad to see how this quick negative experience for some, walking into the auditorium, dampened their mood. Creating a welcoming, positive start didn't seem like rocket science but I could visualize how this negative greeting might play out in a classroom setting.

As various other educators from my school helped get things set up for the presentation, I chatted with our incredible speaker. Hunter, who has interacted with the best and worst leadership examples in the world is keenly aware of organizational climate and culture. He's the kind of guy that listens uber closely and sees even the things you're trying to hide. When Hunter speaks, there is no wasted thought as every word has meaning and intention behind it. I expect he noticed part of the scene when educators were arriving as at one point, he leaned over toward me and said,

"Man, you have a lot of servant leaders...no wonder you're playing above the rim."

Hunter's basketball analogy was a compliment to the Award Winning Culture that we've worked so hard to create by fostering classroom leaders rather than classroom managers. Additionally, his brief comment conveyed how powerful it could be, to intentionally focus on a culture of character, excellence, and community. As I sat down, in my freely chosen front row seat, prepared to be dazzled by a master servant leader, I felt a warm sense of gratitude toward the inspiring freedom of our Wildcat Nation culture.

ENGAGEMENT

Are you leading with power or AUTONOMY?

What educational-related word do you currently despise? While several come to my mind, my MOST hated word in education is: COMPLIANCE. In order for students and staff to reach for excellence, schools must move away from compliance, control, and power. In *Live Your Excellence*, Jimmy Casas refers to the "compliance trap" and explains how educational leaders must shift their mindsets to truly invest in a positive school culture. In future driven schools, perhaps the new AI isn't artificial intelligence but instead - Autonomy and Influence.

Autonomy:

Autonomy and compliance are mutually exclusive. Asking permission is an indication of past compliance. It takes time, trust, and practice for people to learn to run with their own ideas. When we began shifting away from compliancy in favor of autonomy, we examined student behavior in the context of adult expectations.

For example, students used to be forced to raise their hand at lunch time to indicate they're finished and ready to clean up and head outside or to the library. This "rule" originally came about because we were having a compliance issue with students leaving a mess in the school cafeteria. Thus, we saw a behavior concern and believed that increasing rules, expectations, and detailed supervision was the answer to preventing lunch time mess. It's such a common pitfall for schools to misidentify the real problem by attacking compliance rather than teaching Character, Excellence, and Community. It was not that students did not know how to clean up after themselves, but they did not understand the "why". When educators are in a mindset of catching students doing something bad (leaving a mess) you can absolutely bet that some students will rise to the occasion of a power struggle.

I can vividly remember students receiving referrals for being insubordinate because they refused to clean up their mess or repeatedly gnored the new rules. On the other hand, there were certainly students who followed the rules out of fear as educators watched over them. But the relationships were forever rooted in power and control and these rule-following students would ultimately struggle to take initiative ard demonstrate leadership in other situations. Thus, their ability to generalize cultural excellence across settings without adult supervision was compromised. It was almost as if we were training the leadership skills right out of these compliant students.

Our breakthrough with lunch time behavior came when we began focusing on the why. And in the case of lunch time clean-up specifically, the why was teaching empathy for our custodians' job. Each day leadership students help our custodians clean up the cafeteria during each lunch. Naturally, reinforcing the subtle message that this is OUR cafeteria and EVERYONE'S responsible for cleaning it up. Additionally, students are now on a first name basis with our custodians. They see them as humans rather than an unspecified person whose job it is to clean. By intentionally providing connection between custodian and student body, students understand the why behind cleaning up after themselves.

Furthermore, adult educators have shifted their lunch time interactions from supervision to connection. When adults stand with arms crossed waiting to catch students being bad, that's all they'll find. On the contrary though, adults who change their mindset away from supervision into connection, began to foster positive relationships. These relationships heavily impact student's willingness and interest to do their very best in the cafeteria. When our staff took the time to change adult behavior and add in some intentionality around the why of clean-up, lunch time autonomy was a natural offshoot for us. Thus, the need for students to raise hands and follow power driven rules became obsolete.

ENGAGEMENT

Autonomy also shows up in our school library. A place traditionally steeped in silence, compliance, and order has now transformed into a flexible learning environment that's full of educational zest. Students can collaborate, use innovative technology, and are fully engaged in elevating their own learning space. The library is no longer a place to simply check out books or read quietly. Engaged learners are active, messy, and energetic. Our librarian plays culture building podcasts and tv shows or fun music while students lead their own learning. It's incredible to walk into this once museum like space to see students diving head first into full autonomy. Careful observers might also notice the intentional furniture arrangement into flexible learning pods designed for human interaction. While the library used to encourage silos of individual thought, much of the space has specifically been reimagined to facilitate group work, while still maintaining options for individual tasks. All of the resulting efforts provided a future ready facelift to the library through student autonomy.

This same restructuring of rules has shown up with our cell phone policies. Banning a technologically advanced learning tool such as a phone is the answer for many schools. But it's a policy that often becomes hypocritical at best and erodes relationships at worst. On our Award Winning Culture podcast, George Couros reaffirms the notion of using this innovative tool for positivity and the potential to impact culture when he says,

"Some kids are benefiting from (cellphones) and some kids are distracted so educators take them away from everybody and actually hurt the student who benefits from the device...when teachers hang signs that say no phones, the first thing they're insinuating to kids is I don't trust you. As everyone knows trust is a very important part of relationships."

This short-sided approach to forgoing student autonomy pits adults and students in a catch me if you can approach to student management. I look forward to the day when adults' first reaction to a new stimulus isn't solely focused on rules, management, and compliance. We've learned that teaching students how, why, what, and when to use their phone and then modeling appropriate cell phone use is a wonderful way to provide student autonomy while ensuring engagement. Furthermore, restricting student's cell phone use limits the opportunity to make healthy and profound learning choices that may not otherwise be possible without these devices.

Student autonomy isn't just for elaborate innovative learning tools. At Wildcat Nation, the pencil is a conduit to freedom. While some teachers berate, penalize, or scold students who fail to have a pencil in class. Teachers in an Award Winning Culture intentionally provide these necessary supplies as well as empower students to grab additional supplies when needed. Therefore, they avoid time wasters of "I don't have anything to write with" or "my pencil is broken" because students are intentionally taught to problem solve supplies restrictions within the classroom. They know where extra supplies are kept and have the freedom to stand up and go get what they need to be successful.

> **Award Winning Culture removes systemic barriers that hinder students learning by giving them autonomy over school-wide and classroom decisions.**

For instance, in middle and high schools, the master schedule can be a complicated and political landmine that's centered around who gets to teach what and when. Some school leaders use master scheduling as a reward and punishment for veteran or rookie educators. They believe deeply that things like seniority should weigh heavily in scheduling decision making. And while some schools believe they are making decisions based on what's best for students, I'm surprised how few schools make students the drivers of their class options.

ENGAGEMENT

Years ago, our office team traveled to a master scheduling conference. While a good team bonding experience, it was markedly uninspiring as we slogged our way through doubletons, singletons, and other master schedule jargon. However, one ridiculous moment made the entire conference worthwhile. During one session, an educational attendee was asking the presenter a question about how to handle teachers who are upset with their class assignment. The question was rooted in honest vulnerability about how to please her staff while doing what's best for students. Before the presenter could even finish her response, an older heavy-set male administrator in the back row stood up and began barking about what was most important. As he spoke about the need to give students freedom to build the schedule they want, he got so worked up spit flew from his mouth as he pounded his fist on the table. To be frank, I was shocked anyone could be this passionate about master scheduling. Finally, he put his hands in open palm way up in the air as he belted out,

"WHAT ARE WE HERE FOR?"

The administrator's loud overpowering question was meant to remind everyone that he believed we should make decisions based on what students wanted, not what was convenient for adults. In fairness, he muttered those words three or four times before the presenter called for a break. As he burst out of the conference room to cool down, my teammates and I stood in shock at this man's voracious and unexpected filibuster on student autonomy. Honestly, we laughed at this scene for years. Anytime our office team seemed to consider deviating from making a scheduling decision based on students vs. teachers, we reminded ourselves that students must be front and center of decision making, while reminiscing about this crazy story.

Through the years, we have used registration forms, surveys, group and individual interviews as a way of gathering student interest for a subject area. And then ultimately, base our overarching schedule on student needs, wants, and numbers that are student driven and data informed. But Award Winning Cultures are motivated to remove barriers to deliver optimal experience.

During one recent survey, we learned that students cesired a guitar class. We had never offered guitar at our school or across the district at the middle school level. And ultimately our district said they could not support a guitar class because it could not be offered at the other schools.

Intentional Tip:

If you're going to survey folks and then not act on the survey, you will lose people's trust really quickly. So, find a way to follow through.

Our team could not pretend to un-see our students desire to take guitar, so we got creative. We learned an unspecified "music" class was on the district approved roster and thus our guitar class assumed the "music" identity for the purposes of district mandates. Students were informed that if they signed up for "music" they were really signing up for guitar. The class was a smashing success and is still embedded in our current master schedule. After all, we cannot let current district systems impede our students' experience.

But the point of this section on student autonomy is not to give readers an exhaustive list of ways to build in freedom. Instead, I hope readers re-examine school rules, expectations, and procedures with a lens of shifting from managing behavior to leading behavior, even when student autonomy intersects with adult autonomy.

A while back, I was asked to review and write an endorsement for Jimmy Casas and Dr. Jeffrey Zoul's OUTSTANDING book *Stop. Right. Now*. It's the type of book that entices you to examine educational practices with clear vision by offering 39 culture killers coupled with an exceptional how-to guide to avoid common pitfalls. Well, I would like to add **#40** to the list: **LET THEM IN.**

In my district, secondary schools start at 7:55 a.m. Many students arrive at school around 7:15 a.m.-7:45 a.m. with the bulk of students showing up by car, bus, bike or foot by around 7:30 a.m. each morning. Other parts of the country operate on different daily bell schedules but the overall timeline of students arriving approximately 20-30 minutes prior to school starting seems to be fairly universal.

There are schools around the country that intentionally lock students out of hallways in the morning until the first bell. This leaves most of the students unsupervised, unconnected, and out in the cold weather for nearly twenty minutes or more. Some schools do allow students into the building (usually a cafeteria or gym) but do not let them down the hallway or into classrooms until the first bell rings.

While some buildings seem to recognize the need to open hallways for students, they instead provide teacher discretion as to when they unlock their classroom doors. In schools with this form of teacher autonomy, some students find their teachers rooms available while other students are forced to cram into hallways, nooks, and crannies. I've even heard stories of libraries, counseling centers, and health rooms that do not open until school begins. There is a belief that this non-class time of the workday should somehow be protected for adult educators to get work done. Obviously, there are meetings, emergencies, and other factors that occasionally need to be attended to; however, when we shut students out of school during unstructured time, we're sending a strong unwelcoming message while perpetuating students lack of autonomy.

WHY MUST IT STOP?

Educators are missing a golden opportunity to greet, welcome, and connect with students. It's the perfect unstructured time to check-in, ask questions, and build rapport among students/adults. Many students need this positive attention and energy to reset from difficulties at home, online, or from the school bus. By skipping out on this informal communication, students may not be ready to fully focus on learning.

Additionally, why would it ever be a good idea to leave large groups of students unsupervised by adults. Ironically, the practice of keeping kids out of classrooms, hallways, or specific locations only ensures the need to establish a supervisory plan. When adults find themselves in supervisory roles rather than humanistic openness, the attitude, behavior, and feelings inevitably steer negative for both adults and students. When setting up a 'gotcha' culture, educators should not be surprised by elevated discipline, disconnection, and decreased student preparedness.

HOW CAN EDUCATORS DO BETTER?

Let them in! Invite them into our schools for breakfast. Encourage them into libraries to read, study, or explore. Open up classrooms, offices, and gym spaces for students to be...LEARNERS. Facilitate maker space and/or computer labs available to kids. Put the busy work aside and engage with students. This is not me time...it's **WE** time!

Get off your device and have real life connections with young people who DESPERATELY want your attention, help, and feedback. SMILE. Make it rain high fives, fist bumps, and compliments; as you intentionally seek out as many students, adults, and parents as possible. Use Names (not just students names but adults as well). Move around. Get out of your chair, room, or comfort zone to make school a fun place to be. MAKE EYE CONTACT. Play music. Shoot hoops. Start a morning club. Capitalize on YOUR strengths as you welcome others into your sphere of influence. Do groups of students naturally congregate to your space each morning? If not...you're probably doing something wrong.

> **Award Winning Culture actively seeks to STOP bad practices, programs, processes, philosophies, and people who are no longer advancing school culture forward.**

Providing students autonomy, options, and love during unstructured morning time intentionally teaches students that school is an inviting place to be and they have the freedom to engage in awesomeness all around them.

Gum Rule Debacle

Occasionally, student autonomy comes into direct conflict with adult autonomy. As was the case in our staff's most highly contested adult disagreement in school history. Years ago, our school's focus on rules and routines landed us in the middle of a discussion on whether or not to allow gum in the classroom and/or school. What started off as a quick side item on a staff meeting agenda became a full-fledged chewing gum war.

Some teachers believed that gum was such a problem in their class environment that they wanted to ban it school-wide. They believed there was no place for gum near school computers, desks, libraries, or band instruments and thus should not be tolerated anywhere on campus. Other teachers felt that gum chewing gave anxious and active kiddos a chance to release energy in a healthy and less disruptive fashion. They saw no issues with students chewing gum while they read, worked on a history project or created a drawing in an art class. There was even a band of educators who didn't care much about either end of the spectrum, but the ultimate crux of the heated discussion soon devolved into: is it ok to make a school-wide rule for all classrooms when not all teachers agree?

In essence, is it right to create a rule that one teacher might need in his classroom and force another teacher to enforce that rule in her classrooms? Those of you who are astute political observers will recognize the age-old debate of the essence of this conflict play out in political arenas all over the world: *Is it fair for your freedom to interfere with my freedom?*

After much debate, anger, and frustration, our school ultimately decided that a school wide no gum rule was a violation of teacher freedom and that decisions on gum would be left up to individual class teachers. But the interesting thing about this was how this transformed the problems we actually had with gum. While teachers came into this discussion having written frequent referrals for gum, being upset with their colleagues for allowing gum, and being absolutely exasperated with the thought of gum in school, 12 years later, gum is completely a non-issue. Many teachers moved away from micromanaging student gum chewing and those that didn't just set a strong expectation up front.

Additionally, those educators who most vehemently opposed gum were forced to examine the "why" behind gum not being tolerated in their learning environment. Because they were forced to articulate the why and become crystal clear with how this impacted student safety, school property, and/or student learning, they found themselves in an excellent place to intentionally teach students "why" gum chewing would not be acceptable in their class environment. It was as if the exercise of gum debate helped them to clarify their own feelings, thoughts, and concerns regarding gum.

Students are now allowed to chew gum in many places around the building but also have learned that there are places that it's not ok.

When schools facilitate healthy civil discourse through a lens of student autonomy, the outcome can be extraordinary. Furthermore, educators in favor of gum are now in a position to reinforce appropriate gum behavior (i.e. where should gum be thrown when finished chewing, avoiding noisy distractions with gum in the learning environment, who has to clean up gum that's not properly disposed of). As you might suspect, empathy is a bridge to school excellence. The gum rule debacle has become a school wide fable like metaphor that's shared with new staff and retold to old staff, in an effort to remind us of the need for reflection and the importance of providing teacher autonomy to their class culture. Ironically, in this example staff autonomy has directly led to student engagement in non-gum chewing classes and increased student autonomy in the gum chewing environments. Beyond student outcomes like decreased discipline for gum chewing, staff cohesiveness has grown. Now, anytime our staff begins to backslide into a similar black or white discussion of rules, fairness, and teacher freedom a simple verbal nod to the now famous gum rule debacle snaps our staff back into an Award Winning Culture focused on inspiring excellence.

Influence

The backbone of influence is intentionality. At Wildcat Nation, we take the time to intentionally teach our students how to do even ordinary tasks. We believe in leading by example but walking them through the specifics of the modeled behavior strongly influences leadership behavior within our students. For example, students learn how to walk through the door in such a way that they become aware of their surroundings in an effort to help others. While teen behavior can be self-serving, Wildcats learn how to look around for others as they are near a doorway. Teachers physically model how to open the door, hold the door, and wait for someone approaching in an effort to positively support other students or adults entering a space. Do all middle and high school students already know how to physically open a door? Yes, but oftentimes they lack the self-awareness to go out of their way to help someone else through a doorway. Our students spend time being instructed on empathizing with others approaching a doorway by learning where to stand, how to greet someone, and WHY waiting a few seconds to hold the door for someone can turn our school environment into a warm welcoming place.

Our staff applies this level of influence by intentionally teaching students how to make excellent decisions. Whether it's how to build robots in our maker space lab, reading during sustained silent reading, or what to do when your work is completed. When adults take the time to positively influence students and then step back and give students room to take ownership over their school experience, young leaders are built, and excellence is achieved!

Autonomy and influence elevate adult educators from being micromanagers into macro-leaders. Micromanaging is rooted in failing to empower with the tools and freedom to do the job. It stunts engagement because it stifles personal growth among students. Micromanaging will often ensure that behavior is acceptable when under the watchful eye of adults, but behavior will rarely be generalized to other circumstances, settings, or opportunities.

For instance, I'll throw my garbage away, if I think you're watching me in the cafeteria. But I'll have no incentive to do my best to clean-up the locker room or my library workspace, if no one is there to observe me.

> **Award Winning Culture is only REAL, when Character and Leadership exist in the absence of observation.**

ENGAGEMENT

Macro leading provides me with the tools to lead my own behavior and the why behind reaching for excellence. If I care about the custodian, then I won't want to make his job harder. If I have school pride with my library, locker room, or hallway, then there's no need to leave it a mess. Naturally, doing my best and being engaged in learning, socializing, creating, experimenting, etc. is a sure-fire way to approach excellence.

Once again James Kerr inspires us in *Better People Make Better Leaders,* to foster excellence and character in ourselves and others as a way of reaching a winning culture. In other words, people who put in deep personal work to improve their own character build their sphere of influence. Teaching macro, leading outside of the classroom in settings like the library, locker room or cafeteria have a direct impact on what happens back in the classroom. Helping to crystalize these leadership skills in youth can build their confidence, self-esteem, and purpose.

When students are engaged, they have the opportunity to become inspiring leaders for their peers. I'll never forget one high poverty, academically struggling student who shared with me that her band teacher had pointed out her instrument technique, in front of the class. Furthermore, the band teacher called her technique outstanding and asked her to demonstrate her finger positions and detail it for her classmates. She was so overwhelmed by this experience of influence and autonomy that she said to me,

"I'm not used to being told I'm OUTSTANDING or treated like a leader! I love Mr. Miller and love being in band."

When we look for student strengths, intentionally teaching autonomy and leading with influence, student engagement can become excellent. An example of influence is with our student aides. We allow our 8th grade students to apply to be teacher, office, counseling center or library aides. These students do much more than busywork. They are student mentors who are held to a high standard of excellence and help our school run smoothly. Our student aides might find themselves tutoring a peer, setting up for a lab, checking out a book, or helping a student organize their binder. Participating students are highly engaged in serving the adults and students they work with each day. They know that their work matters to others and they take great pride in raising our school culture.

Sometimes student leaders pop up from unplanned circumstances. Recently, we took advantage of a group of 8th grade native Spanish speaking students, who were crushing it in their high school credit elective. After giving them the final and letting them test out of Spanish, we approached them about tutoring some of our English Language Learners who were also beginning readers. Rather than continuing to fall victim to a district ELL deficit we turned our student Spanish-speaking leaders into student 1:1 tutors. This model has been so successful to our ELL support culture, we're now applying this way of thinking to other groups and content outside of Spanish.

One example of harnessing student strengths to influence our entire school culture is with our STAT team. As many adult educators recognize, students generally are much better navigating technology and innovation than their actual teachers. We also realized that some of the students who were particularly tech savvy did not seem to fit into a mainstream sport or school activity. In an attempt to connect these students to other passionately like-minded peers and to capitalize off their unique gift for technology the STAT team was born.

Essentially a team of students was assembled in much the same way a Geek Squad might be created to assist students and staff on common technology needs. Students were taught Chromebook fixes and repair, smartboard and document camera troubleshooting, as well as customer service, ethical decision making, FERPA, and Tech safety. Our STAT team has t-shirts and badges and are recognized servant leaders throughout the building who help staff, substitute teachers, and other students by utilizing their innovative influence and the human passion to connect and support others. As a result, these joyful leaders are frequently buzzing around the school assisting our entire community.

*What are some examples of Autonomy in your culture?

*How are you fostering other's influence in your educational space?

CHAPTER 14
EMPOWERMENT

"Any problem, any issue, any quandary, or any adversity can always be solved with a little student-voice elbow grease."

-Rebecca Coda & Rick Jetter, *Let Them Speak*

Voice:

Amplifying student voice begins with eliminating hierarchy in learning. In traditional models of education, teachers are the keepers of knowledge and thus students are asked to be quiet as knowledge is passed down to them. Even the phrasing of "passing down" content, ideas, or information inherently suggests that education is something that someone does to someone else. This passive and non-collaborative journey has kept schools and educators from reaching the cultural excellence they strive for. Luckily great educators fight to add student voice into all aspects of the learning environment. So, it should come as no surprise to empower-focused leaders that this same application of excellence magnifies school culture. The archaic belief that school culture is ONLY defined by it's top down leadership is short sided and flat out wrong.

> ### In order for schools to reach Award Winning Culture status, all stakeholders must have a meaningful voice.

In the classroom, voice may show up in discussions, ideas, and suggestions on a daily basis. But an authentically empowering culture is uncovered by how educators respond to WHAT IF questions. It's imperative for educators to allow and even encourage critical thinking, problem finding, and analytical reflecting in the form of inquiry. This form of deep thinking leads learners to eventually connect to creativity and the production of meaningful content.

> ### Educators can implement relatable content by seeking student feedback, putting students in the driver's seat of personalized learning, and making them co-directors of their own educational show.

Outside of the classroom, students must have their voices shared in ways that impact the greater school. Within our leadership classes, students plan and run assemblies, school spirit days, orchestrate elaborate student and teacher recognition, and quite literally become the daily voice on the morning announcements. In fact, morning announcements is one of the biggest mishandled student voice opportunities by school leaders. Many traditional thinking administrators believe that morning announcements are their time and place to shine. They see the value in having their vision shared in an inspiring and unified way to all stakeholders. But one of the truest outcomes of great leadership is BUILDING leadership capacity in others.

Award Winning Culture fosters positive leaders at all educational levels.

I highly encourage forward thinking administrators and leadership teams to intentionally teach students how to take over speaking roles like morning announcements, assembly presentations, staff meetings, and celebration and recognitions. One easy way to begin building capacity with your student leaders is to organize regular monthly meetings with a group of student leaders. Ideally, representation from not only student government but clubs, activities, and other non-traditional factions of the school.

These meetings can give adult leaders a chance to listen to concerns and ideas that may not normally bubble to the surface in traditional school settings. Not only are the student leaders empowered to develop their own leadership skills through these forms of student voice but the underlying message to the entire school of students is that YOU matter. Your ideas and thoughts matter! During these meetings, resist the urge to facilitate, manage, and TALK. Work hard to shut your mouth and listen. When talking is necessary, use open ended questions or paraphrasing student ideas to check for understanding. Adult leaders can model great listening as a leadership technique and have the added bonus of supporting student voice in the mission, vision, and direction of the school culture.

As mentioned previously, advisory classes are an excellent school move toward teaching character and building community. Additionally, they're a wonderful way to enhance student voice in smaller family sized groups. At Wildcat Nation, our students spend three years together in their advisory classes focusing on character, college and career exploration, and academic skills. Due to the nature and depth of the relationships

EMPOWERMENT

that develop, these safe spaces provide a weekly platform for students to share feedback with each other, staff and the school. I highly encourage building leaders such as administrators, counselors, psychologists, and librarians to observe and interact regularly in advisory classes. Several years ago, I walked into a character lesson where two girls became emotional as they detailed who/why the person they looked up to most in the world was the other girl. They talked about horrible family experiences that they had helped each other through and how they loved each other, as if they were sisters. Despite a room full of squirrelly boys and girls it was completely silent. People sat in respect as they attuned to the two girls' beautiful moment. The safe, relationship-building culture that the teacher had created was MAGICAL!

Student voice, for the sole purpose of advancing school culture should also show up in anonymous reporting of concerns, dangers, or bullying. No matter how safe educators try and make their school environment, negativity will occasionally find its way even in award winning schools. Beyond traditional barriers to student reporting such as disconnected, shy or introverted students; sometimes situations arise where students are unable to report concerns either out of fear or inopportunity.

> **Sexual harassment, bullying, oppression, and injustice are probably microcosms of the bigger workplace and societal inequalities that are fostered in unsafe cultures and climates.**

Schools have an OBLIGATION to drive societal conversation as the leaders in safe and welcoming organizations. Our humanistic intentional work with creating positive learning spaces should STRIVE to be widely considered the gold standard for all industries on how to create an Award Winning Culture.

We use a Safe School Alert App to avoid some of these barriers. Anyone can report a concern from any location. And that report goes directly to our dream team so we can act on that information immediately. The ability to share their voice through an online system ensures that students can report potential threats or danger from the bathroom, classroom, locker room, home, etc. While physical reporting boxes in the counseling center or office might be advisable in elementary schools, online reporting systems are far superior in secondary settings. At the very least, offering both a physical reporting space and virtual reporting site supports student voice while improving school safety.

Hiring Teams: Including students on hiring teams is an excellent way to infuse student voice into your school culture. Students can help design and ask questions for interview candidates, give student-led tours to get an informal peek into prospective candidates' personalities, and offer unique perspectives during hiring discussions. Furthermore, many schools have candidates actually teach mini lessons, as part of the hiring process. These mini lessons obviously include administration and/or team observation. But perhaps the greatest source of feedback about a candidate's lesson is from a quick informal follow-up chat with students. Unaffected by potential interview bias, students can provide authentic insight in relationship building potential of an interview candidate.

Committees/Other Professional Learning: Students should be included on all types of committees: leadership, curriculum adoption, PBIS, etc. Culture-minded educators must realize that students have the most important voice when designing successful learning.

We've even had a few students in book study groups. Imagine what can be learned by chatting with students about some of the top literature on leadership, character, relationships, wellness, innovation, and culture. I loved when one of our students joined a staff book study on Elisabeth Bostwick's book, *Take the L.E.A.P.* After reading several sections of her book to prepare for an interview with her on our Award Winning Culture podcast, one student felt compelled to join the weekly discussion about Bostwick's incredible work. Her student perspective was invaluable in helping teachers infuse creativity, curiosity, and empowerment into their classrooms. Our environments are strengthened by having diverse representation in all settings.

Team Meetings: IEP/504/Health/Behavior/Attendance/Plans should always include student voice. Whether this is during the actual meeting or some type of pre-meeting or staffing, students' ideas, feelings, and perspectives must be at the forefront of creating a successful plan.

Many years ago, we got a new 6th grade student transferring to us with a 504 plan for severe peanut allergies. As part of the plan, the student was removed from the lunchroom and had to eat in the nurse's office. The previous school believed that sequestering him away from other potential food threats was a sure-fire way to prevent him from coming into contact with a life-threatening reaction. Additionally, there were concerns that the student didn't enjoy eating very much and thus the nurse was assigned to watch and encourage food consumption due to concerns about low body weight.

Upon my first hearing about this plan at the beginning of the school year, I immediately set up a meeting with the nurse, family, and student to review these unusual procedures. To be honest, this entire thing sounded like a violation of student rights and discrimination and I couldn't imagine that the student was on board with this plan. During the meeting, the student voiced that he hated eating in the nurse's office throughout elementary school, away from his friends, and never felt hungry because there weren't many food choices that appealed to him in elementary school. He also wasn't hungry because he was sad not to be included with his peers at lunch.

Using his voice as a catalyst for change, we created a new plan where he could be in the cafeteria at lunch time, throughout middle school and sit at a table nearest an adult supervisor. Additionally, with increased autonomy of food selections, he ate perfectly fine and gained weight rather quickly. After a month into school, the need for any adult supervision became unnecessary as he sat and enjoyed his lunch with his peers each day.

Ironically, giving him a voice, eliminated the need for ridiculous use of compliance and in general made him a happy and healthy boy. By semester of 6th grade, he was completely off his 504 plan, and both parents and the student wrote me a handwritten thank-you card for empowering him to be the leader of his own lunchtime.

Choice:

Talented educators are realizing the positive impact of adding in choice to the classroom. However, increasing learner agency has the positive byproduct of substantially influencing classroom culture. That which impacts classroom culture influences the entire school culture. Much like creating voice, choice not only enriches learning experiences but has a deep impact on the way students and staff actually behave and feel within the overall school environment.

> **Award Winning Culture intentionally builds in student choice as a means toward learner agency.**

Here's a few examples of building in choice within the classroom that directly impact school culture.

Flexible Seating: Flexible seating can completely change the feeling in a classroom, library or common space. Allowing our students to pick their optimal learning space has provided a level of choice that ensures

EMPOWERMENT

student's behavior aligns with their ideal learning state of mind. However, there are two intentional points that some teachers overlook when diving into flexible seating in the classroom: Number of Seats and Lesson Design.

As a rule of thumb, educators should plan for 10 more seats than their highest roster total. In other words, count the number of students in your biggest classroom and add 10 more seats than that number. Along those lines, offering variety is key. Bringing in 35 wobble seats is a mistake. We've found that seating should be malleable and moveable. Additionally, students might opt for one seat during one task and a different seat during a different task. Winning educators encourage students to try out a wide range of seating options and then ask students to reflect on their feelings, thoughts, behavior, and academic performance within various seating areas. The goal is for students to learn how, when, and why to choose their best learning location. Obviously, bringing in additional seating requires teachers to rethink their own items, furniture, and classroom stuff to optimize space. Our most successful teachers utilizing flexible seating removed any non-essential stuff and prioritized student furniture. While most teachers still had a small workspace, teachers also had flexible workspaces as they moved about the room to connect and interact more with students. Gone we're the days of the teacher at their desk, physically warded off from the learners. Our teachers now work in and around the students as learners create.

Secondly, simply putting in non-traditional seating and then continuing to teach traditionally is a recipe for behavior problems and distractions. Teachers who stand up and deliver extended periods of time using classic instruction while students sit in fun learning pods will invariably feel frustration when students aren't on task and listening. When making the culture changing decision to introduce flexible seating in the classroom or whole school, educators must also move toward learner centered and learner empowered models. Our teachers who attempted flexible seating while failing to switch to a more 'innovator's mindset' felt immediate frustration about flexible seating and deemed it inappropriate at the secondary level. Our advice would be to slowly transform instruction before diving head-first into flexible seating; however, when a school community successfully implements flexible seating, the positive school culture can be felt in the ripple of joyful learning throughout the building.

Flexible seating is a strong culture builder, outside of school as well. My wife works best on the sofa at home, while I prefer a stand-up desk. Educating parents about the impact of students picking the ideal learning environment is a winning approach. Just because studying and homework were traditionally done at a desk and chair, doesn't mean that's the uniformly right way for every student to learn at home today. Teaching young people how and where they learn best is just as important inside and outside the school building.

Note Taking: For years, EMS was an AVID school and we made the mistake of expecting all students to use Cornell notes during opportunities for note taking. It was the only note taking strategy taught by teachers and while some students enjoyed and benefited from this notetaking model. Other students grew to hate Cornell notes and ultimately resisted applying their best efforts when taking notes. Over the last few years, we've changed our instructional practice to include intentionally teaching a variety of notetaking. We realized that the goal was not to have each student leave middle school with the uniformly same approach to note taking. Instead, the goal is to allow each student to find value in some form of note taking and to identify their own unique style and strategy to retain information. Thus, we promote sketchnoting, book snaps, outlines, transcription, highlighting, bullet style, Cornell, etc. Building in choice in how students capture and synthesize knowledge ensures students are in the driver's seat of their own learning and makes for a classroom culture rich in purpose.

Readers Workshop/Writers Workshop: Truthfully, any instructional strategy that builds in choice, has the potential to positively impact school culture. For instance, in a reader's workshop, students choose any possible book to read. They are not assigned by genre or AR # or score. They essentially select something that will benefit them the most. While the teacher may present a mini lesson at the beginning of the class period, most of the time is dedicated to students reading and documenting their thoughts during class. This model frees teachers up to walk around visiting, interacting, and connecting with individuals and groups discussing their book. By providing students the freedom to sculpt their learning, teachers move into a support role empowering students to become lead learners.

Demonstration of Learning: We've found that providing students the academic freedom to demonstrate their learning in unique ways empowers students to learn. Rather than them giving up on cell theory or fractions because they've deemed themselves a poor test taker, we encourage personalized learning when we develop student choice in how they express what they've learned. Learning is learning no matter the form. The quicker that schools update to this line of thinking the more positivity school officials, parents, and stakeholders will experience in student centered classrooms. Empowering all forms of student expression of knowledge creates a culture of life-long learning.

Mastery Learning: Thanks to Chad Ostrowski, creator of *The Grid Method*, and CEO of the Teach Better Team, schools are in a position to empower student choice in how they master their own learning. The Grid Method is "a self-paced, learner driven, mastery and standards based educational system that utilizes tiered learning targets and aligned learning tasks to maximize learner achievement."

But what impact does mastery learning have on school or classroom culture? When students deepen their understanding of foundational knowledge before moving on to more complicated concepts, we provide students built in control over their own learning and encourage a gradual release of responsibility as they further develop their skill set. As they transition to a high level of learner agency, students have increasing responsibility over the direction of their own learning. Obviously, increasing agency speaks volumes to enhancing internal motivation. A class or school filled with highly motivated students creates cultural excellence.

Restroom Use: As a general rule of thumb, PLEASE let students use the restroom when they need to. Don't give points or extra credit based on being able to limit bladder function during a specified time period. If schools are truly interested in providing exceptional school culture and climate, we need to recognize that it's IMPOSSIBLE to learn at an optimal level, when we need to go to the bathroom. I understand that restroom use on occasion can be an avoidance behavior but rather than banning, scolding, or discouraging this safety net for select students; perhaps, a winning approach might be to investigate the why behind work avoidance. Regardless, LET STUDENTS GO TO THE RESTROOM!

Water: My mom used to tell me about a time when I was a baby and had an ultimate meltdown, while we rode a train from New York to New Jersey. Apparently, mom had forgotten to pack a drink and while it was a short ride, I got very thirsty which led to a full-blown crying meltdown. The story stood out to my mom because she claims I was a very easy baby. After that train ride, she always made sure I had something to drink. Ironically, my first word was "juice." It's become a funny thing that my friends and family still notice and joke about even today. Anytime I go ANYWHERE, I bring a bottle of water. My friends sometimes tease me that I'll show up to their house, or some event where they have an obvious variety of beverages, with my own beverage (just in case). I've learned that I'm not my best self, if I don't have something to drink. Kids are no different. Similar to the restroom, thirsty students are not ready to learn. Whether we're allowing them to bring a water bottle to class or move about to get a drink from a drinking fountain, Award Winning Culture allows for students to determine when they're thirsty and take steps to quench that need.

Regulation/Timeout Room: For years, we operated with a traditional timeout space. It was a combination of in school suspension coupled with students who were sent by classroom teachers mostly because of off-task behaviors. For all intents and purposes, it was punishment as students were missing instruction, required to fill out a negative reflection form, and parents were called.

After examining our school-wide trauma invested systems, and reflecting on current empowerment practices, we've revamped our old timeout space to become a regulation room. Students can take self-timeouts or be sent by an adult to meet a need: Relationship, Responsibility, and/or Regulation. This shift to a space that offers everything from snacks to mindfulness has helped create a positive space for students to quickly meet a need and return to the learning environment ready to go. We've changed the lighting, furniture, and feel of the room. The space now includes fidgets, soft music, yoga mats, sand pits, comfy chairs, and other sensory relaxers.

It's no secret that when every student has the power to identify their own needs and a means to meet those needs, the collective school culture becomes a more effective, compassionate, and caring environment as seen through the behavior of learning.

Earbuds/Music: Some students greatly benefit from wearing earbuds and/or listening to music to ease distractibility, anxiety, and increase focus. Schools should actively work to build in these types of student choice to raise successfully regulated students. Students in an Award

Winning Culture can be found wearing earbuds in the lunchroom, library, hallway, locker room, and of course classroom. Don't wait for students to show up with a 504 or IEP plan to tell you they need this accommodation. Make this a best practice for all students and then adjust as needed if a particular student is not being successful with his or her choice. Eliminating this successful tool for all students out of the fear of possible classroom management issues that may arise for a couple students is a failure to empower classroom leaders, build in student choice, and meet kids where they are.

Snacks: Would you like to know a really, really, really big secret? Kids are hungry. Like really hungry. ALL THE TIME! I know, I'm dropping all kinds of amazing knowledge here. But seriously, expecting kids to wait around all day until some arbitrarily determined food time, is archaic and flat out wrong. Plus, this doesn't even take into account our students of poverty or students who woke up late and missed breakfast. Ever been to a staff meeting, PD session, or training with no snacks, coffee, treats. I'll bet you started freaking out, while you planned your early departure. Students are hungry. Let them bring a snack in. Let them share snacks. Provide snacks. Do whatever you gotta do but let kids eat, when they are hungry. Period. Your school and class culture will be better off when you give students the choice to eat when they are hungry.

Free Time: Intentionally teaching students what to do when they're done with a task, assignment, or activity improves overall student behavior during unstructured or free moments by giving them a choice in how they use their most scarce resource: TIME. Obviously, this looks different in different classrooms or settings but teaching students appropriate free time behavior is a practice that should exist in K-12, as its school-wide reach is seen as a function of positive behavior.

Bulletin Boards/Walls: Who determines what gets hung up on bulletin boards and walls? The answer to that question probably depends on whether you believe that a classroom is the teacher's space OR the student's space. Educators who work in an Award Winning Culture realize that every choice...even what goes on the walls...should include students' thoughts, feelings, and opinions if we are seeking students to classroom connection and student meaning. The best classrooms I've been a part of, not only provided student choice in WHAT is hung up but also empowered students in HOW it was hung up. Let's make each classroom feel like their space!

Of course, this list is just a starting point as innovative teachers are constantly seeking out new ways to offer student choice, within their content area. Choice can also be built into school-wide arenas. Here's a few examples outside the classroom:

Lunchroom: At EMS, we've built choice into lunch options (4 different lunch lines plus the option to bring cold lunch) as well as student choice in where students sit, and how they spend their time throughout lunch. Students can use their phone, Chromebook, head outside or visit the library. There are two different school stores that provide additional items to purchase. Finally, we offer leadership games, STEM activities, clubs, and other culture building fun during this student break time.

Additionally, we've even created places for anxious students to enjoy their lunch outside of the large crowded space in our commons. These lunch time freedoms are a large cry away from the compliant mess hall like lunch experience we offered years ago. No more raising your hand to go to the bathroom or assigned seating. It's amazing how well students can behave when we expect mature positive behavior rather than building in safety precautions that undermine student choice.

Library: Our library is a flexible learning space with uber choice in seating, media, and tools. Students have a wide variety of interactive options that they can enjoy on their own without adult supervision or interference. They even have full library access from home. Tapping into these resources remotely ensures that even distance learners can utilize these media centers.

Visiting the Counselor: Students have multiple ways of signing up to see a counselor at EMS. We have physical sign-up sheets on our door where students indicate name, date, and reason for seeing a counselor: schedule, friends, college/career, personal, or other. Students can sign up before or after school, at lunch time or in between classes. Additionally, we have an online signup with google form, that allows a student to communicate a need with their counselor at home, during class or any other time of the day. By empowering students to choose when and how to see their counselor, students take ownership over their own guidance.

Dress Code: I know this'll be controversial to some. But we don't have dress codes. I mean, don't get me wrong, there are certain clothing that is deemed inappropriate, offensive, or too revealing. However, aside from these select items, students and staff can wear whatever they want. We believe that a person's individualism should allow for students and staff to come to school in whatever they find comfortable. Whether it's jeans and t-shirt, shorts, or suit in tie we believe that freedom of wardrobe and teaching an acceptance for whatever outfit stakeholders wear is more important than "dressing professional." How can we ask teachers to roll up their sleeves and sit in flexible learning spaces with students on the floor and then require them to put on uncomfortable garbe? On the other hand, I recognize that some schools find success with compliant focused dress codes. I do wonder; however, how the underlying message of student empowerment or learner agency might be impacted with so many specific clothing rules.

Teacher Request: If a school is truly reaching for excellence and we want EVERY student to have the optimal learning opportunity, then why would we refuse to match student and teacher in the most appropriate

EMPOWERMENT

way. For the past 20+ years, we've allowed students and parents to request specific teachers. And, assuming there isn't a block to a student's schedule (I.E they need band at the only time a teacher teaches a math class) we continue to successfully grant all teacher requests.

We see this stakeholder choice similarly to how businesses utilize a money back guarantee. Few people actually follow up on the money back guarantee to return an item. However, just knowing this is an option gives consumers a relative peace of mind coupled with purchasing power.

The same is true for granting teacher requests. Students and parents can identify a specific teacher request during the time of registration. Thus, when we're building the master schedule and ultimately begin both mass and hand scheduling individual students, we incorporate said requests into planning and executing schedules. Additionally, this information is helpful feedback to both administration and teachers on student and parent perceptions. Thus, every teacher is striving to offer a classroom where stakeholders WANT to learn in.

School Supplies: We provide all school supplies to our students. In fact, we even let them pick them out, on the first day of school. We set up school supplies assembly lines in our cafeteria and then give students a choice in what color notebook or binder they select. We've effectively leveled the playing field by providing supplies to everyone and then allowing them to restock throughout the year. No more teacher dilemmas about giving students a piece of paper or a notebook. When a student needs something, they know exactly where they are...so they go grab it. Plus, we limit one equity issue by ensuring everyone is prepared with the supplies. Obviously, students have the option of bringing additional or alternate supplies from home but ensuring all students have what they need is such a powerful cultural builder!

Drills/Assemblies: Some students are negatively impacted by loud assemblies, anxiety provoking bells, sirens, or evacuation procedures.

We take the time to create plans, options, and choices in how impacted students handle drills and/or assemblies. For instance, we notify these students about fire drills, arrange for alternative seating in assemblies, provide earbuds during loud events, and in general work to empower these students to lessen triggers to anxiety and/or outbursts. By making them co-conspirators in safety drills or assemblies we turn them into leaders who do some of the following tasks: check classrooms, count students, turn lights on/off, keep track of class rosters, unlock doorways, etc.

> **Award Winning Culture intentionally builds in leadership opportunities during our most anxiety inducing school-wide activities.**

Therapy/Emotional Support Animals: Five years ago, I never would have considered this a part of our culture; however, times change and schools must adapt. Our district currently has a partnership with local support animal agencies. Handlers bring in dogs to work with our district's students in the following ways: reading, calming, grief support, behavior management, etc.

I do not include these support animals as a way of offering best practice for creating an Award Winning Culture. Instead, I include these animals as a reminder that schools that are focused on excellence are always pushing the envelope in ways that may benefit school culture. Bringing therapy dogs into our schools meant rewriting district policy, establishing procedures, parent permission, examining student and staff allergies, and designing a plan for how to use the dogs. It is not as if we just opened up our doors and provided Scooby Snacks for every classroom. Intentionality, thought, and pre-planning have allowed us to maximize the benefit of having therapy dogs interact with students.

EMPOWERMENT

Mediation: Long before restorative circles became in vogue, EMS had offered student mediation as a successful way to resolve conflict. Our counselors and administrators are all trained in facilitating these experiences for students. However, we don't force, mandate, or require mediation to work through interpersonal issues. Students must opt in to this intervention strategy. Providing students with choice and some autonomy over how this looks, make mediation circles actually become more effective. Authors Nathan Maynard and Brad Weinstein explain the power of teaching empathy using restorative justice in their book: *Hacking School Discipline*. Maynard and Weinstein lay out a 9-step plan for implementation and the ensuing societal impact of not simply suspending kids and instead giving them voice and choice over making positive relationship repairs.

When students choose to voluntarily work through a difficult discussion with adult guidance, they tend to be more open to listening, empathizing, and problem solving than if they were required to be there. Additionally, if they successfully resolve their issue or concern, word of mouth among students spreads that participating in a mediation is a valuable opportunity. This increases the likelihood of making a positive choice toward mediation instead of a negative behavior retaliation during conflict.

Furthermore, mediation is not just for student to student issues.

We've found success with these types of circles in student to teacher conflict, teacher to teach conflict, and parent to teacher conflict. The key is to model authentic communication while empowering choice with participation.

Clubs/Activities: We have such a wide variety of formal and informal clubs and activities that we offer at EMS, it's almost impossible not to find something that you're interested in. However, our school wide caveat to students is, if there's a club you wish we had at EMS, that doesn't already exist, come see an adult educator and we'll help you create it. Over half of our clubs and activities came about because students (not adults) saw a need and were intentionally taught how to go about starting a new group at our school. When schools give students almost unlimited choices of activity design, we greatly enhance student connection to peers, adults, and school.

How will you amplify voices throughout your school community?

What are some current examples of choice in your classroom? school-wide examples of choice?

Are there downsides, barriers or issues with infusing more voice and choice within your culture?

How might you mitigate or combat those concerns?

CHAPTER 15
EXPERIENTIAL

By now you're starting to see the impact of providing experiential learning opportunities within the school culture as this buzzword continues to permeate this book. Experiential excellence raises the bar by creating education filled with purpose and meaning with an authentic audience. Here's a few Wildcat Nation examples of students creating their very best content, through intentional experiential moments:

Student-Led Podcasting

With over 700,000 podcasts ranging in every topic imaginable, it seems that anyone with a microphone has a ready-made platform to share their ideas with the world. Naturally, this societal endeavor has led to an educational surge of project-based learning that filters into the classroom. My favorite educational podcasters invite me into an inspiring conversation and then hold a mirror up, for me to self-reflect. Student-led podcasting has become an educational wave as teachers explore creative ways to incorporate STEM into their content area. However, few schools realize the school culture impact that can be had by building an authentic audience outside the classroom with a culture focused podcast.

At Wildcat Nation, we've created a student-led leadership podcast called Award Winning Culture, that is centered around Character, Excellence, and Community. Our student leaders interview best-selling authors, keynote speakers, athletes, educators, and other leadership students and then offer reflections at the end of each podcast episode. Our school-wide podcast focuses on the following types of culture building topics: leadership, innovation, character, kindness, empathy, community building, service, mindset, self-care, wellness, mental health, etc. This isn't a laid-back platform for students to chat about their favorite food or sports teams. It's also not narrowly focused on a specific classroom content area. For example, some educators who utilize student podcasting have students discuss topics specific to only a particular class. Thus, the best-case scenario is that students and teachers are the only reasonably interested audience of this work.

When thinking about building an authentic audience, educators with a mindset for experiential excellence realize that traditional assignments, projects, etc. follow a familiar path. Students turn in assignments. One person sees the assignment: the teacher. The teacher hands the assignment back to the student with a grade on it. And the assignment usually ends up in the garbage. Whether the assignment lands in the garbage that day or at the end of the semester, the longevity of the work is generally short lived. Some teachers manage to build in class groups or peers into viewing a student's work. Perhaps, the student shares the work or project through a presentation to the class. However, once again the impact of the student creation is generally limited to the 4 walls of the classroom.

By contrast, a student created podcast that offers rich culture building content that's not limited to a specific class has allowed our passion-based learning project to reach a vast audience. Each week, students, staff, and parents are listening to our podcast. Thus, lessons, reflections, and connections that directly impact school culture are driving conversation throughout our community. When student podcasters began to realize the impact of their words on behavior, thoughts, and feelings far beyond the classroom we've embedded natural meaning and purpose into what students are doing. For example, preparing for an interview with leadership expert Jon Gordon meant students watched his viral videos, read his inspiring books, and carefully crafted intentional questions that might center around a joy filled theme. This work might sound like homework, but the truth is, there is no grade. There is no requirement other than students' self-desire to be ready for the interview. When students feel a sense of intrinsic motivation to learn, discover, and prepare for excellence...we're helping them develop joy. Joy of learning. Joy of life. Joy of creating original and inspiring content.

Origin Story

In February 2018, my wife (Jennifer) and I had the pleasure of taking a small group of students to a state-wide leadership conference (SERVUS) at the Shoeware Center in Kent Washington. What made the four-hour trip worthwhile? SERVUS is an eight-hour conference filled with the brightest middle and high school students in the state. They pack 5000 students and educational leaders in to listen and learn from inspiring leadership experts, speakers, athletes, and celebrities from around the country.

I'm sitting next to my wife, maybe three quarters of the way through this incredible day. And we're listening to a 95 year-old holocaust survivor named Naomi Ban. This frail tiny woman is in a wheelchair on stage speaking in broken English to the arena of teenagers and you could literally hear a pin drop. As I looked around, I saw students leaning forward and educators wiping away tears, while we all hung on her every word. It was absolutely EPIC! Suddenly, I leaned over to my wife and whispered: "we've got to do this." She shot me a puzzled look, like only wives can do, followed by "WHAT?" Again, I reiterated, "WE'VE GOT TO DO THIS!" At the next break, we began to explore how we might be able to create a platform for our students to learn from incredible cultural leaders like Ban. While we were able to bring a handful of students across the mountains to this special event, there were another 750 students, back home, unable to hear and experience these whole child learning.

As Jen and I spoke, the idea began to become fleshed out that maybe we could create an experiential learning opportunity through a student-led podcast. Leadership students would interview experts within the lens of character, excellence, and community and then share reflections at the end of the interview. And if we built it right, perhaps it would be something our entire school community would benefit from. Heck, maybe even communities around the world might tune in. This was the early seeds of establishing an authentic audience with the Award Winning Culture student-led podcast as we forever shattered the ceiling on student voice!

Our student-led podcast allows students to learn from incredible experts on mental health, innovation, leadership, school culture, character, mindfulness, etc. They conduct a thorough research of the guest, generate questions, record an interview, and then offer a reflection at the end of the podcast with their thoughts, feelings, and takeaways from the experience. After the interview, they send a basket of goodies and hand-written thank-you cards to each guest. Our students pick out the goodies

EXPERIENTIAL

and put the baskets together. Lastly, we edit the podcast and send it out to the masses. We have students, educators, and parent listeners, all over the world.

awardwinningculture.com

Here are a few opportunities that podcasting has generated for our student podcasters:

- Podcasting has opened doors to our students such as blogging, creating spoken word raps, and presenting and teaching to both students and educators on how to podcast.

- They were approached by three different companies before agreeing to terms with **CharacterStrong** as an initial sponsor of the podcast.

- Students have been invited onto other educational podcasts to share their unique journey into student voice.

- Guests have sent swag, books, clothing, etc. to our students.

A quick search reveals that the Award Winning Culture podcast is one of the most popular educational podcasts available, but how does creating a cool platform like this actually impact the excellence of a school's culture? I want to highlight a couple aspects that relate directly to creating exceptional school culture.

Obviously, student podcasters learn things like advanced empathy, listening skills, and rapport building while sharing their voice during interviews with amazing people.

It is also no surprise that empathy is a key soft skill that whole child focused schools are actively teaching. Thanks to whole child initiatives, empathy is becoming a point of emphasis in the same vein as core subject areas (Math, Science, ELA, etc.) have always been. Indeed, in an ever changing, unstable world filled with technology, fear, and a me-first mentality, empathy and kindness seem to be a revelatory anecdote to hate.

Andrew Sokatch, is the Founding Research Director at the Character Lab with Angela Duckworth. Sokatch's previous experience includes teaching elementary, middle school, college, and graduate school students, and spending over a decade leading teacher quality research at Teach for America and The New Teacher Project. Sokatch says,

"End of the year test scores are the floor of what we need to expect from schools and we're mistaking that floor, for the whole house."

Dr. Clayton Cook, is the John and Nancy Peyton Faculty Fellow in Child and Adolescent Wellbeing at the University of Minnesota and Associate Professor in the School Psychology Program. Dr. Cook co-founded the School Mental Health Assessment, Research and Training (SMART) Center at the University of Washington and is a core faculty member within the Institute of Translational Research in Children's Mental Health at the University of Minnesota. In addition to his research, he consults with several school and community systems throughout the US to improve practices and outcomes for students to meet the demands of civic, work, and home life. Dr. Cook shares,

"If we only focus on academics then we're only giving students 30-50% of what they need to be successful after high school."

When we design platforms of learning that are built upon authentic audiences, the students involved in the platform are not the only ones to benefit from the experience. The brilliance and true impact of projects like Award Winning Culture are measured in the cultural shifts happening school-wide, district-wide, and system-wide. For instance, students at our school regularly reach out to our student podcasters to share thank-yous, appreciation, and gratitude for putting a voice to difficult topics. I remember one podcaster sharing,

EXPERIENTIAL

"My friend came up to me today and said how much this week's podcast meant to her. She said that she had been struggling with being bullied and feeling alone and LOVED the guest's perspective on how to deal with bullies. But her favorite part was my personal reflection on how I've felt bullied before."

When students lead with vulnerability and brave leadership on platforms like student podcasts, other students can learn vicariously through our podcasters firsthand account. But cultural impact at EMS isn't limited to students.

Teachers and parents have been some of our biggest listeners and subscribers. Adults are tuning in to learn and understand more about how middle schoolers think, behave, and feel. It's as if we're providing a window into the inter-psyche of 12 and 13 year-olds. After having international parenting expert and empathy guru, Dr. Michele Borba, on the show, parents reached out to say how much it meant to them, to hear student reflections on specific parenting advice. One parent explained,

"My own kid won't open up to me, so it was awesome to hear what middle schoolers actually think about social media expectations, rules, and the ideal way to approach a teenager to have difficult conversations."

Additionally, teachers have been given a front row seat to learn real feedback on what does and does not work in student/teacher relationships, homework, innovation, and autonomy of learning. Many teachers have found it empowering to learn that a particular lesson, risk, or strategy was well received when student leaders shared in detail about how and what they learned in class.

I was surprised to hear one student's reflection that her favorite relationship building strategy employed by teachers was to seek feedback. It was fascinating to learn how adults' willingness to ask for and then incorporate specific feedback played big in the minds of teens.

Student-led podcasting has also helped me uncover another powerful form of measuring the cultural impact of this far reaching platform. This additional impact, I call Secondary Experiential Learning. Educators know that essentially experiential learning is doing and then reflecting on the doing. But when students share their reflections with the world, we create the opportunity for a secondary cultural impact as well. I first became aware of this tertiary impact within the first couple months of establishing the Award Winning Culture podcast.

In our second podcast interview, our guest, James Hunter subtly challenged our students to *be the student who goes and sits with the kid who's all by him or herself at lunch*. Hunter didn't make a big deal out of it but just dropped a small challenge to three podcasters near the end of the interview.

About a month later another one of our podcasters mentioned this during the end of an anti-bullying podcast. She reflected about how she had listened to Hunter talk about sitting with isolated students and that she and her friends had taken it upon themselves to go sit with students

EXPERIENTIAL

who seemed alone. She talked about how it felt, what was challenging and overall how much she and her friends enjoyed lifting others' mood at lunch. At the time, I felt this was a cool reflection but didn't give it a ton more thought.

Approximately a month later, some students from a middle school on the east coast (thousands of miles away) started messaging us on Instagram. They explained that they had listened to the episode that detailed her lunchtime seating changes. They loved the idea and started doing something similar at lunch, to positively impact their own school. They thanked us for creating the podcast and Audrey for sharing her experience.

Now to be honest, as adult educators supporting the project, Jen and I had some idea of the reach of the Award Winning Culture podcast already through social media, website, podcasting downloads, impressions, and reviews. However, up until that point, our students had no frame of reference to their real impact outside of our own community. When our podcast students realized that the words they say into a microphone in West Richland, Washington impact student

behavior in Cedar Crest Pennsylvania---LIFE-CHANGING!!

The energy, effort, and enthusiasm to forever shatter the ceiling on student voice became magnified for our student podcasters. Their interest in positively influencing school culture shifted from only focusing on our community to the world. Since then, we've seen dozens of examples of Secondary Experiential Learning with this intentional shift towards excellence through podcasting.

Near the end of the first year of podcasting, we planned a podcast retreat. Part celebration of current podcasters and part onboarding of new podcasters, we believed that it would be a unique experience for everyone involved. It was so cool to watch students teaching other students, the finer points of speaking, editing, writing, etc. One of our BIG surprises was a video we created for our podcasters to watch from listeners, supporters, and fans all around the world. Such a POWERFUL message to show our students the far reach of their words and actions. Knowing that they've inspired students to try podcasting, had authors use their work in writing projects, and impacted educators' views on leadership and learning—UNFORGETTABLE!!

AWC-TV

Many schools offer video production classes or clubs. However, at Wildcat Nation we've carved out video and audio platform design that focused exclusively on the 3 overarching wings of school culture: Character, Excellence, and Community. With this lens, student created projects offer audiovisual content that directly impacts school culture. By creating content that focuses on things like mental health, parenting, growth mindset, grit, poverty, learning disabilities, assessment, trauma, tolerance, kindness, and empathy our students are directly impacting the very same culture that they currently exist in.

Blogging

Student blogging is a wonderful platform to empower students to use their voice on school culture related topics. These and other examples of writing can be created by students and promoted by students and staff around the school. Thus, any student can become involved in writing a powerful piece to an upcoming topic that fuels their life's purpose. Blogging is a special personalized journey to open your mind to yourself and your heart, with the world! This is a big departure from traditional student newspapers with a regular working committee. Again, the goal is not exclusion of student writers. Instead, we're welcoming and inviting all students with an interest in sharing a message, idea or viewpoint that directly moves the school culture conversation.

EXPERIENTIAL

> **When we take the time to support student literary work that's directly tied to school culture, we essentially invite the most important stakeholders to a seat at the table of positive change.**

Thus, students who may not be our most vocal or extroverted leaders can still have incredible influence within the school community. I really appreciated one student's blog about the need to make a change to our old SEL curriculum. She voiced what many educators weren't able or willing to see quite yet. Through her brave writing she challenged people like me to find a better social emotional curriculum that students and staff would enjoy. And her hot take on the necessary pivot towards something better was right on!

Cavalcade of Authors

I'm fortunate to work with some outstanding literacy leaders including our incredible librarian. Our librarian is a forward thinking literacy advocate who has created an absolutely unreal annual event called Cavalcade of Authors (COA). Since 2007, she and her team of volunteers have been planning, organizing, and leading a writing conference where secondary students across our region are given access to some of the best Young Adult authors of our modern era. There are writing contests, featured book talks, panel discussions and autograph sessions. COA provides students a chance to learn and interact with the very authors whose books they are reading.

Students at a recent COA conference said:

"Cavalcade of Authors was the chance of a lifetime to meet authors and ask them questions."

"Everything around us is an inspiration!"

"I learned that at any age you can be a writer."

"The workshops are a lot of fun and are very interactive. Plus, the authors are super cool and very friendly."

Students aren't the only ones who are thrilled to be a part of this unique mentorship experience. Writers around the country are clamoring to be part of this annual event. Author, Jennifer Donnelly, said,

"I loved every minute of Cavalcade-from the enthusiastic school panels, to high-fiving the writing contest winner, to the workshops attended by super-dedicated young writers."

Furthermore, Author Justina Chen reiterates her literary peers' excitement when she shared,

"I'd like to give a personal shout out for organizing a fantastic Northwest book festival. Through Cavalcade of Authors, thousands of teens have been able to meet with their favorite authors because of her, her vision, and her team of literacy-minded volunteers."

> **Award Winning Culture thrives when educational leaders create special experiential opportunities designed to promote personalized literacy exploration.**

The authors are given the full **Wildcat Nation** treatment with an adult event the night before, red carpet entrance, and all of their needs met with exceptional hospitality and service.

EXPERIENTIAL

How might you turn up the dial on your school's passion for literacy?

College and Career Day

This year we're finalizing details for our 6th annual College & Career Day. We host 50+ community volunteers in our two gyms, cafeteria, and outside space for kids to roll up their sleeves and interact, test out, and ask questions with the very careers and colleges they aspire toward. Each year, we turn a three-hour half day in February into an experiential opportunity for all students. In order to invite the student desired professionals, students complete a WOIS career interest inventory and a four-year high school planning tool that ensures we know what careers students are particularly passionate about.

My fellow counseling partner has spearheaded this impactful Wildcat mainstay with an intentional vision of servant leadership, student voice/ choice, and student reflection. Our office team, in partnership with our leadership teachers and students help elevate the experience to the next level. Student leaders meet and greet volunteers prior to the event, carry vendor and company supplies in from the parking lot and physically help them set up. We provide breakfast snacks, coffee, and refreshments delivered to each booth, throughout the event. Additionally, we provide individual handwritten thank-yous, treats, etc. at the conclusion of the event. The communication that she and her team provide to our volunteers complete with maps, event vision/mission, details, video, etc. help set the stage for a special experience for our entire community. But the experience for students milling around the booths is even more top notch. Our volunteers, vendors, and career experts deliver larger than life hands on moments of learning, fun, and connection that helps students uncover their own joy.

Editing Authors Work

An example of experiential learning has been the opportunity to have our students edit and interact with authors work in progress. Thanks to our connections on social media, we've found avenues to bring real world writing revision to our classrooms. By giving students a chance to practice editing, revising, and feedback to professional authors, students connect to the writing process in a meaningful way.

Recently, some students edited Allyson Apsey's new book, *The Serendipity Journal*. This experiential learning opportunity fueled their class to work on the writing process while learning about human relations, empathy, and understanding trauma. Reading and creating great literature is wonderful. But helping support the creation of great literature is exponentially more meaningful!

Skyping with Experts

Mystery Skypes, Virtual tours, and Class to Class chats are all wonderful ways to infuse a level of experiential learning to reach a level of excellence in the classroom. Anytime we remove the four walls of the learning environment, we expand student minds, hearts, and relationships. Learning about culture in other parts of the world provides students with ideas and insights to improve our current school culture as well as a level of gratitude for this special atmosphere they've worked hard to develop. Additionally, inspiring curiosity in others leads directly to empathy.

STAT

As previously mentioned, our Student Technology Assistance Team (STAT) is a strong experiential opportunity to practice technology skills in the real world, with built in leadership and character-building moments.

As you can imagine our district innovation and technology department has been highly supportive of this experiential empowerment move.

Teachers and students who are struggling with a routine technological challenge have an immediate in-house lifeline to support their needs. For substitute teachers, this form of student leadership has become invaluable! Furthermore, our STAT facilitates fun STEM-focused activities such as maker-space events at lunch time. Without a doubt their unique gifts coupled with a desire to give back to our school have made them a school culture game-changer!

> **What if we celebrated kids who could add value to other's lives, in the same way we celebrated kids who earned straight A's?**

Experiential learning gives students a chance to practice and live moments that reach and teach the whole child. By moving beyond academic content and practicing soft skills, character, and leadership development schools craft meaningful learning that's rooted in big ideas like purpose, joy, and love.

What would it take for you to design some experiential moments for your students?

What impact to school culture do you anticipate as a result of increased experiential opportunities?

CHAPTER 16
EPIC

Essential **P**ersonalized **I**ntentional **C**uriosity

Creating a culture of excellence starts with planning through a lens of EPIC. Striving for an EPIC culture includes all of the following: Essential, Personalized, Intentional, Curiosity. By breaking down big ideas, decisions, and potential outcomes through this framework, school personnel have the ability to create powerful moments that leave imprints of positivity on the soul.

Essential

When designing a powerful culture building moment, it's critical to start with the essentials. Essentials are the requirements, expectations or points of emphasis that need to be covered. There are always aspects of every profession that are out of our control. In education, we sometimes run up against systemic restrictions, expectations or policy that presents challenges that might keep us stuck to only focusing on mandates and failing to reach cultural excellence. Fostering EPIC moments in culture begins with identifying the essential parts.

For instance, perhaps your planning parent teacher conferences. There are specific elements to the experience that are required. In some districts, union and district leaders have negotiated certain mandates for secondary conferences: time of day, style (arena style), not student-led, etc. In many ways, the district and union bargaining choices have created a less than desirable experience for parents, students, and educators. By focusing exclusively on compliance and sustainability both parties have undermined the most important aspect of an effective parent teacher conference: open and healthy communication about a learner's progress. Additionally, we've unintentionally put the entire focus on grade reporting and academic progress which can exclude the impact to the whole child.

Within the academic world, teachers might recognize essentials as the standards, EALRs, or Common Core. Those important pieces are universally recognized to be critical to learning. Teachers may also have required curriculum or key points of emphasis that are outside of their control. However, innovative educators around the world are creating very unique learning experiences while operating within the same set of standards. We all have teachers in our building that are provided the same curriculum, expectations, and district/state requirements but yet create completely different cultures of learning. The talented educators pick apart what's essential and then infuse personalization, intentionality, and curiosity to reach unforgettable learning experiences.

Coaches might view essentials as the rules, restrictions, or universal athletic guidelines that drive competition. Some inherent essentials to a sports team might include number of practices, time of practice, required playing time, dates when practices can begin, location of practice, schedule of games, rules of the sport, etc. There are numerous aspects to a given sport that may create challenges to a coaching staff. Just like with academics, a key to creating the best team is to first understand all the essential elements of that sport. Figuring out what's in their control and what's out of their control helps coaches create exceptional teams.

By disseminating essentials, students and staff can begin to personalize a culture building moment. A couple examples of essential questions for designing powerful experiences might include:

- What is the food restriction laws or policies?

- What are the district rules for using student faces on social media?

- What time does the teacher we want to celebrate have a prep period?

- Are there FERPA considerations when having leadership students decorate the inside of student lockers?

As you can imagine there are an endless number of questions and considerations of essentials, when designing an EPIC moment of excellence. Once educators have a firm grasp on any and all parameters of a potential culture building experience, they can begin to explore personalization.

Personalized

We all recognize that one size does not fit all. This is why education has Individual Education Plans (IEP'S), Personalized Learning, Mastery Learning (The GRID Method), Universal Design for Learning, Flexible Seating, Genius Hour, etc. It's also why Howard Garner's work with multiple intelligences led educators to redesign learning experiences to address individual differences in students. This same approach to classroom instruction can and should be applied to culture building moments. Why would we assume that all people want to be recognized in front of the school, in an assembly? Or that every staff member would want their class interrupted for a Wildcat Snack Cart. People are different. They have unique personalities, style, tastes, and previous experiences that ultimately shape their desired love language. In 1992, Gary Chapman identified *The Five Love Languages*: Receiving Gifts, Quality Time, Words of Affirmation, Acts of Service, and Physical Touch. While the book was initially geared toward romantic relationships, these ideas are absolutely transferable to relationships in schools and organizations.

Beyond a person's identifying love language personalization of powerful culture building moments implies a bit of research. In an earlier chapter on the Wildcat Award, I mentioned students need to do recon. Imagine how a school that focuses on learning what drives others would be in constant empathy mode. And as my friend Barbara Gruener says, "Empathy gives Kindness it's WHY." We can use empathy to inform the optimal way to express kindness to others.

Students and staff that truly want to create EPIC moments of culture are committed to asking questions, listening, and being genuinely interested in HOW, WHAT, WHEN, WHY, AND WHERE to brighten others day. EPIC focused cultured builders know that it's not enough to decide to do something nice for the secretaries, basketball team, or band teacher. They must learn everything they can about a target of affection, in order to elevate the experience. This is why a handwritten card means so much more than a store-bought greeting card. When it's handwritten, the personalization is left up to the writer.

Intentional

"When you become intentional about adding value to people and make it your priority, anything and everything you have can be used to help others."

-John C. Maxwell Intentional Living

Positive Intentionality is a deliberate and purposeful plan of action to bring about a desired result. Indeed, all actions either contribute to or detract from others overall cultural experience. I first became aware of intentionality, while working on my masters.

The Tissue Lesson

I was fortunate to attend one of the best counselor prep programs in the northwest. Central Washington University (CWU) in Ellensburg Washington is highly distinguished for 3 specific programs of study: Accounting, Teaching, and Counseling. Indeed, their counselor prep program is second to none, in my part of the country! Perhaps, the biggest distinction between CWU and other universities' counseling programs is the experiential practicum experience that students receive in a real-world clinic. While some programs are grounded in role playing, scenarios, and fake setups, CWU required me to complete nearly two years of individual and group counseling with actual live people. It was insanely rigorous and inordinately challenging. All 50-minute sessions were videotaped for us, our supervisor, and our student teams to review, analyze, and critique. We spent hours transcribing words, interpreting non-verbal cues, and examining feelings or thoughts. If you've ever recorded yourself doing anything, you recognize that the camera catches everything. Frequent questions arose during viewing sessions that would make the most confident individual re-examine their future counseling path:

"Why did you cross your legs there?"

"How come you leaned forward there?"

"What message are you sending to the student with this greeting?"

"How might you more accurately capture this person's story?"

"What transference or countertransference was observable in that clip?"

As you might imagine, every little component was picked over. In fact, I believe the saying, "leave no stone unturned" could have come directly from CWU's clinical counseling program. It was a challenging and awesome experience and I loved everything about it! Frankly, we all knew that if we survived this program (and not everyone did) we'd be ready to flourish in the helping profession. Of all the memories, learnings, and take-aways from my time in the program, the one I continue to come back to is something I call *The Tissue Lesson*. During one unforgettable review session, my supervisor (Dr. Collins) took a close look at a session I was confused by. During the session, the student and I seemed to be connecting well. We were building rapport and the student was slowly opening up. At one point, she began to cry and started to share some intense feelings. Suddenly, she stopped weeping and put up an emotional wall. It was clear that she no longer felt comfortable exploring her feelings at that moment. On video tape, it became obvious as she quickly clammed up and returned into her own head before moving the conversation into a different direction. As our team zeroed in on this piece of the tape, we tried to determine what might have gone wrong. Dr. Collins, an expert in human behavior and a passion for teaching future counselors made me replay a 20-second clip probably half a dozen times.

"What do you see Hans?" Collins questioned.

"Ah, I don't know. I gave her a tissue as she started to cry," I stated as I tried to make sense of his nonsensical question.

"How did you give her the tissue," Collins probed.

"Ahhh, I handed her the box" I said with slight annoyance, as I looked around the room at my fellow peers trying to understand the point of this inquiry.

"Anyone else see anything?" Collins posed to the other students.

Silence.

At that moment, Dr. Collins reached for the tissue box next to him...slowly and methodically pulled out one tissue, presented it to me with an open posture flourish and then set the entire box gently next to me.

"Hans, let's consider how you presented the tissue to her instead," as Collins gathered the box back with an air of excitement, as if he knew, he was about to forever change my way of thinking.

"When you handed her the box, there was no compassion, no feeling, no warmth. You simply picked up the box and set it down coldly next to her, as if to say, 'dry your tears now.' Obviously, that wasn't your intended message, but you didn't present the tissue in a way that encouraged her to continue to explore her own feelings. It's critical to create a safe culture where our students can tackle real emotion because that's where real learning and insight comes from."

We went on as a small group to discuss and practice something I've come to dub *the tissue display* for another 15 minutes. During this time, we determined the optimal spot in the room for the tissues to reside. We reconfigured the chairs to better meet the demands of immediacy. We worked through just how close the box should be to both the student and counselor. Additionally, our group delved into a thorough examination of how to offer the tissue, how much eye contact to give, what to say and not say. Let me assure you, there are literally a zillon ways to hand someone a tissue. We played around with subtle differences that might be awkward, funny, or strange ways to offer up the tissue. I can only describe the scene, as if it were an image from an improv group such as SNL or Second City blocking and choreographing potential actions for a performance.

Near the end of this experiential learning discussion, Dr. Collins asked the group,

"So, what's the big takeaway from Hans' session today?"

Naturally, we all started yammering on about tissues, feelings, safety... when Collins stopped us sharply,

"No, No, No" Collins explained. "It's not about the tissue. Although don't get me wrong, the tissue matters. Obviously, knowing how to respond to someone in tears is critical. But that's not ALL! It's about the DETAIL and INTENTIONALITY OF THE MOMENT. Exceptional educators think through EVERY aspect. The lesson moving forward is that you each need to analyze, consider, and reflect on every action, communication, and facet you present in a helping or learning setting. Furthermore, you must consider the space, environment...right down to the furniture layout and choice of the room. Will you have background music, what type of lighting is best, what will you hang on your walls, etc. No detail is too small!"

This entire review session is burned in my memory forever. Years later, I've used the tissue lesson with school counseling interns to great success. Obviously, it's a beautiful way to illustrate the need to establish a growth mindset towards reflection and to think in terms of student experience rather than educator perception. When we're trying to create the perfect culture for humanistic growth, Collins was exactly correct in that every detail smatter. The tissue lesson emphasizes both practice (how to present a tissue) and theory (application of a detail focused mindset).

> **Award Winning Culture establishes a mindset for continual exploration of details that impact thoughts, feelings, and behaviors...and hereby LEARNING.**

But are these levels of consideration actually necessary in education? I so admire intentional educational thought leaders...not just for their ideas...

but for their willingness to step outside the proverbial tissue box and wrestle with the intricacies of student experience.

As we start breaking down routine educational events into the tiny particular choices, decisions, and aspects that form your work, you realize that the great educators have a different level of thinking that goes into creating their educational ecosystem.

Additionally, the tissue lesson teaches us that there is no perfect way to present the tissue to every person. Former school counselor, author, and creator of *Character Speaks*, Barbara Gruener says:

"Mindfulness is being where your feet are."

When educators are willing to be in the moment and are committed to getting outside of their own heads to take an empathic stance on others cultural experiences, educators find themselves in the perfect position to serve the whole child.

Perhaps the greatest lesson from Dr. Collins' tissue experiment is to never stop reflecting on our own work. And if you think about it, modeling a lifelong pursuit of learning might be our greatest gift to our students, families, and colleagues.

Step back and take a wide-angle view on something you've been struggling with...

Might there be a more meaningful way to offer
THE TISSUE?

What unintended outcomes might YOUR actions be yielding?

What current educational practices might you dissect to recreate a better character-infused experience for others?

How might you fine tune an event, lesson, or daily occurrence to maximize the positivity within your school culture?

Curiosity

Fostering curiosity in the classroom is a widely recognized goal of effective instruction. Curious students go way beyond guidelines and expectations to become driven by a need to learn. What if we applied this strategy to creating excellence in culture?

The curious culture influencers are focused on constant improvement, tweaking, and moving forward. They recognize that school culture is not in a forever state of homeostasis. Instead, school culture is an ever-adapting mix of behaviors that are influenced by literally everything that exists in the schoolhouse. Therefore, students and staff must be relentless in their pursuit of cultural improvements. Thus, a program, an event, or just a way of doing things might not be ideal a year from now. Adopting a growth mindset that's curiously seeking a better way of advancing culture and climate EVERY DAY is critical to a school's success.

Consider social media. Prior to social media's existence, no educator believed that a social media presence was necessary to its culture and climate. However, there are many schools who have failed to jump into the pool of school branding by way of social media. Their unwillingness to take on a mindset of curiosity about social media, in terms of school culture, has created systemic barriers to reaching all families.

The need for cultural curiosity isn't just limited to innovation. Curiosity is critical in relationships. Jason Treu, author of *Social Wealth*, says that

"Just asking questions can increase and enhance a relationship."

The more we take the time and energy to express meaningful curiosity, the more connected we become.

> **Award Winning Culture promotes curiosity in relationships, intentional and personalized culture building moments, and as a means to improve the daily school experience of all stakeholders.**

Let's examine a basic example of non-EPIC and then EPIC kindness. If a student drops a pencil in the hallway and I bend over and pick up the pencil and return it to him I've done something nice for that student. Nice is a REACTIVE form of positivity. However, let's assume that I walk up and down the hallway handing out pencils to random students. In this case, I would be offering an act of kindness. Kindness is PROACTIVE and a much stronger form of positivity than simply being nice.

However, this random act of kindness (handing out pencils to students) does not actually ensure that I'm connecting with someone who truly needs a pencil. I might get lucky and accidentally hand a student a pencil who really needs it but I'm also just as likely to miss the student who desperately needs some positivity today. If we combine kindness with EPIC, we get the highest form of positivity. What if we re-examined the act of kindness through an EPIC lens of culture building excellence?

Essential: I only have a window of time today during lunch to do something really special for a student. My day is so busy that I'll only be available to do this act of kindness during 7th grade lunch.

Personalized: I may ask around to 7th grade teachers, which student really needs a win this week? Maybe they're worried about someone in their class who's been struggling. Several teachers identify Weston. Weston doesn't always come to school. I know he's on the free lunch program as his home situation is less than ideal. Weston eats pizza every day.

He already has all the pencils he needs, since he could easily help himself to a pencil or other supplies, in any of his classes. We've sponsored Weston's family for thanksgiving and Christmas before so I know food and snacks are something he might enjoy. Weston is not shy, he's a pretty outgoing kid who craves attention.

Intentional: What if I took a little treat into the lunchroom, at the beginning of 7th grade lunch. I could give it to the lunch lady and ask her to give it to Weston, when he comes through the pizza line. I could instruct her to say "Weston-this is from someone who really cares about you," as she hands him the treat. Who wouldn't like a little surprise treat!?

Curiosity: I might follow up with the lunch lady later in the day to see what Weston's reaction was. If it seemed to be a genuinely joyful moment, I'll remember this for future reference. If it fell flat, maybe I can learn why. Did he not enjoy that treat? Does his desire to seek attention mean that I should have personally handed him the treat? Did I miss an opportunity to make this an even grandeur moment with the triangle of Joy?

Don't miss the obvious point of excellence here though! This easy to do, act of kindness took me maybe 5 minutes to plan and execute. But I hope it's obvious to you, that the impact will be a far greater act of intentional kindness toward a student who desperately needs some positivity than picking up a student pencil or handing out pencils to random students.

Combining intentionality and kindness doesn't only impact the target of our affection. Tamara Letter in her treasure of a book, *Passion For Kindness*, explains "making intentional choices to bless others with kindness shifted many aspects of my life." In a chapter about Sandy Hook, she emphasizes the "jubilation" and connections that make intentional kindness life changing.

This form of kindness can and should exist within distance or virtual learning worlds as well. In referring to Sandy Hook, Tamara talks about researching the victims of that horrific tragedy and pairing her own kindness act with the inspiration of global positivity. Even though she was far removed from both the people and events of Sandy Hook, she didn't let geographical location deter her ability to work within essential elements while personalizing, Intentional moments of magical balloon giveaways in honor of a 6 year-old victim. Because she was curious about how she might serve the Sandy Hook community, she made a huge impact on her own community, the Sandy Hook community, and herself. Tamara's incredible act is a wonderful reminder of the power of intentional kindness in a time of school closures, increased distance learning or COVID-19 social distancing.

How might you apply the EPIC framework to events, activities, and practices at your school?

How might relationships grow as a result of becoming an EPIC classroom, school, or district leader?

CHAPTER 17
PETE

"Closing the caring gap in education requires relationship development to build trust!"

-Don Epps

I'll never forget Pete. Pete was a freckle faced, tall thin young man with thick coke bottle glasses. He had buck teeth, a goofy smile, and an impish disregard for following the rules. He was completely disinterested in traditional education and took painstaking opportunities to avoid work. Prior to middle school, he had been 'gifted' the labels of ADHD, Tourettes, Oppositional Defiant Disorder, Learning Disabled, Behavior Problem, and in general pain in the butt. He had tried counseling and medications throughout elementary school with little to no success. His parents were excruciatingly demanding, critical, and combative with their son's school system. In all my years working in education, Pete was one of the most challenging students I have ever worked with. If I'm being honest his mere name mentioned in some teacher circles brings about grunts and groans before eventually giving way to tiny smiles. Surviving Pete and his family was a badge of honor for some educators who had their patience, commitment, and forgiveness tested on a regular basis.

My first encounter with Pete was in the spring of his 5th grade year as his elementary school led a transition meeting to get him "all set up for success in middle school." I distinctly remember him openly explaining to all of us (probably 10 adults in attendance) that there was "no point in middle school" because:

"I'm going to play video games for a living."

It's the same type of grandiose proclamations we've all heard: *"I'm gonna play in the NFL," "I'm gonna marry someone rich" "I'm gonna be a Youtube star."* One time, I even had someone say to me: *"I don't need school cuz I'm gonna be a drug dealer."* (I CRINGE typing that last sentence—A story for another time).

In all transparency, I NEVER thought Pete would go on to play video games for a living. Back then, I'm not even sure I knew that was a potential career path. Certainly, I wanted to believe that Pete was capable of success. However, at 13 years old, I couldn't fathom what success might look like for him.

In his time with us, Pete struggled academically, socially, and behaviorally every day. We tried support classes, remedial classes, and no classes. We implemented behavior plans, academic plans and 504/IEP plans. In three years, we probably had dozens of parent meetings, staffing, and brainstorming sessions. While I could write about some of the crazy days I had with Pete (and there were plenty) and his family, there's no need to do that here. You had or currently have a Pete in your school. He or she may look or sound slightly different. Probably goes by a different name but I'm confident you recognize the at-risk signs of despair. Your team of educators have identified him or her as a kid, who you fear, for many reasons, may not make it. You worry about him or her dropping out, passing state testing, and even getting mixed up into unhealthy or unsafe choices. But beyond school, you worry about his or her ability to function in society. Will they be capable of forming relationships or holding down a job? There's little doubt that your Pete keeps you and your educational team up at night, as you theorize ideas, solutions, or options to support him or her.

Pete isn't a story in how our Award Winning Culture saved the day or turned him around. This isn't an opportunity for me to pat myself or my colleagues on the back. Truth be told, we never figured out how to help Pete. It was a struggle for three years just as it was the next 4 ½ years in high school. Luckily, our refusal to give up, his parents hard work, and our high school's commitment to graduate Pete, kept him afloat. In 12+ years of public education, schooling never got easier for him. He found little to no success as he squeaked and suffered through. Having barely graduated from high school, college was neither of interest nor opportunity for Pete.

So, why do I include Pete in my development of an Award Winning Culture? By now, you might be curious to know how Pete actually turned out?

Pete is currently a video game tester and designer who lives in the San Francisco area. He makes over 3 times what I make and flies all over the world working on the latest video game roll outs. He's a highly sought out technological expert who no longer requires therapy or unhealthy amounts of pharmaceuticals. Although he takes a mild dose to help with Tourette's, he's basically support free. He's uber happy, passionate, and filled with gratitude for the RSD educators and parents who never gave up on him. Because I had stayed in occasional contact with his parents, I was able to follow his meteoric rise to life success. However, I still longed for the opportunity to visit with him in person.

Several years ago, he finally stopped into Enterprise Middle School to say hi to myself and a few teachers. Behind the corrected teeth, and updated eyewear, Pete was still a smiling, bundle of energy. Sitting still was obviously difficult but his heart shone through as he bounced around the school. While he made no attempt to see every educator he had in RSD, he was purposeful in seeking out a handful of folks in each building.

If I'm being honest with myself, I feel like he succeeded DESPITE all of us and part of me wondered WHY he would ever want to come see any of us...let alone me. His words explained it all,

"Thank-you for not giving up on me Mr. Appel, you always challenged me to reach for excellence."

We shared some laughs about some of the ridiculous antics that Pete routinely found himself involved in and I relished in the opportunity to hear a first-hand account of how he made his dream of playing video games come true. He absolutely beamed as I gushed praise and admiration for all he had accomplished!

Pete is the type of unexpected success story that causes reflective educators to take pause. How should school have been set up differently for Pete? Would he have benefited from Flexible Seating? Student-Centered work time? Project Based Learning? STEM focused education? The Grid Method? Student Choice? Student Engagement Strategies? Universal Design for Learning? STAT Team? Passion projects? Genius hour? Coding? Etc.

Of course!!

How many other students slip through our educational systems' because they lack supportive parents, a singularly focused life vision, and the unapologetic insight to recognize their own strengths? How many students give up before they find their WHY? Does it scare YOU? It scares the heck out of me!

In hindsight, EVERYTHING we tried was the wrong approach. I'd like to think that Pete's educational experience at EMS might have been much different now as we work so hard to help every student find their joy in life. But Pete isn't an example of excellence because of our "perfect" school. He succeeded in spite of all our best efforts at the wrong interventions, treatments, and fixes. However, **Pete is a shining reminder that refusing to give up on a student's ability to reach excellence is perhaps an Award Winning Culture's most important intervention.** Probably more than a few educators were moved to tears, anger and frustration during Pete's 12 years of education. I know I was.

Other educators may have become indifferent and/or oblivious to his lack of school success. They may have chalked it up to a lost cause and put their energy back into other "savable kids." On the other hand, Pete's success and positive attribution to a band of educators that refused to admit defeat is a perfect illustration of why educators in an Award Winning Culture simply don't quit on kids.

> **Award Winning Culture adopts a mindset that EVERY student can realize success if we refuse to give up.**

> **Furthermore, if we know our current systems are NOT set up for our next Pete to succeed...what's preventing us from changing our culture NOW?!**

Since Pete successfully foreshadowed a future career in gaming, I've helped other students understand and explore the gaming world. In fact, for the past 4 years, we've brought DigiPen (from Redmond Washington) in to speak to our students about summer opportunities, distance learning options, and discovering a college experience at the #1 Video Game Design School in the country. Since 1988, DigiPen Institute of Technology has been preparing students to succeed as skilled engineers, artists, and designers in the growing technology industries. They were the first college in the world to offer a bachelor's degree in video game technology and development. With the help of DigiPen recruiters, and students like Pete, blazing a trail of gaming hope; I feel more equipped than ever to support my students' dreams of 'playing video games for a living.'

Of course, the lessons with Pete, have little to do with video games and everything to do with relationships. My challenge to educators is to relook at your school's student-version of Pete with fresh eyes and an open heart. If we assume that EVERY kid is one adult away from success, are you willing to turn over every stone, to be THAT adult? Maybe it's not always about getting the right intervention, program, or strategy.

Sometimes it may be as simple as getting the right adult. Just think... if enough of us create an Award Winning Culture, within our spheres of influence, perhaps there's a tipping point where our educational ecosystem becomes flourishing...better yet EXCEPTIONAL for all the Pete's out there.

I urge you to start TODAY! Don't wait for the system to change. Change the system. The next Pete is already waiting. He might be in your office, classroom, or hallway. Heck, he may even be living in your own home.

"Every Student. Every Day. Whatever it Takes."

~ Jimmy Casas, *Culturize*

Which of the 4 E's of Excellence (Engagement, Empowerment, Experiential, and EPIC) do you think are most critical to your students' success? WHY?

How might one element of Excellence, support another element. Share an example of how fostering one of the 4 E's might also strengthen another?

What are your next steps to raising a culture of excellence at your school?

SECTION 3

COMMUNITY

What Will You do for Others Today?
SHAPE our Community

(**S**ocial Media, **H**ouse Rules, **A**uthentic Branding, **P**ersonal Outreach, **E**xperience)

- S: Social Media
- H: House Rules
- A: Authentic Branding
- P: Personal Outreach
- E: Experience

What will you do for others today?

CHAPTER 18
SOCIAL MEDIA

"When the student is ready the teacher will appear"

-Buddha

Mentorship is the guidance provided by a mentor, especially an experienced person in a company or educational institution. We typically associate mentees in schools as interns and/or practicum students. The underlying implied outcome is that the intern benefits from the mentors' wisdom.

This is only part of the story. While being an effective mentor takes time, patience, and a dedicated willingness to examine one's practices, the outcomes for the mentor are equally rich.

When I decided to take on a counseling intern, a few years back, I had no idea that I'd grow as much or more than my intern. Thus, I've created a new working definition of mentorship:

> ## Educational mentorship is a mutually beneficial endeavor that promotes growth, insight and learning for both parties.

As I enjoyed breakfast one Saturday with my former intern, it dawned on me, just how educationally meaningful this experience had been for me. As Nate and I caught up on his recent attendance at the ASCA national conference and debriefed both last year and his plan for next year...I realized how far both of us had come.

Having an intern forces one to take a deep dive into relooking at everything you do. With fresh, open eyes, interns can often unintentionally cast a light on outdated procedures, programs, and policies. Their very presence initiates the kind of necessary introspection that often gets pushed to the side, in favor of mandates, routines, and requirements. While my takeaways from my time with Nate were plentiful one has really stood out...

In the spring of Nate's 2nd year of a 3-year internship, he approached me about doing a survey of all our stakeholders. He wanted to create a way for us to gain some feedback from parents, students, and staff about our counseling program. I liked the idea and believed we were overdue to take our school's temperature on the effectiveness of our work. We spent time crafting questions, put it out to folks and then began to sift through the data.

Overall, we had very positive results! Getting a great response was very reaffirming to what we were doing. However, in one category we got absolutely destroyed. The data was very clear on this part of the survey; people did not feel we successfully communicated about our counseling program and the happenings around the school. I remember feeling a little like I'd been punched in the gut. It was as if people said to us, 'we love what you're doing but we don't always know what you're doing.' As Nate and I reviewed the results and attempted to make sense of how everything could be so positive and yet have this one giant black eye on the entire program, Nate expressed something profound to me,

> *"I think there's a shroud of mystery that*
> *inherently surrounds counseling."*

I'm sure I looked at my intern like he had three eyes that morning. Shroud of Mystery?

He went on to remind me that much of what counselors do tends to be removed from observation. One on one counseling sessions often happen behind closed doors. Even in small group work, other stakeholders are rarely invited to peek behind the curtain. The very nature of the counseling relationship, confidentiality, and much of the direct service counselors provide is not easily open to public viewing. Thus, it's probably crucial to share whatever program aspects we can with students, staff, and parents. In his own way, Nate was basically telling me...we needed to tell our counseling and/or school's story. BOOM! Mic Drop!

The truth is...there's a little bit of mystery that surrounds all educators. It's easy to get compartmentalized and disconnected from other educational professionals if we don't intentionally seek out collaboration, communication, and teamwork. This form of alliance can take place by departments, school or district wide. Additionally, we can collaborate on a global level. While our school family was a tight knit group, communication outside the school (to parents, community, and the greater education world) wasn't even on my radar. Education is so much stronger when we share ideas, support, and experiences.

I'm not afraid to say, this was a new way of thinking for me! If only I had already read Beth Houf and Shelley Burgess' *Lead like a Pirate*, George Curous' *Innovator's Mindset*, or David Geurin's *Future Driven*. Perhaps, this wouldn't have been such a revelation to me, but the truth is, I was completely unaware how necessary it is to share our school's story with the world. Until that moment, I believed that doing good work was enough. It's not! We have to share the work that we're doing. Not only does sharing help education move forward but it ensures our community has the opportunity to emotionally, mentally, and physically invest in our school's journey.

Since this conversation, our counseling team has moved all in on our social media outreach. We revamped our counseling center website, took over our school's Facebook, established Instagram/Twitter, and a YouTube Channel. We've even ventured into blogging, rolled out a student-led podcast and started AWC-tv. Many of you are thinking, *So what? You started social media. What's the big deal Hans?*

Now here's what's truly interesting from a personal standpoint. Prior to a few years ago, I had NO social media accounts. None. Let that sink in for a moment. So for all the anti-social media folks (and believe me I was the strongest of the bunch)...or the educators who have personal social media but haven't yet ventured into interacting at the educational level...let me assure you that telling our school's story has been worth every minute. And beyond that, the relationships, feedback, and learning that I've encountered from my own Professional Learning Network (PLN) are life changing! I quickly learned that it's not enough for me to share my school's counseling story...I also have to take interest in other stories around the country. Because the work that's happening in education is award winning! There's so much to be inspired by, when we open up a window to our collective educational soul.

SOCIAL MEDIA

But the truth is, it's not about specific social media. Social media is just a tool and that tool may change over time. It's about having an open communication with the world about what you're doing, your school, and your vision. Pulling our counseling program, our school, and myself for that matter...out of the shadows was about having the transparency, vulnerability, and confidence to share our school's journeys. I've realized the power and impact that sharing our **#WildcatNation #AwardWinningCulture** brand has had on ourselves and others. It really is worth all the time, effort, and energy!

Of course, none of this EMS story happens if our counseling team didn't first take our school's pulse on the current state of our program. Having a willingness to look critically at your own practices and stakeholders' experiences is humbling. But growth only comes from reimagining our mistakes into possibilities. Possibilities become realities with a sprinkle of action. Who knows when we would've been ready to create a survey if we had no intern prodding us? Indeed, my willingness to take on a mentorship, almost guaranteed educational improvement.

In *All In: Taking a Gamble in Education*, Kristen Nan and Jacie Maslyk share part of my story about how my time with Nate directly led to the eventual creation of our student-led podcast, which has had a profound impact on our school culture. I wrote, "my mentorship journey is a wonderful reminder that when we cash in on life's opportunities and willingly lean-in to professional risk-taking, we have the chance to forever shatter the ceiling on student voice!"

> **It's truly amazing what personal growth and learning can occur when we open ourselves up to mentorship.**

Observing all the critical success **#WildcatNation** has had Nate is now creating a vision of how he'll help share his school's story...So cool that the actions that he helped inspire now inspire him.

> **What new educational RISK or adventure are you BRAVE enough to explore to ensure your classroom, school, or district has NO MORE "Shrouds of Mystery"?**

Social Media Intentionality

Who: Everyone should be involved in storytelling, personal development, and modeling positive behavior on social media. Award Winning Schools believe that every stakeholder and at every level should play a part in social media. This means school accounts led by students. Teachers and support staff posting things to school hashtags. And parents and community send out daily awesomeness.

When: Ideally, school storytelling exists all the time. When we send out learning, moments, and reflections in real time we not only unify our school community, but we offer learning beyond the classroom. But messaging can also have a higher degree of intentionality tied to it. For instance, we try to be mindful of the optimal times that students, parents, or staff might be on social media for targeted releases. A school reminder for the day is highly effective between 5:30 a.m.-6:45 a.m. (for a school that starts at 7:55 a.m.). Very often this is the first post that students will receive and thus it goes to the top of their list when they get on social media for the first time that day. Live streaming assemblies on Facebook, Instagram, or Twitter can be super special for parents who can't attend. Are you sending a message that you want all students to see during the day? Send it at lunch time, or at the end of class, when they're freed up to check social media. Monday and Wednesdays are particularly good days to send out blogs and podcasts to parents? In our community many families attend church on Sunday. Thus, there's a window of time when church gets out and before the Seattle Seahawks start that targeted social media can be super effective. The point is, experiment with different days/times/types of media or messaging and then pay attention to when you have the most community traction.

Where: When first beginning social media, one of my biggest mistakes was capturing video and photos from the school day and then sending them out in the evening from home. As I reflected on this practice, I think I was doing this because I lacked proficiency with technology and I somehow felt guilty about posting to social media accounts during the school day. Social media can and should be uploaded in real time. If we're truly capturing our school's story, stakeholders shouldn't have to wait 8 hours to access that story. Additionally, posting social media directly in front of students during the day, allows us to intentionally model appropriate content, systems, and application of media to our students. If we're not directly and indirectly teaching students what acceptable content looks like at the moment...the real question is, how are students learning how to reconcile real life vs. social media? Furthermore, when we post at school (whether it's 1st period in the science teachers' classroom or after school at the basketball game) we also indirectly model school storytelling for other adults (teachers, parents, and community). Lastly, social media should not be seen as an additional requirement or duty. Social media should NOT feel like a homework assignment for educators to complete at night. True educational storytelling through media must be part of the everyday educational process.

What: Our middle school students are primarily on four platforms: YouTube, Instagram, TikTok, and Snapchat. While they use others periodically, these are the best and currently most reliable places to reach middle schoolers. As our students shift toward high school and beyond, they seem to also add in Twitter and Facebook. Most of our parents are on Facebook and Instagram. While we have a strong school website and counseling center website, we've found that these static places for information don't get frequented very often on their own. Instead, we use social media, e-mailing, podcasting, blogging, etc. to drive stakeholders to important information on our website. Furthermore, one post is not enough per item. If we're announcing a Donuts With Dudes event, we post it on multiple days and times, over multiple platforms. We've found that stakeholders are so inundated with media stimuli, that it takes repeated attempts for students, staff, and parents to interact with the information.

> ### Intentional Tip:
>
> *I would highly recommend educational storytellers check out principal Mariah Rackley's work with social media. Mariah was the 2018 NASSP Digital Principal of the year, lead learner at Cedar Crest Middle School, and a champion for a platform called Wakelet. Wakelet pulls all social media and school storytelling into one unified spot for families, staff, and community stakeholders to enjoy.*

How will you more intentionally use social media to shape your school culture?

CHAPTER 19
HOUSE RULES

Award Winning Culture creates, displays, and infuses *House Rules as a community-wide truth which influences and inspires life-long learners to be their best version of themselves. We often think about rules as a set of explicit or understood regulations like mandates, laws, and requirements. Some schools aim too low as they simply target specific behavior: I.E. keep hands and feet to yourself. Whereas, other institutions focus on rules that are too general: Students will respect themselves, others, and ongoing learning. While behavior expectations are critical. And having solutions, consequences, and or designed coaching when there's a failure to meet said expectations is important, it's not enough. Furthermore, schools must create big universal ideas that all classrooms, homes, local businesses, and groups can get behind. While classroom rules or family rules might differ from environment to environment, house rules are the thread that binds a community to exceptional school culture.

As mentioned before, our Wildcat Nation House Rules are:

Will you do the right thing? (Character)

Will you do your very best? (Excellence)

What will you do for others today? (Community)

No matter what your background, religion, experience, politics, personality, or position in life...these are hard to argue with! Additionally, you might notice that they don't just apply to students. Another big mistake schools make is creating overarching rules that don't pertain to educational staff. These house rules are equally applicable to both youth and adults. In and out of the schoolhouse.

Schools share their vision, mission, and values within their house rules. It's an awesome responsibility to ensure our community message to all stakeholders is a positive reminder of who we are, what we believe, and what we're becoming.

Furthermore, we post, display, and promote our house rules as often as possible. Every space in our school has a poster with these three ideals, front and center. On social media, we regularly send out reminders of these three house rules. Even during winter, spring or summer breaks social media offers culture focused educators a chance to reach out to intentionally influence our community. Our house rules show up in new teachers' interviews, reader boards, ASB and TA applications, and staff decision making. They are simply everywhere.

My friend, Taylor Armstrong, who's an Information Technology Specialist for the Vestavia Hills City Schools in Alabama, believes that we can inspire others to model their life's direction when he says,

"Educational leaders can be the compass to help others find their true north."

Whether students are in school or not, the house rules offer a visual compass to help others remember who they strive to be.

By shaping our rules to relate to our entire community, sharing and promoting the rules to all stakeholders, and then living those rules into existence on a daily basis, we begin to establish an authentic brand.

House rules have mattered immensely during a recent COVID-19 outbreak. Thanks to school closures, educators are working harder than ever to maintain a strong school culture in a whole new virtual world. By having a clear-cut community-wide belief system, we've managed to thrive by reinforcing Wildcat Nation expectations regardless of being homebound.

What are YOUR house rules?

How are you living those house rules out each day?

CHAPTER 20
AUTHENTIC BRANDING

Years ago, a high-level administrator asked our staff: *"what's the point of middle school?"* At the time, it felt like an insulting question to a group bound together with the crazy singular purpose of teaching young hormonal minds and hearts. But at the core of the question was: **WHO** is Enterprise Middle School? And maybe more importantly: **WHY EMS**?

What is your school about? I'm not asking you to recite some mission or vision statement that no one in your community even believes in. What makes your building unique? How do you convey that message to your various stakeholders? What perceptions do students, staff, and community really have about your school?

Branding refers to a name, term, decision, symbol or other feature that distinguishes an organization or product from its rivals in the eyes of the customers.

We can all recognize uber popular brands like Nike, Apple, or the LA Lakers. We've grown up on McDonald's, Coca-Cola, and Disney. Through the years, our world has been turned upside down with brand giants like Google, Netflix, and Amazon. However, for years, education circles stayed away from intentional branding. Perhaps this avoidance was deliberate or even unknowing.

In recent years, there's been an exponentially stronger push in public education to effectively brand individual schools, districts and even classrooms. Perhaps, this marketing need is in response to negative public perceptions about education. Or maybe it's correlated to increased numbers of private, charter, and independent schools. It could be that in some areas, there is increased competition for enrollment. While all of these may be factors, I think it's most important because branding our school allows others to see the magic that we see every day.

> **Branding isn't just about school choice, it's a way of creating a community and shared belief system for your school culture.**

There are schools doing incredible work with branding. Mandy Ellis, principal of Dunlap Grade School in Illinois has created a school wide movement centered around literacy. In her book, *Lead with Literacy*, Mandy details the power of infusing and fostering a culture of reading into the fabric of her elementary school. She encourages educators to integrate literacy in aspects, locations, and messages of the school. Her book should be required reading for any Humanities teacher, administrator, or librarian. And at the heart of her work is branding her school with something that's hard to argue with: Reading and Writing.

Slackwood elementary school in New Jersey believes "we're all part of one golden heart." Jay Billy, former Slackwood Principal and author of *Lead with Culture*, suggests that culture is what really matters. And Slackwood's brand is evident to all visitors as illustrated by a recent blog post from Tara Martin, *All the Feels-Lead with Culture*. who says educators must BE REAL (#REALedu) and that Billy and Slackwood's brand of putting culture front and center is as real as it gets. But Billy and Martin both know that if our brand only "exists' ' when parents or other school officials are visiting our building ...then it's not a brand based in reality. Dr. Joe Sanfelippo, author, speaker and superintendent of Fall Creek School District in Wisconsin says,

"Your brand is what people say about you,

when you're not there."

Great leaders like Billy, Martin, and Sanfelippo recognize that creating a brand of culture-first takes time and a commitment towards leading with the heart. Branding often begins with a vision in mind.

Some schools have parlayed successful hashtag visions into unique school brands to create a shared vision for success. Beth Houf's #fmsteach, Sean Gaillard's #CelebrateMonday or Matt Bush's #GFC have provided their schools with intentional avenues to recognize and celebrate awesomeness in their schools.

In other examples, entire districts are branding themselves. In Washington State, Selah school district cultivates lifelong learners through *"the Viking Way."* They utilize specific social media, videos, and messaging to communicate who and what they are and WHY they do what they do. Key forward-minded educators like Susie Bennett and Marc Gallaway have helped lead the *"the Viking Way"* into a community masterpiece.

When I first started becoming aware of the rise of branding in education, I actually thought we were already ahead of the curve. We were heavily involved in creating yearly themes centered around success on state testing: "Rock the Test", "Construction of Knowledge", and "Learning is a Marathon". We made t-shirts, had door decorating contests, and made assessment important throughout the year. We actually had a lot of fun with it! [*Although I still have nightmares of our PE teacher dressed up as 'marathon man', complete with short shirts, an 80's Rock Band wig, and portable loudspeaker*.] We took something that was inherently stressful, boring, and overwhelming to students and staff and attempted to create whimsey. Our teachers were spending time, money, and energy to infuse positivity around high stakes assessments. And to a degree these manufactured efforts worked. Our test scores and community positivity toward the assessments increased. But these positive changes were temporary, and it quickly became apparent that they weren't based on anything real. And therein lies the biggest mistake schools often make. Education has historically focused on creating themes rather than brands.

A theme is a topic or subject of a talk, a piece of writing, a person's thoughts or an exhibition. Themes are short lived often designed by a handful of folks or committee for a specific purpose. This year's 8th grade party theme might be Winter Wonderland or Paradise. Whereas a brand is built by everyone and grounded in the organization's "Why." Indeed, branding helps garner community support.

> **School brands must go beyond mascots and logos and be rooted in authenticity.**

Some educators from my school might argue that in addition to our yearly themes, we had a defacto brand. For years, we used a slogan called "it's great to be a wildcat." I think we believed that if we said our school slogan out loud then people might act it into existence. This along with our WOW PBIS program felt similar to a brand. Our school's PBIS program was even so popular we had the opportunity to present at several conferences laying out the details for other educators. And while there are many elements of that program that were successful and still live on at EMS, it was never really quite a brand. Here's the thing...if you're going to say that it's "great" to be a wildcat...then it better actually be great! And the truth is, back then, it wasn't really great for everyone. While we were a good school, many students, staff, and parents would eagerly acknowledge that we were coming up far short of great with our overarching school culture.

> **When comparing themes and brands this chasm of Wish vs. Reality can haunt the authenticity of schools.**

Perhaps the ultimate test of a brand is what happens to it, when a new regime takes over. With staff and leadership turnover, does the "brand" live on OR does it get cloudy with educator change? Ours got cloudy and quickly devolved into nothing more than a thematic gimmick.

Our current EMS leadership really gets it; and they equate branding to building a structure. We ask self-imposed questions like: *"What are your stakes in the ground?" "What is your school built upon?" "How do others know what your school believes in?"*

We've been working on our brand for years...and over time...we've slowly grown toward something special. Branding isn't something you arrive at or something that you suddenly wake up to. It takes time, intentionality, and humility to ask stakeholders for input in an effort to seek your school's truth.

After all, a school is only as good as the EXPERIENCE of its students.

Our **#WildcatNation** brand is rooted in *Character, Excellence, and Community* with the three school wide questions driving who we strive to be everyday:

Will you do the Right thing?

Will you do your very Best?

What will you do for Others Today?

> **Award Winning Culture yearns to be branded for all stakeholders to appreciate sustained efforts towards something special.**

School branding considerations include all of the following: Physical Spaces, Identity, Internal Events/Rituals, Marketing Channels, Internal Stakeholders, and External Stakeholders. These key considerations can offer a wonderful entry point to evaluating and crafting one's on school brand.

Physical Spaces: Entrances, Classrooms, Hallways, Gym, Cafeteria, Bathrooms, Stairs, Floor, ceiling, Front Office, Lobby, Staff Offices, Conference Room, Library, Outside Signage.

Identity: Logo, Mission/Vision, Slogans, Mascot, Name (Both Full and Abbreviated), Positioning, Key Messages, School Colors. I reference homemade cookies frequently throughout the book. My wife loves to bake and so we create sugar cookies for many instances at school. Several years ago we purchased a sugar printer. Sugar printers allow you to take any computer logo or image and print the image on edible wafer paper that can be put on deserts such as cookies, cupcakes, muffins, etc. We print out Wildcat Nation wafer paper to reinforce our brand at school. Furthermore, our sugar printer has come in handy when we have a desire to personalize treats with other images to highlight programs, people or events: Character Strong, PBIS Rewards, Community Strong, Award Winning Culture Podcast, etc.

Internal Events/Rituals: Assemblies, Parent-Teacher Conferences, Orientation, Open Houses, Tours, Graduation Ceremony, Drop-off/pickup, Community Strong Event, College & Career Day, Carnival, Movie Night, STEM night, Dances, etc.

Marketing Channels: School website, Class website, Library website, Counseling Center website, Personal Outreach, YouTube Channel, Instagram, Facebook, Twitter, Wakelet, PTSA Newsletter, School Podcast, Morning Announcements, Clothing line (t-shirts, hats, socks, sweatpants, leggings, PE uniform, sweatshirts, etc.) SWAG (water bottles, bracelets, pens/pencils, stickers, pop sockets, posters, backpacks, etc.) Announcements, Business Cards, Brochures, Email Signatures, Letterhead and/or school paperwork.

Internal Stakeholders: Students, Administration, Administrative Assistants, Support Staff, Teachers, Counselors, Librarians, Psychologist, Classified employees, Food Services, Coaches, Custodians, Volunteers, PTA/PTO, Parents, Extended family (Grandparents, Siblings, Aunts/Uncles, etc.).

External Stakeholders: Local media (print, television, etc.), Realtors, Online Review sites, District office staff, Business/Community leaders, Elected or appointed officials, School Board, In-District employees, Educational Peers out of district, Neighborhood groups, Community Mental Health Specialists.

If we return to those slightly irritating questions from before and make a slight alteration to the verbiage:

What's the point of YOUR school?

How might you communicate that point?

What steps will you take to evaluate your school's current brand?

CHAPTER 21
PERSONAL OUTREACH

Morning Greeting

At EMS, we start everyday with students and staff greeting everyone who comes in the three entrances of the school. Smiles, high fives, fist bumps, and heart to heart connection offers a meaningful overlay to the daily musical accompaniment that raises the collective heartbeat of our school community. Leadership students, highly impacted special education students, police officers, teachers, and everyone in between link metaphorical arms to literally welcome and embrace all who enter Wildcat Nation. On special days our jazz band even replaces live streamed radio with a well-rehearsed musical set from their award winning band program.

As highly sought out hubs of Wildcat Nation pride, these three entrances become a gathering place of school-wide love and a b-12 shot of positive energy for all stakeholders. Indeed, it's simply the place to be. Regardless of rain, wind, sun, or snow, our students and staff are out greeting every day. They hold doors open, compliment passerbyers, and establish real relationships with students and staff. There are special handshakes, inside jokes, and silly nicknames that all provide evidence of the school wide impact to positively flipping a person's day as they enter the school.

- **Imagine the power as a student or staff member who may have had a challenging morning at home instantly feel LOVED as they approach the school.**

- **Imagine the staff member or student who doesn't quite feel like being at school only to have their mood brightened by the feeling of serving their school through intentional outreach.**

- **Imagine the relief, safety, and comfort of a parent dropping their kids off at school for the day, when they're met with a scene demonstrating that kindness is normal at Wildcat Nation.**

- **Imagine the impact on neighbors, new students, prospective families, local businesses when witnessing our tapestry of awesomeness.**

Indeed...Greeting is the gateway to BELONGING.

We've purchased heaters, portable speakers to play music, and hand warmers to combat the weather elements. We take the time to intentionally teach students and staff that this is time to put the phone away in favor of human connection. We make specific efforts to learn and use names. We even teach students and staff how to stand in an open posture, while being careful not to block the doorway. Young leaders intentionally model a daily commitment to greeting and how to enhance other people's morning.

> **When talented youth are armed with empathic hearts, educators create generational positivity that ripples throughout the world.**

It's also critical to teach students that some folks are not ready for kindness. Perhaps, they don't trust its authenticity, maybe they struggle with social anxiety, or human touch and may opt to not give or receive a high five as they enter the building. We've seen several students over the years take an entire school year before opening up enough to give a high five or smile. Still our students and staff recognize that being a true servant leader requires patience and a commitment to consistent daily kindness, even when it's not reciprocated or outwardly appreciated. On rare occasions we'll surprise our morning greeters with donuts and hot cocoa for their steady and continued service.

Once a month we have morning staff meetings which pull staff away from the doors for an entire morning. We've set up an arrangement with our parent group to have parents replace staff welcoming everyone on those select mornings. While we have leadership, students sign up to hold certain doors and a core group of dedicated adults, we invariably find that students and staff from all over the school join the daily party.

Recently, a parent from another neighboring school, pulled up and parked outside all the festivities. She walked up to me, introduced herself, and began sharing her story. Apparently, her son was struggling at a nearby private school and she was considering transferring him to her local public boundary school, down the street. However, a friend of hers was a teacher and had encouraged her not to transfer her son to the brand-new STEM school. Instead, the teacher had recommended that this parent transfer him to EMS. According to mom, she had been mulling over this information for weeks and finally found herself driving near our school that morning. After seeing and experiencing our Wildcat Nation morning greeting, she immediately enrolled her son at our school. And, he's been flourishing with us for the past year.

With the new temporary crisis of COVID-19, we've modified our physical contact to lean toward elbow or chicken wing and foot tapping as opposed to potential germ passing high fives. But more so, it's forced us to not simply fall back on physical contact. Students and staff have had to revisit how we're connecting with people as they enter our building or classrooms.

This meant an increased effort toward using names, handing out compliments, smiling, and making eye contact. It also meant pausing in the hallway to have a little longer conversation than we might normally choose to. And you know what, these are actually more important forms of connection than a well-placed fist bump.

> **Award Winning Culture values CONNECTION over contact.**

COVID-19 will probably come and go but I'll remember this lesson for a while. Connection isn't about physicality. Connection is about uncovering our HUMANNESS.

Connecting the Unconnected

"Connection is why we're here; it is what gives purpose and meaning to our lives."

-Brené Brown

We make every attempt to identify disconnected students and then intentionally connect the unconnected students. We do a yearly connection survey that focuses on clubs/activities, identifying a trusted adult, friendships, and the overall perception of climate for each individual student at the school. Additionally, we create giant poster size lists of student names and each staff member identifies, rates, and ranks how connected they are to every student in the school as well as how well they

PERSONAL OUTREACH

know each student's story. These lists and surveys are then poured over to find patterns, insights, and trends during staff meetings. When comparing survey results, staff connection perception and cross referencing this data with participation in clubs/activities, grades, attendance, behavior, and assessments, we begin to form a picture of students who are at risk for being unconnected at Wildcat Nation. This initial deep dive into personal connection helps drive critical work with a subset of students.

For example, one year we followed up with this population to learn that many students did not relate to any of the clubs and/or activities that we offered at the time. We quickly implemented a multi-faceted approach to increase student connection to clubs and/or activities. In one year, we generated numerous new clubs based on student passions. Additionally, we taught students how to form a new club or activity so that all students felt like there was something for them. During that year our ASB leaders were recognized by our school board for creating an explosion of student participation, which was best punctuated by our 55% increase in student involvement in extracurricular activities.

We also learned that many of them had transportation issues involving coming early or late to attend clubs and/or activities or simply couldn't afford the fees for participation. Because of limited family income, parent work schedules, or physical proximity of home to school, we had unexpected hurdles and built-in in-equities that prevented student involvement.

Interests: After developing a list of disconnected students, we made personal connections with each student. By having one on one conversations with disconnected students we learned what activities they actually wanted. We added numerous NEW clubs like Archery, Board Game, Dungeons and Dragons, Harry Potter, Guitar, Equality Club, Fellowship of Christian Athletes, Magic the Gathering, Sewing, Quesadilla (yeah...that's right...they eat quesadillas!!), Lego, etc. Adding additional offerings was amazing! Our archery students hosted and won our statewide tournament including a national recognition for one boy. Our guitar club originally made up of many of our at-risk students morphed into an actual music class that all students can sign up for, as part of their daily schedule. And students learned how easy it was to start a new club based on their own specific interest. Furthermore, our district added soccer to the athletic rotation for all middle school students. More options meant we were reaching more students!

Transportation: We successfully lobbied for a 4:30 p.m. activities bus to allow more students to stay after school for clubs, activities, sports, and even tutoring. The ability to remove systemic barriers preventing participation meant we began reaching every student. During this heartwarming process of student equity, we learned that all students want to belong and become connected to something bigger than themselves. By eliminating barriers outside of student control they jumped at the opportunity to become more connected to Wildcat Nation.

Beyond the increased fun connections with clubs, activities, and sports our attendance in after school tutoring skyrocketed so much that we had to seek additional volunteers to help with tutoring. Eventually, we reached out to a local college to have future educators earn practicum hours for volunteering as our tutors. Again, by pouring intentional energy into our after-school tutoring program, the overall value and student benefit increased beyond measure.

Fees: While there are fees associated with all ASB related clubs, activities, and sports we uncovered state funding (InvestEd Funds) designed to level the playing field for students in poverty. Thus, by forming relationships with students and knowing which students are struggling financially, we're able to use funds to support their passions. Additionally, we offer targeted giveaways to students in need. For instance, we'll provide free tickets to school events and then personally give tickets, coupons, etc. to the student.

> **Award Winning Cultures assumes every student has a desire to be connected to the school community. And educators must be relentless in uncovering why a student might be temporarily disconnected from that community.**

Summer Home Visits

Every June, our office dream team along with the help of our EMS teachers and elementary feeder school teachers identify students to reach out to in August. We're looking for students who have poor attendance, might be disconnected, or just need a little boost of intentional positivity before the school year starts. Typically, we put together little backpacks of Wildcat Nation Swag (bracelets, pens, pencils, stickers, etc.), some candy, and handmade Wildcat Nation cookies. We ask for staff volunteers to break into teams (usually two or three people per team) and drive to identified student homes to bring them a little something. The day before we go on our home visits, we have two paraprofessionals who call home to let families know, we'll be stopping by to deliver a little fun surprise. It's hard to put into words just how much fun this brief activity is! The smiles, hugs, and thank-yous help inspire our staff as they make their final summer push toward opening the school year.

The main goal of the activity is to make personal connections with potentially at-risk students. We want to infuse positivity and excitement about their return to the new school year. However, this also provides a strong reminder to staff how some of our most impacted students truly live. In other words, seeing our students, in their natural environment gives adults an extra layer of empathy to build upon throughout the year.

For instance, one of our students lost their family home in a horrible fire. Ironically, one of the biggest supporters during this crisis was a teacher who had met the family in August, on a summer home visit. Despite the fact that he taught a completely different grade level and did not have the student in class, he viewed her as HIS student. The personal connection to the family compelled him to deliver furniture, food, clothing, and other essentials to the family on multiple occasions. One could argue that he's just a great guy but there's no denying that his heart for the family was significantly affected by the empathy building that began on a hot summer day in August.

Check-In

In an interview with Phil Boyte on the *School Culture By Design* podcast, high school teacher, Bryan Slater shared an innovative approach for regular outreach with his students by checking in with them using google forms three times a week. He uses this to seek feedback on his own instruction and to stay connected to his students' social and emotional needs. Hearing Slater's powerful strategy encouraged us to get creative in our outreach efforts.

Wildcat teachers have found great success with a regular check-in. For instance, we have teachers using a google form entry task to keep their finger on the pulse of student need. The quick intake form asks students to rate how they're feeling that day on a scale from 1-10, why they rated themselves that score, and if there's anything that the teacher can do to support them. Some teachers even embed academic content or fun silly questions (i.e. rank your favorite Christmas movie) to build in some lightness to the activity. Teachers who share their own daily rating, find that they get more authentic information from their students. Typically, teachers will scan through the responses during the hour to gauge who needs additional support. Also, our teachers download the google form into a spreadsheet and email it over to our office Dream Team. This email allows us to personally connect with any struggling students and keep tabs on emotional trends amongst individual learners.

Additionally, google check-ins are an excellent way for educators to stay connected to students during breaks, closures, or global pandemics. Indeed, the ability to stay up-to-date with our learners emotional needs is critical during times of distance learning. And beyond, student check-ins, many schools are using this tool to check-in with families, co-workers, or employees. As principal of Quincy Elementary, Allyson Apsey uses this style of outreach with her staff to keep tabs on how they're doing.

Rolodex of Connection

Personal outreach can even start on day one. Teacher hands out a 3X5 index card on the first day of school. They ask students to write 3 things on the front of their card. Here's a few examples:

- What are you passionate about?

- How do you feel about (subject area)?

- What might you teach me this year?

- How can I support you in (subject area)?

On the back of the card students write their name, nickname, pronouns. Then the teacher keeps all the cards in a little box at the front of the room. Anytime they want to call on a student, they have instance personal information to connect with that student. *For example,* "Ryan-Before you tell us the answer to #7...what do you think about the Yankees baseball season?"

Pre-School Pronunciation

Being able to correctly pronounce student names, nicknames, and/or use appropriate pronouns can be a powerful relationship tool. Some educators are using technology to gain an advantage on relationship building, prior to school even starting. With programs like Synth and Flipgrid, it's possible to send messages out to your incoming class roster asking students to record the proper way to address them. This form of personal outreach can have such a profound impact on connecting early by empowering teachers to learn pronunciation immediately. Additionally, it makes for a wonderful resource for a teacher to refer back to. Imagine the LGBTQ student in transition or learner with an unusual spelling of their name being welcomed in the correct way on day one.

> ### Intentional Tip:
> *Send out your own video to students/families introducing yourself, prior to school starting. Think about crafting your award winning classroom culture before the first day of school.*

With virtual work settings within distance learning, these programs become crucial not only for pronunciation, but for on-going relationship building. The ability for educators and students to see each other's faces, share non-verbal ques, and make personal connections prove to be a lifesaver in outreach efforts in non-traditional school settings.

Personal Invitations

Personally, inviting a student to participate in something has a real impact in their connection to school. We make an intentional effort to invite students to sign up for specific classes, join a club, activity, or sport, and/or come to a school event. When adults take the time to say I see you and I think you'd be really good at XYZ, we've found that students are much more likely to get involved. Incidentally, the same is true for inviting parents, volunteers, local community members, etc. to be involved with your school. Personal face to face contact really increases the likelihood of community involvement.

But Award Winning Cultures go beyond adult outreach. They inspire, encourage, and support student outreach as well. There is no more

PERSONAL OUTREACH

powerful influence in middle/high school than their peers. When students are taught to intentionally learn names/faces, create relationships and then utilize their influence to invite peers to clubs, activities, events and sports...MAGIC happens! After all, everyone loves to feel wanted and accepted by their peers.

Furthermore, our students make phone calls to local companies and businesses and seek support from other community adults. However, it's imperative that student leaders are not only connecting with others when they need or want something. An onslaught of requests can erode a relationship with a school. Instead, students must operate under the umbrella of what will I do for others today while infusing occasional school requests.

Transition Meetings

Each spring, we set up transition meetings with elementary staff for incoming 6th graders and high school staff for outgoing 8th graders. The staff varies from school to school as they have autonomy over who they prefer to be the keeper of the information. Some schools we meet with all teacher teams while other schools offer a mix of admin, counselor, or psych. These are separate from our district mandated IEP and 504 transitions. During these hour-long meetings with school personnel we learn or share pertinent information on at-risk students. Basically, we want to communicate about anything that can support a student's transition to the next academic level. Topics include family dynamics, organizational skills, personal/social challenges, behavior, attendance, interests, passions, strengths, ideas or solutions that have been found to be effective. Sometimes these proactive meetings can trigger transition plans, summer home visits, personal outreach, or future team meetings.

> ## Award Winning Culture creates successful learning environments with the help, support, and guidance of previous year's educators.

This doesn't mean that students or families should be locked into services, support, or interventions that they don't need. Instead, transition meetings provide staff with information. And information is useful outreach to aid school to family connection.

These transition meetings must happen just as often in distance learning schools and districts. Programs like Zoom allow multiple educators to be in a meeting with each other, from the comfort of their own home. Thus, a school's ability to reach out and learn about incoming students is not impacted by physical proximity.

Feeder School Visits

Truthfully, like many schools we'd been doing elementary visits for years. We went out and presented to 5th graders about classes, schedules, rules, etc. But we missed the chance to personally connect with our incoming students. We spent our time talking at students rather than welcoming them with inclusive conversations. And, if I'm being honest, we failed to excite and inspire while relaxing natural anxiety about starting a new school.

With a bit of intentionality, schools can make these visits truly amazing! Changing the tone of these visits began by including current 6th graders. We now take 6th graders because they know exactly what it felt like to be sitting in an elementary gymnasium or classroom thinking about starting 6th grade. Afterall, only a year ago, they were right there, sitting in 5th grade classrooms. While 7th or 8th graders might have more developed leadership skills, sense of self, or Character development, they often lack some of the connection to the specific challenges that 6th graders experience. The presentation, group work, and even accompanying school YouTube video have 6th grade fingerprints, voice, and vision throughout. We take our entire Dream Team, a group of student leaders, and our school Mascot (Willis the Wildcat) and enter each elementary school with an air of whimsy and fun. Our collective mindset being let's light this elementary school on FIRE with our authentic passion for Wildcat Nation.

Wildcat student leaders greet every 5th grader as they enter the gym or classroom with high fives, smiles, and enthusiasm. During our whole group time, students introduce themselves and we show a video which features high impact visuals of fun, mixed with pictures, testimonials, and videos of what it means to be a wildcat based on our house rules. Indeed, we're essentially sharing our school-wide passion for Character, Excellence, and Community during our first face to face encounter with these incoming 6th graders. But make no mistake, we're not focusing on teaching 5th graders about tardies, dress codes, or the consequences of bringing banned substances to school. This is a moment to light the place up with excitement and positive energy. These initial first impressions of Wildcat Nation always create a powerful buzz as they laugh, smile, and spontaneously belt out verses of the pop songs featured in our Wildcat video.

Next, we break into smaller groups with both student leaders and adults where students answer questions and make connections while we share critical information. While there is some paperwork to take home to parents, the focus of our time is on relationship building and easing stress and anxiety on coming to a big new school. The registration forms will be there for them to review, with parents at home.

Award Winning Culture values PEOPLE over paperwork.

We always end with candy, a school-wide cheer, and high fives and fist bumps as we leave the elementary school. As a pied piper of school spirit, we are akin to a rock concert that shows up, blowing the roof off, and then moves on to the next community down the road.

Creating a similar feeder school outreach opportunity with distance learning is a bit trickier but absolutely doable. For instance, 6th graders and middle school staff can record separate video clips for 5th grade families to review. And how cool, that if the family misses something, they can simply re-watch the clip again. Additionally, small group presentations can be scheduled for individual question/answer and relationship building moments through Google Hangouts, ZOOM, Skype, etc. Beyond the appeal during national pandemics, imagine how welcoming this might be for the homeschool family transitioning to middle school, who may not have been able to attend an in-person feeder school outreach. As our society continues to re-imagine school culture in an ever-changing virtual world, educators have to push the envelope in personal outreach techniques.

Lessons in Tragedy

Personal Outreach is not limited to adult to student interactions. Reaching out to fellow educators can be essential to crafting an Award Winning Culture.

My mom was an exceptional person! We were close when I was just a little kid and we grew closer as I morphed into adulthood. After my parents' divorce, my mom moved back to Texas (her family and close friends created a safe landing back for this southern belle). While we didn't see each other nearly as often, as I was thousands of miles away in Washington State; our long phone calls kept us as connected as ever when I transitioned from college to professional school counselor.

In May of 2003, I received a frightening phone call from my mom where she explained that she had stage 4 Breast Cancer and that they would be starting Chemo immediately. She explained that mastectomy was not an option as the cancer was highly aggressive and had already spread. I was 27 years old at the time. While I knew almost nothing about breast cancer at the time, I was aware of one scary genetic fact. My mom's mom died of breast cancer in her mid 30's (when my mom was just a little girl). If I understood anything about this disease, it was that it was incredibly serious.

During the next few months Jen and I traveled to visit my mom. We knew there wasn't a lot we could do from thousands of miles away but were confident that our presence provided a little positive energy for her to endure chemo. Those of you whose lives have been impacted by breast cancer, or for that matter CANCER, know what kind of AWFUL disease it is. But the Chemo used to treat cancer can be almost equally damaging to the body.

Upon our first visit, my mom had lost all her hair, looked very weak but was steadfast with her humor and passion for taking care of others. After much cajoling we convinced my mom to let us clean her house. She was very prideful and used to keeping her home up to a pristine state. But with the illness, her usual house routines had taken a back seat and we knew she needed help. While I visited and entertained mom, Jen took the next few hours and cleaned her entire home from top to bottom...inside and out. It was immaculate when Jen was finished! Afterwards, my mom began to cry and express gratitude; she shared that no one had ever done anything like that for her before. At first, we weren't sure what she meant. Cleaning the house? No, "serving me in such a meaningful and loving way." My mom and Jen spent the next few moments laughing and crying. That experience left a lasting bond for both of them.

As the weekend drew to a close, we committed to our next visit. Throughout that summer, we spent as much time/money as possible with my mom. But at the end of August, school was starting, and it was time to refocus on our lives in Washington. Over the next few weeks I kept tabs on her ups and downs of treatment. On Friday September 12th, 2003 I received a phone call that my mom had passed away in the night due to complications of the cancer spreading to her brain and other organs. It was one day before her 54th birthday.

Flooded with emotion, Jen and I boarded a plane and spent the next week and a half grieving, planning a funeral service, and dealing with decisions outside my emotional capability. For those who have lost a parent, you understand the complexity and multitude of tasks that need to be taken care of. Beyond the pain and loss there were dozens of decisions and items to be completed. Flowers and casket to buy. A house to pack up. Calls to make. Financial decisions to be considered. Death certificates to obtain so that I could send them to various agencies. Being from out of state, provided additional challenges in dealing with the Will, estate, and court system because I had been named executor. There were loans and liens to work through. My mom was an amazing woman but not as financially prepared as one might hope.

Through all the craziness my wife was an absolute rock. I couldn't have gotten through all of it without her love and support. During one of the days, I felt compelled to write something to be read at my mom's upcoming service. I had remembered a few years earlier sitting in a district PD training with LA teacher and Richland High Football Coach Neidhold. (Side note: Neidhold just led his RHS Bombers to a State Championship in 2018).

During the ELA presentation, Neidhold talked about using vulnerability with his students and shared an essay he wrote about his father's unexpected death. He read his moving and powerful tribute about his dad to us that day; in the same way he did for his students when sharing voice in writing.

Sitting on an unmade bed, in Texas, in a pile of tears and anger, I vividly remembered back to Neidhold sharing how cathartic the experience of writing and then sharing had been for him. I figured, if it was good enough for Neidhold, I'd give it a try. I spent the next couple hours writing a short letter to my mom, that would be shared at the service. I think that was the first meaningful thing I ever wrote. I agonized over every word in that letter. This was such a painful writing experience but incredibly helpful in my grieving process. Several months removed from the funeral, I decided to frame the letter and hang it near a picture of my mom, in my house. At first, I couldn't read through that letter without getting choked up. But, over time, I began to look at both the letter and photo of mom with a warmth that filled my entire body. It was my way of staying connected to mom and now years later always makes me smile. Coach Neidhold's solution to grief was spot on and while everyone has to find their own "Path to Serendipity," Neidhold had laid out a perfect blueprint for me to find peace.

September 10th, 2003

Dear Mom,

Last Friday morning, God took you to a better place. You leave us with sadness, memories, and life lessons. You were the teacher... I was the student. You taught me the value of tradition, and I will continue them with my family.

In addition to being a great teacher, you were simply a great person. You were a loyal friend to many, including me. You were a social extrovert who reveled in a funny story. You were a compassionate, warm, and giving woman. You were a talented seamstress who could mend my deepest wounds. You enjoyed cooking, traveling, and listening to music. You collected antiques, flowers, and doll-house furniture. You were a creative artist, who enjoyed the beauty in design, homemaking, and fashion.

YOU WERE A TEXAN THROUGH AND THROUGH!!!

You redefined the words "shop til you drop." You always believed in dressing to the hilt and putting your best foot forward. Although, occasionally your feet would get tangled.

You were afraid of escalators, mice, and growing old alone. Through it all I'll never forget the sweet smells of gingerbread, pumpkin pie, or any other holiday treat that was being baked in the kitchen. I'll always remember the long talks, the laughter, and our uncanny connection.

Now there will be changes in my life. Some of them will take time, some will cause me grief, some will mean risk, and a lot of growing pains, too. But whatever the case I know I will make it. It's having someone like you to see me through both the good times and the bad that makes me so sure of success. Thank you for being my guardian angel.

We miss you and will always love you!

Your Son, Hans

P.S. Thanks for teaching me to believe in magic!

After a week and a half in Texas, with funeral service completed, it was time to return home and get back to school. My first day back fell on a Tuesday. Every Tuesday and Thursday a group of teachers and coaches got together at 6am to play morning hoops. I'm sure that sounds crazy to some of you non-morning folks but you'll have to trust me that it was worth every minute. It was an exceptional way to release competitive

PERSONAL OUTREACH

juices and connect with colleagues. I never missed a Tuesday or Thursday. But my mom's passing meant that I had been gone the previous week's hoop days and I was eager to get back to some sense of normalcy.

My return to school that day meant that the guys at morning hoops would be my first contact with anyone in person, since I landed back in Washington, after an emotionally exhausting week. My typical routine was to show up about 15 minutes early to stretch, shoot baskets, and generally warm up before we started playing. Another competitor always arrived at about the same time with a similar warm up routine each day. Coach Mayer, who was and still is the head boys basketball coach and leadership teacher at Hanford High School, was as usual one of the first people in the gym that morning.

Mayer and I had a highly competitive yet respectful match for years. He was a fierce competitor who left it all on the court! In 10+ years of playing ball together, I'm not sure that we ever were 'allowed' to play on the same team. We invariably found ourselves on different sides of this monumental decade long battle and truth be told I loved nothing more than beating Mayer's team. I have no doubt he felt equally satisfied when they kicked our butts (which happened far more than I wished). That morning, I remember feeling a little awkward about playing basketball and just generally how people would interact with me as students, co-workers, and morning hoopers all knew I had lost my mom. While I was sitting down stretching in this mostly empty gym, I looked up to see a long arm extended out toward me. Needless to say, it was Mayer.

"We missed you man. I'm so sorry for your loss, I can't imagine losing my mom. I'm so happy you're back."

We shook hands, exchanged pleasantries and jumped into another typical basketball game. Mayer's kind words have stuck with me for years. It was exactly what I needed to hear that morning. He demonstrated empathy, humility, and respect. Often people don't know what to say so they avoid difficult conversations. Sometimes people try to make a joke or ignore you. Mayer communicated to me that he SAW ME, UNDERSTOOD on some level, and WELCOMED me back. Years removed from his personal outreach, I can't tell you how I played or who won that game but I know that this warm, positive exchange helped me transition back to school that day. This interaction has also made me very aware of how I greet and interact with students who return to school after going through something traumatic.

I will tell you that I've shared all parts of this story with students over the years. I've described the grit and toughness that it takes to work through Chemo. I've expressed how powerful serving someone can be for both you and the person you serve. I've told them about Coach Neidhold's impact on me using writing to overcome a loss and showed them my dear mom letter. I've detailed what they can say to someone who's transitioning back from trauma or tragedy by reflecting back Coach Mayer's kind words.

> **We have an opportunity to give others a magical gift of outreach if we're willing to be vulnerable, kind, and compassionate while serving their needs.**

Moments of Intentional Outreach

Over the last few years, we've had many examples of personal outreach but sometimes the most impactful examples are less about the creativity of ideas and more about the intentionality of the moment.

Locker Surprise: Lockers are a big transition for middle school students in our area. We have adults and leadership students available to help 6th graders before and during the first week of school. We've created how-to videos, orientation days, and personalized instructions to support this. We've even reached out to 5th grade teachers to have students practice opening locks while they're still in elementary school. Regardless, it's a little stressful and it takes some practice.

One year, a 7th grade boy came up with an incredible idea over the summer. He realized that one of the most stressful parts of starting 6th grade was learning how to open your locker. He arranged and coordinated with our leadership students to put a handwritten note, Wildcat Nation info, and candy into every incoming 6th grade student's locker, before the year started...as a sort of...welcome to Wildcat Nation! His thinking being that it's hard to get it open the first time but how rewarding it might be to have a little treat when you got it open.

You can just imagine the gleeful SURPRISE that these students had while struggling to learn how to open their middle school locker for the first time, on a sweaty August day, only to discover an ENCHANTINGLY thoughtful surprise inside. Parents were overcome with joy! And it wasn't my idea. It wasn't our leadership teachers' or another adult educator's idea. As we all know, oftentimes the best demonstrations of kindness and empathy come from the students themselves. A sign that your school is on a path toward creating an Award Winning Culture is when the epic ideas start coming from students! Since then, this has become a best practice at our school.

Snow Day Kindness Challenge: This past year, our community had record high snowfall. In fact, we had 7 days of school canceled. After almost a week of not seeing our students, we began to get worried about some of the kids. Sure, to some students, it was a day off to play in the snow and not think about school. But for a few of our students the icy roads and school closures meant elevated stress without their breakfast, lunch, and routine of school learning. We decided to intentionally choose

AWARD WINNING CULTURE

20 students who were most at risk and struggled with school/home connection to personally connect with. We purchased 20 pizzas/pop, baked homemade cookies/cupcakes, and wrote a personal handwritten note. The outreach package was made all the more meaningful when our librarian donated 20 brand new books.

We were met with tears, hugs, and smiles as we ventured around the snow plowed roads of our community to deliver a snow day kindness surprise. Our intentional efforts brought real joy to families and a sense of purpose to a school staff tired of snow days. But the evidence of impact was far reaching as thousands of people in the community and across the country witnessed the outreach with our self-made video. The point of creating the video wasn't to say look at us...we're so wonderful. It was intended to spark inspiration to others to ask themselves how THEY might help others...even on a day off. Alas, the triangle of Joy shows up yet again!

> ## Award Winning Culture takes care of each other, even outside of the school house.

The snow day kindness challenge is a perfect example of a culture building outreach that can be done within a distance learning or virtual school. With a bit of creativity, educators can surprise students and families with kindness beyond the walls of the schoolhouse.

I presented the snow day kindness challenge at a state conference last year, in which someone asked me if other students were jealous or if we had received any backlash for choosing only those 20 students. My answer was: no. It was very well received and there was no negativity attached to it. I think the biggest reason being that moments like this are just normal in our school community. Students and families are used to exceptional moments of kindness so ideally, we're reaching EVERYONE with special moments throughout the year.

**What small steps can you take, this week, to intentionally reach out to specific students
or staff?**

What if our schools were filled with students whose self-esteem was directly tied to the positive impact they had on others?

CHAPTER 22
EXPERIENCE

"Where are the Fingerprints of Kindness?"

-Houston Kraft

Houston has such a talent for turning complicated big ideas like kindness into manageable action items that are both easier to understand and readily identifiable. Houston says that schools with exceptional school culture have these special fingerprints that invite others into their daily land of awesomeness. At Wildcat Nation, we refer to this experience as the VIP Treatment and we capitalize on these relationship opportunities.

"VIP" Treatment: In traditional organizational culture, special consideration and care is given to individuals who are deemed to be Very Important People. What if we considered EVERYONE to be a VIP who's qualified and deserving of exemplary treatment? With a simple reframe to Very INTERESTING People, it's easy to shift toward a culture of curiosity and caring, when we're truly interested in others. This shift naturally pivots student and staff mindset into a place of helping, service, and community. But what does VIP treatment actually look like? It looks like exceeding daily cultural expectations through a community lens of asking ourselves what we will do for others today. Here's some daily examples:

EXPERIENCE

New Students

One of the most anxiety-provoking circumstances is being the new kid. We use an intentionally inclusive blueprint to help foster belongingness to all new students. Our recipe begins with a warm greeting and orientation packet from our school registrar detailing the registration timeline, specifics, and expectations over the next couple days:

Day One: Students and parents/guardians fill out all paperwork including registration, immunization, English Language Learners, IEP, 504, free/reduced lunch, sports, and Mckinney Vento qualifications. Day one is not officially finished until all paperwork is completed. Paperwork can be completed in person or online and is translated into whatever language is necessary.

Day Two: Student arrives at 8:30a.m. Intentionally after the morning rush and when maximum time and attention can be provided. Over the next couple hours, the student will take math and reading assessments, receive a detailed student-led tour, and have a chance to chat with a counselor and/or admin about scheduling, behavioral, and attendance considerations. Beyond initial rapport building, these brief chats allow each student to make personal office connections to support their transition. Also, these conversations can lead to opportunity to connect students to a specific program, activity, and or person that they might have interest in (Band Teacher, Football Coach, Harry Potter Club advisor, etc.)

The Detailed Student Tour is led by 1 or 2 trained students from the same grade as the new student and who demonstrate a desire to welcome new students to our school. These leadership students have been intentionally taught to shake hands, make eye contact, learn names, and develop a real interest in the new student. They provide a behind the scenes look at Wildcat Nation which includes personal introductions to key staff members, coaches, teachers, and club advisors that the student may need to know about. Additionally, the trained students make plans to connect at lunch, when the new student officially starts school, the next day. Depending on parent availability, they may also join the tour.

Counselors send a detailed email to the student's teachers and admin providing information on class schedule, locker, test scores, personal anecdotes, concerns, or additional support needed.

Day Three: First official day of starting school. The new student arrives 20-30 minutes prior to the first bell. Leadership and/or other trained students meet the new student in the counseling center. Students receive a copy of their schedule, locker info, Wildcat Nation Swag, and t-shirt. During this time, the students help the new student walk their schedule, open up their locker and introduce the student to more key people.

At lunch admin, leadership students, and/or counselors intentionally connect with new students to check-in, answer questions, and help ensure a smooth transition. *Under no circumstances do we want a new student sitting alone at lunch.*

At the end of the day, the new student is called down to the office for a brief (10-15 minute) overview on school norms. This student-led presentation complete with video, keynote slides, and question/answer format includes all of the following: House Rules, PBIS Rewards info, CharacterStrong and advisory background, Club/Sports info, After School Tutoring, Jolly Rancher Fridays, upcoming fun events, etc. We want them to walk away excited to come back the next day and armed with knowledge about our culture and climate.

Day Five: Counselor calls the new student into their office sometime within the first 5 days they start school to get a sense of how things are going. Sometimes questions or concerns have come up and it's critical to connect early to ensure successful student transition is happening.

EXPERIENCE

Additionally, new students are often intentionally on the office Dream Team discussion agenda to help keep multiple sets of eyes on students in transition. During these discussions, we talk about infusing other adults into the new student's world as a way to further connect them to their new school.

Making new students feel welcome, accepted and loved shouldn't be any different with online schools. The ability to call, video-chat, check-in and provide timely relevant information does not depend on being in a physical school. However, it does require educators to be just as intentional with their efforts to make people feel amazing. What if homeschool students could receive handwritten welcome cards and personalized video greetings upon starting their online journey? How easy would it be to set up a video chat with incoming students to answer questions or relieve anxiety as we served individual distance learning needs? We could also connect new students with other new students so that they might form a bond of supporting each other through distance learning.

> **Let's not use social distancing as an excuse to socially disconnect!**

Prospective Family

When meeting potential new wildcat families, we want them to experience a clear sense of what we're about. Our prospective family packet must include our brand, house rules, and core essentials that make us unique. From the moment they reach out to us by phone or email, their experience is what they will remember about their interaction with the wildcat nation. Secretaries, counselors, administration and a few leadership students might be their first and only contact with our school. Everyone should be prepared to respond by email, phone, or in person with a fervor for helpful service. They may have originally picked our school based on awards, parent feedback, or real estate information but they'll ultimately stay based on their experience. I'm blown away by how many parents I meet that tell me the secretary at another school was rude or that a counselor or administrator did not reply to them in a timely manner.

> **Educators in an Award Winning Culture treat all potential stakeholders as if they are part of the school family, even if the prospective family does not currently attend their school.**

Site Visits

When a school truly begins crafting an Award Winning Culture, invariably other educators, schools, and districts start reaching out to come visit. In hopes of bottling up some of your school's secret sauce, they start showing up in droves. During the past few years our staff has grown accustomed to seeing strangers walk through the building observing our school culture up close and personal. Here's a few of the tips that can turn an ordinary site visit into a master class in school culture intentionality:

Create a site visit packet for each visiting school member. Including site visit agenda, character lesson they'll be seeing, school information (bell schedules, advisory information, clubs/activity brochures, etc.), school swag (stickers, word of the month cards, etc.), evidence of success, links to corresponding websites and/or google form QR feedback information about the visit.

Learn everyone's name/position/ who will be attending your school's visit. Write the person's name at the top of their site visit packet. Also, provide these names to your secretary so that visitor badges can be

EXPERIENCE

created ahead of time and to support staff addressing visitors by name. Be sure and provide details on time of arrival, which school or city they'll be coming from and who the contact person for the group is. Student office aides and leadership students are awesome at creating packets and name badges if given a template to follow.

Provide snacks, treats, water, and coffee to all visitors as they arrive for their site visit

Set aside a specific location for the group to use as a home base such as a conference room, available office, or library sometimes provide a great location for people to set their things down and come in/out of.

During the visit, set up a diverse experience allowing people to observe teaching moments, ask questions, and interact with multiple educators/students; while still building in reflection time.

Even though educators are there to learn from you and your school community...educators with an Award Winning Culture mindset take advantage of all opportunities to soak up knowledge, ideas, and thoughts to advance their own school culture. You may be the expert on your school but you're being gifted a front row seat into someone experiencing your school community with fresh open eyes. Ask questions. Ask for feedback. Learn all you can about what's working well at their school. Some of the best ideas we've gotten have been ideas we stole from other schools who came to learn from us.

After the site visit, send an email later that day with any additional information, thank them for their visit, and ask if they had any other questions that came up on the car ride home. Car rides following a site visit are where some of the richest conversations happen during the entire visit. These moments often lead to additional thoughts, ideas, or questions.

District Office

District office staff may show up on your campus for a variety of reasons. Perhaps, they're there for a meeting with the principal, a classroom observation, or a surprise walk through. We want them to feel the same warmth and openness that we're striving for with all of our school community. Rather than viewing them as a visitor, staff and students should be interacting with them like their part of your family. Again, cueing secretaries, other support staff, and students of names, schedules, and agenda help to prompt a genuine welcome.

In *The Teacher and the Admin*, Kris Felicello and Gary Armida, tackle systemic educational challenges from two different perspectives. It's chalked full of strategies and a unified approach to collaboration. However, beyond the refreshing mix of practicality and educational artistry, the authors deliver such a powerful reminder that trust is the key between administration and all other educators.

> **Award Winning Culture amplifies opportunities to build trust among administration and teachers by remembering that everyone is there to serve students.**

Kristen Nan reminds us that we must open ourselves up to connecting with the "pit boss" or district administration in order to actually build trust. In *All In*, she and co-author Jacie Maslyk retell their first encounter when Jacie (district administrator) showed up in Kristen's 3rd grade classroom. It's a beautiful lesson in being willing to come together for the betterment of students. And truthfully, the authors of *All In* and *The Teacher and The Admin* remind us that risk taking is an implied requirement for game-changing relationship building. The depth of these powerful district admin-teacher relationships not only impact classrooms and building but entire districts as the shared visions can ripple K-12.

However, beyond waiting for district folks to stop by, actively invite, cajole, and initiate district office staff participation at your school. We can do this by including them on personal invitations to school events, regular email, newsletter, and social media outreach, and specific opportunities to see excellence in action both in and out of the classroom. In the same way that telling our school story to families is important, this practice is equally important with district leadership. We can't hope they'll read minds and just know what's happening in our buildings. We must intentionally connect with district leaders to share the school wide awesomeness.

As an added bonus, when difficult situations arise, having first-hand knowledge of a school and its individual staff sets district leaders up with powerful information when making challenging decisions, avoiding political landmines or resolving stakeholder concerns. It's similar to how principals can best support teachers, whose classrooms they frequently spend time in.

Speakers/Presenters

Speakers and presenters experience a wide array of greetings in schools. I've heard many assembly speakers open up about horror stories regarding things not going smoothly because of a lack of intentional planning and preparation, by school personnel. In some schools, these presenters may not have any idea where they're going and who is supposed to be helping them. In fact, I myself have experienced walking in to do a school presentation with nothing set-up, no one aware we were coming, and not a sole interested in helping us. Whether it's a top-notch speaker you've paid thousands of dollars to bring in, the local high school counselor speaking to a group of 8th grade students, or a parent presenting their occupation on career day. There's simply an Award Winning Culture way of working with speakers/presenters:

Confirm Details: A quick email or phone call a week before can really lay the groundwork for an exceptional presentation. Shore up all the specifics including location, needs, who will be greeting them, introducing them, time/dates/duration, and special requests. If they're coming in from out of town, where are they staying, what's their agenda, do they need a ride/pick-up, or area information.

Greet Them: We assign two leadership and/or other interested students, to be each presenter's personal liaisons. If possible, they literally greet them in their car with a smile, handshake, and helpful stance. Otherwise, they meet them at the main entrance of the school. They help carry things in, get them checked in at the main office, help them locate a key adult, and are generally at the presenter's beck and call throughout the duration of their time with us. Many people mistakenly assign this role to an adult. However, while they have good intentions sometimes adult educators get pulled in different directions. For instance, they get busy with working with other presenters, students, staff, parents, etc. Our student leaders take great pride in this sense of responsibility and love the personal connection with a perceived VIP. One student might forget or be sick that day but giving them an accountability partner ensures a successful greeting.

Treat Them: We put together personalized baskets of treats, refreshments, and wildcat swag. While the content and elaborateness vary depending on the type of speaker, the intentionality always rings true. From personalized handmade cookies to handwritten notes of thanks, speakers and presenters are treated exceptionally. We've provided lunch to folks whose presentation coincides with the middle of the day. We've grabbed coffee orders and breakfast to folks presenting in the morning.

EXPERIENCE

> **Intentional Tip:**
>
> *Ask during booking about things like t-shirt size, coffee preference, etc. To be honest, they'll forget you ever asked but believe me the gesture will go a long way to making for a wonderful and personalized experience.*

On some occasions we've even surprised out ofv town presenters by leaving their welcome basket at the front desk of their hotel lobby. I'll never forget chatting with one speaker about how he was moved to tears after showing up in the middle of the night at a hotel to discover a beautiful welcome basket from Wildcat Nation. He explained that he had lost his wallet, missed connecting flights, etc. Just a horrible day of travel. And in roughly a thousand school assemblies no other school had ever set up a welcome basket at his hotel lobby. Needless to say, his performance at our school assembly the next day, EXCEEDED all expectations!

But maybe you don't really care about their experience. Perhaps, some uninformed educators believe we are already paying this person or this is their job to present this. How might an exceptional experience by a presenter in our Award Winning Culture alter the impact of their presentation? If they're in a great frame of mind, heart, and soul there's nothing stopping them from crushing their presentation. And who benefits? Students, Staff, and School Community.

Time: Understand that students may have questions, want to take pictures, get autographs or just visit with your guest. Don't forget to be mindful of their time as they may need to be somewhere else. Our student leaders also are trained to help usher them out so that speakers and presenters don't get trapped with student fans or a barrage of educator questions and unable to leave.

Feedback: Seek feedback on all things including students, venue, mics, their experience, etc. This can be done following the event or activity and can include both positive and critical feedback. I love asking if they presented again next year, how might you all make it even better for THEM.

Follow-up: The goal is not to simply have them do their presentation and move on. This presentation is an open door to an ongoing relationship. Perhaps, you'll bring them back next year or maybe three years down the road. There may be other things they can do to support your school. For instance, we've had presenters skype with our classes, appear as guests on our student-led podcast, or provided follow-up materials and/or workshops because they were so emotionally moved by their time with Wildcat Nation. Rather than looking at a presenter as a financial transaction, it's critical to conceptualize the opportunity as relationship building.

Parents/Volunteers

In working with parents and volunteers, I always try and remember that their experience at my school may determine the extent and willingness to be involved in both EMS and all other future school related activities, at other schools. Thus, reaching out, using names, recognizing faces, and creating warm welcome educational spaces is essential to a positive Wildcat Nation experience. Some key considerations are: Communication, Climate, and Follow Through.

Communication: Parents and Volunteers love regular communication from a variety of different channels (phone, email, social media, reader boards, newsletter, etc.) but nothing replaces face to face human interaction. Award Winning Culture builds in specific formal and informal communication opportunities throughout the year. Beyond predetermined parent-teacher conferences, parents and volunteers value schools that intentionally keep communities in the loop. Events, Activities, Awards, Recognitions, Safety Concerns, Schedules, as well as Daily Occurrences are all opportunities to communicate with these big-hearted stakeholders.

Climate: Parents and volunteers can almost instantly feel what you are school is like, when they walk in the front doors or show up for an event. They might notice things like how your student body behaves at sporting events, how are they greeted by students and/or secretaries as they enter the building, or how organized are your school events, assemblies, or activities. Parents and Volunteers may not always be able to or choose to put their observations into words, but you can be sure the feeling of your building drives their experience in your space and will be shared out through word of mouth, social media and in casual social settings. Try to imagine: would I want my child attending this school?

Follow Through: When concerns, questions, or ideas are brought to your school...does someone follow through with the parent or volunteer, in a timely manner? I hope so, because these stakeholders notice when problems or thoughts aren't addressed. Even acknowledging areas of improvement can provide a positive experience and ensure future feedback. We regularly seek out feedback from parents and volunteers through surveys, e-mails, or personal conversation. But if folks don't see efforts to incorporate feedback results, they often grow weary of speaking their truth; which can ultimately result in disengagement, disillusionment, or discontent.

Classroom Rituals

An awesome way to increase the community experience within the classroom is to establish classroom rituals for excitement, celebration, or aahh learning moments. I've witnessed teachers creating rituals around cool classroom moments like ringing an oversized bell, doing a lap around the classroom, being allowed to ask the teacher one crazy question, or the entire class doing a quiet golf clap. I love walking by one of our ELA teacher's classrooms and hearing a large cowbell being rung. It's always proof to me that something spectacular just happened in his classroom. Teachers who add fun and energetic rituals to the classroom benefit from increased cohesion, engagement, and connection.

What are the collective experiences of people entering your culture?

What stakeholders might you be currently missing the mark with intentionality?

How will you SHAPE your community after learning the 5 keys to improving others' lives?

SECTION 4
CULTURAL MAXIMIZERS

CHAPTER 23
THE Y OF SCHOOL CULTURE

(Yet, Yes, and Yah)

When reshaping our school, three Y's can greatly influence a positive culture. Teaching students, staff, and parents to operate from a position of YET encourages a growth mindset that fuels mastery learning, sustained effort towards excellence, and belief to trust the process. Schools who foster growth mindsets among youth and adults create life-long learners who refuse to let barriers, setbacks or challenges deter them from their pursuit of joy.

Organizations with game changing cultures often adopt a mindset of YES! For instance, top customer service companies like the four seasons practice client-centered support that's highlighted in the following moto:

The answer is YES...now what is the question?

When educational spaces intentionally operate from a place of YES and leaders actively help stakeholders reach a yes, schools foster higher rates of creativity, curiosity, and risk-taking. When faced with a difficult request, the best educational leaders offer the following question: how can we make this a yes? This positional pivot reframes conversations from a compliance driven structure to an ownership of both the culture and the learning.

- Imagine the teacher who says yes to the student request to demonstrate their learning in some funky crazy way, order or location.

- Imagine the administrator who says YES to a teacher's request to modify pacing, deviate from the curriculum, or go gradeless.

- Imagine the District leader who says YES to a principal who wants to carve out time in her building to teach the whole child or move toward self-directed professional development for her staff.

Cultures of YES breed educational leaders who have the autonomy to make a difference every day.

Lastly, when schools emphasize a YAH or celebration atmosphere, students and educators can accomplish impossible feats. For instance, for years, we've celebrated growth at our school. Each quarter our dream team plus other available educators enthusiastically go into our Tier 2 and Tier 3 academic classes to high five, cheer on, and congratulate students on their hard work. Reading and Math support teachers give personal heartfelt speeches about their student's effort, grit, and perseverance as a precursor to an end of the quarter party which highlights a student's great work.

But our commitment to celebrating students, parents, and each other shows up on a daily basis in hallways, staff meetings, classrooms, and assemblies. Our staff literally is in constant pursuit of a YAH moment. A YAH moment is an opportunity to showcase someone being awesome. It might be planned out with all the wonderful moments of intentionality or might be a spur of the moment. Regardless, when educators get out of their own heads and actively seek out moments to celebrate students, parents, and peers, school culture is transformed into a place that everyone can feel proud of.

How might you keep focused on the three Y's of Culture?

CHAPTER 24
ANY QUESTIONS?

Asking questions is one of the best ways to grow as a human being.

-Michael Hyatt

As a counselor, I frequently find myself in a position of talking to students who need help...although, sometimes the help they need isn't actually from me. Ironically, they seek my guidance or thoughts when they should be talking directly with a teacher. Maybe they're struggling to understand a concept. Or perhaps they're having a conflict or feeling disconnected with a teacher. Other times, they may have a desire to make a change to some aspect of their learning. While students hopefully view their counselor as a safe advocate, we often work to empower them to plug back into their own student/teacher relationship and follow-up directly with the adult who can help them.

However, students' avoidance of asking teachers questions makes me wonder where does this inquiry-based trepidation come from?

Would you like to know the most frequently uttered statement by teachers to parents during conferences: *I'd really like to see him or her ask me more questions*. What prevents students from seeking help? Ok, sure, at the secondary level, there are a multitude of factors that play in with peer acceptance near the top. *"People might think I'm stupid if I ask this question."*

Fair enough. Social pressures for teenagers weigh heavily and can greatly influence their willingness to seek help. Yet, the reality is, there are so many opportunities to ask for teacher assistance, in quiet, non-observable to others sorts of ways. Students can talk to teachers during work time, before/after school, lunch time, over e-mail or google classroom. Some of my introverted readers might be quick to point out that Susan Cain's *Quiet* would remind us that personality types impact their boldness to ask questions. YES! A student's outgoingness absolutely affects their frequency to ask verbal questions. Although, I'm not quite as convinced that a propensity toward being introverted precludes online questions. Indeed, teachers have found exceptional ways of eliciting student participation from our quieter students, through the use of technology.

If I hadn't witnessed an overt discomfort to seek help by consistently ALL ranges of personality type over the last 20 years, I might have been content to conclude that peers and personality were the only driving force preventing inquiry. Rick Jetter and Rebecca Coda, authors of *Let Them Speak* so eloquently explain that if we want to know WHY kids do something, why not just ask them! So, I have...for most of my career. What keeps you from asking the teacher? While there is no denying personality and peer influence has impacts on students' willingness to seek help, fear of teacher response is clearly involved. There are actually three categories of this fear: **Witnessed**, **Perceived** or **Experienced.** A major fear factor that students cite--I'm afraid the teacher will make me feel stupid.

Now, before I get a litany of hate mail from all educators for saying that teachers make their kid feel stupid. Let me clarify. There are actually three categories of this issue: Witnessed, Perceived or Experienced.

Thus, I don't think for a minute that most teachers ever TRY to make a student feel stupid. Just the opposite! Most teachers WELCOME student questions. So, for the most part, let's assume good intentions on behalf of the classroom teacher.

We've all witnessed a student asking a question that has already been asked. As teachers know, sometimes the SAME questions are repeatedly asked again and again in front of the entire class. How do YOU respond to this repetitive inquiry?

Do you SHUT IT down?

Do you elect to use SARCASM?

Do you openly MOCK or point out to the class that this is the same question?

Do you WARN the entire class not to ask the same question that has been answered already?

Is there a general implication that this is somehow a 'stupid question'?

On the other hand, maybe a question has been asked in a quieter moment (work time, before/after school or even lunch time). Have you ever said any of the following?

- *Come on, you KNOW how to do this?*

- *I don't think you're even TRYING right now.*

- *You don't know HOW to do that?*

- *I thought you would've known how to do this one.*

- *That's an EASY one.*

The interesting takeaway is that it ultimately doesn't matter if an educator said this directly to a particular student or a student simply WITNESSED any of these responses; ultimately, their comfort level to ask questions might be impacted.

Additionally, you may have NEVER said or even thought of these above responses. However, the problem with education is that students often predict YOUR behavior on what they've seen or experienced previously from another educator's behavior. (i.e., a teacher I had in 4th grade said this so now I'm concerned that my 7th grade teacher might respond in the same way.)

Are counselors, admin, and other educational professionals immune to this unseen barrier for help? Absolutely not! In the same way that teachers must actively overcome certain past student experiences to find real connection, all educators must work tirelessly to create positive moments within our sphere of influence. Trust me, I see this in counseling relationships every year. People have preconceived notions based on previous elementary counselors, outside therapists, social workers...or even doctors. Additionally, because I have an office in a similar location as the school administration sometimes new students anticipate a disciplinary encounter, when entering my space.

In this teacher question scenario, a student's EXPERIENCED moment impacts their comfort level on asking a question. And again...it can be both personally experienced and witnessed. For instance, a student's self-dialogue might include remembrances of students in middle school being mocked and now their gun shy to ask a question of their high school teacher.

Lastly, students may PERCEIVE a negative response to questions based on a limited ability to predict your behavior due to low levels of connection to you. Thus, if I don't have a strong connection to you, I may postulate that an interaction will be negative even if I have no evidence to support this. In some student's minds, a lack of a relationship almost never suggests positivity. Therefore, I won't ask questions of educators who I'm not connected to. I know this sounds very gloom and doom. I'm basically saying that students bring all previous educator interactions, relationships, and perceptions to your classroom, office, or school.

Do you think this is just a kid problem? Having worked with thousands of parents over the years, let me assure you that they bring all the same types of biases, expectations, and concerns from both their childhood school experiences AND their child's experiences. Some parents can be incredibly skeptical of school systems, educators, or programming based on previous challenges. It can take years of relationship building to overcome tightly held school beliefs.

Beyond, students and parents, educators themselves can unknowingly be 'taught' not to ask questions, share opinions or generally speak up. I will NEVER forget witnessing a well-respected teacher get publicly berated for offering an answer in a staff meeting. The administrator at the time asked for a volunteer to answer a question. This bright, leadership team member, who was outgoing and confident was made to feel small and stupid in a quick throwaway moment during an August inservice meeting. Years removed from this, I don't recall any of the actual words used during the public exchange but the feeling in the room and the teacher's reaction later were burned in our collective memory. The teacher confided to a small group of us that afternoon,

"I'll never speak in another staff meeting again!"

It took two different principal changes before this wonderful teacher did choose to speak again in an open forum. Additionally, everyone who witnessed this uncomfortable exchange, was also in some small way traumatized and given information on how questions, answers, and responses would be welcomed by this leader. People often say they encourage risk-taking and mistake making environments, but their actions illustrate a completely different story. In this one fleeting moment by an administrator, the culture and climate of our staff meetings were negatively altered FOR YEARS!

For those that think this type of educator's negative moments must be specific to public forums, in order to do real damage, I'll share a common pitfall. Many professionals claim to have an open-door policy. They believe that physically having an office or classroom with an open door ensures that feedback is welcome. The real test of this, comes from how we handle critical feedback. If we immediately shut down criticism, opinions or insights that vary from our own perceptions, the proximity of the door to door frame will have NO consequence on whether anyone will actually walk through again. On the other hand, maybe criticism isn't the anthesis to a failed open-door policy. What if we're busy, distracted, or preoccupied in such a way that the staff member, parent, or student recognizes that our open-door policy might be held back by convenience. Essentially, we're saying to the world, I have an open door as long as it's a good time for me.

Furthermore, talented educators realize that relationships are built outside of their own space as well. Getting outside the classroom, office or even school is critical to forming relationships that invite others to seek your help.

> **Educators in an Award Winning Culture recognize current and past barriers toward seeking help and ACTIVELY create safe and welcoming conditions to support students, parents, and educators.**

For instance, one small thing our counseling group has done to increase connections and openness to others seeking help is to stand out in the hallway during passing time. Our purpose in the hallway isn't to monitor or supervise students. It also isn't about just visiting with other adults. It's an intentional move to connect with students as they pass outside the counseling center. It's incredible how much more approachable you seem with a smile, fist bumps and saying hi to students by name.

As highly trained professionals, we invariably find ourselves in a position to SERVE, SUPPORT, and SCAFFOLD people on a daily basis. Our actions both directly and indirectly impact our ability to help others find joy. Education can reach incredible heights when we intentionally reach for excellence in our interactions with others.

Obviously, we can't change the past, nor can we control what others have already experienced.

How will you intentionally create systems of support for your QUIET students?

How are you measuring and evaluating your current relationships with students, parents, and other educators?

What are some positive ways to respond to repeated questions or incorrect answers?

What non-verbal cues might YOU be giving off to certain folks that make you seem unapproachable?

How might you demonstrate HUMILITY when working with others?

Upon reflection of past experiences, who might you need to APOLOGIZE to TODAY?

CHAPTER 25
EDUCATIONAL CROSS TRAINING

Twenty plus years ago, when I began my career, I was a counselor who worked in education. But time, experience, and perspective have a funny way of changing your sense of self.

Warning to educators reading this, you might be upset by what I'm about to say. Ok, here goes:

> **In my experience, SOME educators spend too much time focusing on what their role 'should be' and not enough time living WHO they want to be. Aligning our WHO with our WHY helps us integrate into the school system, and more effectively reach the Whole Child.**

I know. I told you this might feel controversial. But far too often I hear things like "that's not my job" "they can't make us do that" and "this is not what we really should be doing."

Don't get me wrong, I would LOVE to have a 250 to 1 student/counselor ratio; which the American School Counselor Association (ASCA) recommends. I fully believe in the ASCA national model of Academic, Personal Social, and College/Career focus. Additionally, I think it's my job to educate students, staff, and parents how I fit into the school system. But, educating others about what I do isn't enough and certainly doesn't ensure me to *Be REAL* (Thanks Tara Martin!) within the school system. In her incredible book, Tara argues that educators might strive to be:

-R Be Relatable

-E Expose Vulnerability

-A Always be Approachable

-L Constantly Learn through real-life experiences

If educators were focused more on being REAL, perhaps our profession would be even stronger! In Heidy LaFleur's book *Hop on the Clue Bus*, LaFleur succinctly invites educators to a common sense approach to leadership. LaFleur inspires through age old futuristic concepts like listening, empathy, and relationships. She reminds us that integrating ourselves into a school system isn't rocket science but instead: human science. Her style is transparently refreshing as she abandons games and mind tricks and falls back on compassion, accountability, and love. She's the kind of educator who seems to have worn many hats throughout her experience and understands others' roles expertly!

One of my favorite educators, Meghan Lawson (who's the Coordinator of Instructional Services at Hamilton County Educational Service District in Ohio) recently started a new leadership position. She decided that prior to the first day of work she wanted to learn more about her teammates. She arranged coffee and casual time with co-workers prior to her official first day. WHY? Meghan is a positive dynamo who understands the power of relationships and identifying individual strengths. By taking a little time to ask questions, learn about each person's job, personal life, etc.: Meghan is better prepared to support and serve her team into the future. What if we intentionally connected with new educators to help their transition to our schools and districts by learning about each other?

In *Path 2 Serendipity*, Allyson Apsey reinforces this servant leadership approach to education as she explains "leading while walking alongside others is good for all of us." She talks about the need to ask questions and learn about others' work, when she started her principal position at Quincy Elementary School, in Michigan. Rather than focusing on her role being: I'm the principal and I need to have all the answers; she integrated into the building by learning about others.

A while back I had the pleasure of reading David Guerin's epic book *Future Driven*. In *Future Driven*, David has perfectly modeled the premise of his book as he resists spoon feeding readers all the answers on creating optimal learning environments but instead creates conditions for educators to do real thinking about how to create learning experiences for the future. In the same vein as the *Innovator's Mindset* by George Couros, it's the kind of book I anticipate being relevant 30+ years from now. David inspires by saying "we must create schools that reflect the world we live in, not the one we grew up in." My question to David was if this should apply to educators' own learning as well as student learning. While I'm confident that compartmentalized job roles served our school admirably for years, perhaps there's a need for more overlap of roles than previously thought. Or at the very least, an overlap in understanding of said roles.

After working through David's powerful insights, I began to wrestle with the idea that perhaps some of our professional development might be better focused on learning outside of our present job title. In other words, empathy, proficiency, and competency of educators could be vastly improved with a willing dive into other colleagues' skill zones.

Imagine a teacher who can expertly meet a student's emotional needs, within the classroom? How might student experience be different if the adults they worked with had varying skills? Are teachers the only educators in schools offering instruction? Would there be times a counselor might use direct instruction when working with an at-risk student or group of students?

Are counselors the only adults qualified to teach social emotional learning and or character ed? Many schools have moved toward teaching the Whole Child through advisory and/or leadership curriculum implemented by teachers. These schools realize that an intentional focus of Social Emotional Learning and Character Ed, coupled with the strong relationships (Teacher/Student) are a recipe for success.

Think about it another way: is it reasonable to leave all leadership tasks to administrators? Perhaps the key to creating an Award Winning Culture isn't about finding new or better people.

> **Award Winning Culture fosters positive leaders at all educational levels. Students, Staff, and Community.**

We can't sit back and put all the onus of leadership on the shoulders of a few people with the title: administrator. How can we build leadership at all levels? Maybe it starts by creating an environment that encourages risk taking, leap jumping, and comfort breaking.

Consider this, are coaches the only adults who need to give the occasional inspiring pep talk? Would other adults benefit from learning the customer service skills of our most talented administrative assistants? How might the overall school synergy change if we all had some greater range of skills in teaching, leading, serving, counseling, etc. Imagine *ThePepperEffect* (Thanks Sean Gaillard!) that could be generated with bandmates who possessed a diverse skill set. I guess the underlying question is:

Are we willing to concede that all adults in the schoolhouse are "educators"?

One of the best ways an educator can become "REAL" is through cross-training.

Cross training is the idea of training in one field with the purpose of raising one's effectiveness in another field. We often understand cross training in terms of sports.

Since I'm a huge football fan, I'll start with that "field" (pun intended). My favorite football player BY FAR was Walter Payton. When he retired, he was the all-time NFL rushing leader and a sure fire 1st ballot hall of famer. They even named an award after him: The Walter Payton Man of the Year, for his exceptional character. For years, people wanted to know the secrets to his stamina, agility, grit, and "sweetness" on the gridiron. Payton was legendary in his workout regime, which included running an intense hill each day...later renamed "Payton's Hill." By pushing himself beyond his limits running up and down, and even backwards, Payton stretched himself beyond what other running backs were doing to establish new success in cross training. Ironically, running hills is now considered a common place for running backs. But in the 1970's and 1980's this form of intense training was very cutting edge.

In the past 10 years, football organizations are continuing to push the boundaries on cross training with ideas like ultimate fighting, boxing, and wrestling. Defensive and offensive linemen work on such hand to hand combat skills in an effort to develop an advantage when lined up against other gigantic athletes across the line of scrimmage. It's not that they will be physically assaulting the other team (although some have described football as an organized car accident). However, football coaches understand that games are won in the trenches. Essentially one man trying to impose his will on another man. One player tries to protect the person with the ball and the other player tries to tackle the person with the ball. Hand placement can be crucial to gaining leverage on another oversized human being. Teams have incorporated a host of physical cross training to strengthen key elements of the game.

Perhaps the newest and most outside the box cross-training is mental conditioning. NFL athletes like Seattle Seahawk quarterback, Russell Wilson and Houston Texans' Deshaun Watson, have become synonymous with Mental conditioning coaches like Trevor Moawad. Moawad has been deemed the "best brain trainer" by Sports Illustrated for delivering advanced mindset solutions to the most driven leaders in competitive sports. Moawad's team helps motivated individuals reach peak performance by training their minds.

While I'm clearly obsessed with football, cross training isn't limited to my favorite sport. Basketball players like Kareem Abdul Jabbar prescribed learning yoga to increase flexibility and recovery from the pounding their bodies take on the hardwood. Basketball coaches like Phil Jackson, even facilitated group meditation exercises during practices. Some baseball players have even been known to study ballet. Furthermore, gymnastics has been shown to be helpful to competitive swimmers.

But cross training isn't limited to athletes. Chess players are frequently encouraged to take up soccer. Actors sign up for comedy improv classes. And most educators are aware of the positive student connection between math ability and learning to play a musical instrument.

Even the business world has jumped on this future driven mindset. Companies routinely cross train employees by having cashiers and/or customer service representatives learn a variety of aspects of company operations to help ensure empathy for both fellow employees and customers. Some tech specific companies even pay employees with bonuses for becoming certified in branches of the business, outside of their daily work routine. Indeed, mega successful companies like Netflix, Starbucks, and Amazon are so passionate about training employees outside of their companies, they are willing to lose good folks for the betterment of company morale. Amazon even pays up to $12,000 for tuition, fees, and textbooks to allow employees to pursue education unrelated to Amazon.

I recently saw an enlightening Instagram post from Danny Steele, former principal at Thompson 6th grade. Danny is a speaker and author of multiple books and passionate about all things related to school culture. *In Essential Truths for Principals*, Danny and Co-Author Todd Whitaker share,

> *"School Culture is not about the big things; it's about the little things."*

A while back, Danny had sent a picture of himself working with the custodial staff to clean the floors with some kind of cool machine. Danny had included an inspiring commentary on how outstanding his custodian staff are and how much fun he had getting his hands dirty, on that warm summer day. A cursory look at the post may have yielded the conclusion that Danny's time spent working with the custodial staff was a brilliant relationship building opportunity. Yes! I think that's definitely true. But further interpretation of Danny's experience also revealed that Danny gained an understanding of the complexity of his staff's job. By developing personal insight and empathy into the custodial world, Danny is a stronger leader in his ability to anticipate and understand staff needs. A bonus of the activity is increased positive influence with key educational staff. Danny's willingness to learn outside the "principal space" is certainly a brilliant expression of vulnerability and a perfect example of cross-training.

What if administrators were willing to answer the phones for an hour or two, while the secretaries did classroom observations. What insights into the front office culture might be gleaned for the administrators? How might specific classroom knowledge impact a secretary's job to interact with parent concerns in the future?

At my school, our outstanding secretaries even cross train each other; thus, they ensure that they're all capable of being the critical cog that makes the front office run smoothly. By being able to do each other's jobs at a functional level, they ensure all stakeholders are met with exceptional customer service. Have you ever reached out to a company or organization for help, only to be told that the person who could help you is at lunch, doesn't work on Tuesdays, or has the day off. It's a maddening experience! This form of siloed expertise can seriously erode culture through poor customer service.

Are we willing to integrate ourselves into the entire school system? Or are we DEFINED by our job title?

Recently, at the National Principals conference in Chicago, no surprise to anyone...it was almost all principals. However, the experience and takeaways were pure M.A.G.IC even for a non-administrator like me. How incredible would it be to send a team of teacher leaders to a conference like this?

At last year's school counselor conference, most of the participants were...school counselors. What if school psychologists or administrators were wrapped into these opportunities. What if we intentionally ventured out to conferences outside of our job title or role? Imagine the learning.

What books are you reading? Who do you follow on social media? I hear prominent educators speak glowingly about their TRIBE. But does a Tribe have to be made up of a homogenous group? If we're only surrounding ourselves with people of similar educational experiences, we're probably not pushing ourselves into uncharted waters. It's ironic to me that as I've begun to build my own PLN, I'm mostly drawn to non-counselors. Invariably I love interacting and learning from teachers, coaches, administrators, paraprofessionals, authors, consultants, speakers, etc.

> **Remember growth only occurs when we go beyond our comfort zones.**

Why not participate in a new twitter chat? Locate a new educational blogger. Listen to a non-educational podcast. Challenge yourself to learn a new skill or concept.

During the past 5 years, I've made a significant push to learn outside of the counseling space. One summer I spent my time learning amazing new concepts from the HiveSummit with Michael Matera. He's pushed virtual PD to epic levels with teachings from incredible educators on concepts like #BookSnaps #Gamification #Sketchnotes and much more. To be truthful, much of the content wasn't specific to counselors. But the chance to learn about cutting edge instructional tools, strategies, and outside the box thinking was worth every minute! I'm a better counselor for my time spent BEE-ing in the HIVE!

Last summer, I discovered the Teacher Success Summit, created by Chuck Poole as a fun alternative style to professional development. Chuck and his team shared out video content from incredible educators around the world in a streamable format that makes learning easy. But cross-training implies that I don't simply skip over non-counseling related content but instead fully engage in all parts of education. Naturally, some of my biggest takeaways from the TSS weren't parts where I was even the targeted audience. Learning advanced leadership or instructional strategies was such a gift to my own development.

Additionally, I've attended principal specific and teacher specific national conferences. I recently got back from presenting at the Teach Better Conference. A conference that was largely geared toward teachers ended up being the best conference I'd ever attended. The Teach Better Team is founded on a growth mindset vision of personal and professional development:

Teach better today than I did yesterday. Teach better tomorrow than I did today. In their book, *Teach Better*, the authors state,

> *"There is an important truth in education that is often overlooked: We do not teach content. We do not teach history of the American Revolution or the mechanics of bone and muscle. We do not teach grammar or how to add fractions. WE TEACH KIDS"*

Therefore, my time spent learning how to teach kids, reading teacher focused books and learning more about pedagogy, instruction, and best practice in the classroom has helped me become a stronger counselor.

My time in Twitter chats is mostly centered around discussions that have very little to do with counseling. I've intentionally sought out inspiring educators who are not in the same role as me (Here's a few favorites: #MasteryChat, #TLAP, #PrinLeadChat, #Rethink_Learning, #LeadUpChat, #EduAR, #SuptChat, and #LeadLAP).

I have read business, leadership, and self-help books to expand my understanding of what makes success. I'm proud to say that I've researched and implemented ideas in my life that focus on self-care and wellness from top authors like Dan Tricarico and Sarah Johnson.

But perhaps my greatest professional development through cross training is facilitating our student-led leadership podcast. This opportunity has given me a front row seat into learning from our most important stakeholders: STUDENTS. As an invited guest to peak behind the teenage current, I've learned what students actually value in teacher student relationships, how student agency can drive intrinsic motivation, and the role that fear plays in preventing student learning.

On the flip side, we need experts within a school building. The training, personality, and specific talents that we all bring to the table should and could not be overlooked. I'm not suggesting that we all become interchangeable parts. We've all been drawn to certain aspects of education due to our own personality, education, and prior experience. But imagine if we all understood each other's work on a deeper level. The type of service we might provide our students and families of the future could reach award winning heights.

> **My challenge to educators is to learn our colleagues' strengths, skills and needs so that we can effectively support the educational ecosystem.**

This only happens if we're willing to listen, ask questions, engage, and occasionally cross train outside of our comfort zones. While it's great to communicate your role and how you fit into the school, it may be even more important for you to reach out and discover more about your peers and co-workers. Who knows, maybe you'll also discover something about yourself?

Are you a Principal? Administrator? Coach? Teacher? Psychologist? Therapist?

One of my favorite teachers to follow on social media is Nicholas Ferroni, whose bio reads,

"As a kid, I wanted to be a superhero, psychologist, philanthropist, philosopher, actor, and comedian...So I became a teacher."

I might also add to Nicholas' bio: **Educator**.

After years in education, I no longer see myself as a counselor who works in education. **I'm an EDUCATOR who works as a counselor.**

Who are you?

What types of cross-training do you need to become a better version of yourself?

How are you teaching others about the work YOU do?

CHAPTER 26
GRATITUDE

A few years ago, I remember having a conversation with a colleague and sharing that I would NEVER leave education because of the students. We all have those students who push us to our core. They test our patience. They require us to learn new skills and strategies. They're just not easy. In fact, some days we're not sure we're making a difference at all. But no matter how challenging a student might be, the successes and overall mission always inspire us to keep moving forward. We remember the students who come back and share incredible stories of success. We hold dear letters, e-mails, and conversations of how we made a difference in some young person's life. Years ago, my former assistant principal encouraged me to create a file folder of these memories. Keeping a running record of gratitude and joy kept me in love with education. Educators all over the globe have some version of this well documented reminder of what this profession is all about. On those, less than stellar days, I can look back and recall how I impacted someone.

Check out this heartwarming video from Sumner School District on "The Heart of Teaching." Good luck not getting choked up!

https://youtu.be/IQNo5oeJNRM

Go Ahead...I'll wait.

However, I went on to explain, to my friend, that the one variable that could drive me out of education might be the adults. Teachers that are less passionate than we wish them to be. Politicians who just seem to "care" a little less about education than everyone else. Or maybe it's the parent who disagrees with everything we believe. Perhaps, it's a district level administrator shoving some new initiative down our throats. I was convinced that there would never be a time that students would push me to leave but that the adults……might!

So, I started thinking.

Educator turnover is at alarming rates! Educators begin their careers as inspiring change agents and too many walk away because of systems, peers, bosses, politics…in other words adult issues. Indeed, few adults ever leave the profession because of the kids. I wanted to find a new way of loving the adults I worked with.

On the other hand, I'm lucky to work at a school with an Award Winning Culture. We've got rock star teachers, administrators, and support staff. Let me tell you about a few of them:

GRATITUDE

We have a science teacher who might very well be the **KINDEST**, sweetest teacher in America. She's like a warm blanket on a rainy day! She oozes comfort and compassion as she connects with her students. She frequently gives up her student-free lunch to share her time and classroom with students who may not fit in with their peers. She's universally loved and I feel so lucky to have her at EMS.

Or maybe I should tell you about a math teacher who works with our struggling students with equal success to the brightest of the bright. His class load consists of gifted math students and students who have such low skills they hate math. He's that teacher who refuses to give up on a student. He gets to school at 5 a.m. when school doesn't start until 7:55 a.m. His **COMMITMENT** is unmatched. He believes in the power of education, has a passion for math, and the art and skill to coax greatness out of his students.

I should definitely mention our 60 year-old PE teacher ...who was incidentally MY middle school PE teacher. She has more energy in her little finger than I have in my entire body. She's a positive force of nature, who is the poster child of **HUMILITY**! It's impossible not to smile when you're around her. She sings happy birthday to each individual student throughout the school year and then relishes in demonstrating her badminton or b-ball skills. In 30 years of knowing this woman, I've never heard anyone say a negative word about her.

Our speech therapist who provides humor, **PATIENCE**, and high expectations all rolled into a 5 foot frame. She works with all levels of students with ease and grace and instills hope in each student. They simply leave middle school with a belief in themselves because of this woman. She brings IT every day and she treats each student with the respect and dignity they deserve. #Thankyou

We have a leadership teacher who we simply give the toughest students in school and tell her to "turn them into leaders." She has a knack for

RESPECTING those challenging, hyperactive boys in the same way that she can gently connect with the quiet anxiety ridden girl. She's all in on teaching kindness, service and empathy in and out of her classroom by modeling what it means to be Character Strong. She has no kids of her own, so her students are her children.

I'm not ashamed to admit that one of our ELA teachers recently brought me to tears as he presented and celebrated his students outstanding growth on a recent standardized test. His heartfelt, intentional, **HONEST** words had everyone in the room, reaching for the nearest tissue. He's the guy who greets every student at his door with a unique handshake and personalized hello. He's special because he recognizes the need to put relationships first and then focus on challenging the best out of his kids. #Authentic

There's a 20-ish year old history teacher who infuses technology and innovation in the coolest ways. He's always trying something new or pushing himself and his students in an exciting new direction. He makes history come to life with stories, personality, humor, and conviction. Beyond that he's **SELFLESS** when helping others learn how to integrate technology in the classroom. And EMS is better off for having him.

We have a special education teacher who works with our most behaviorally challenged students in the entire district. He chooses **FORGIVENESS** every day for the choices they make by giving them a fresh start to make it a great day. His laid-back style of relationship building ensures these students have the best possible chance for success.

Any parent would be thrilled to have their child connected to these incredible educators and countless others. I'm leaving out stories about our team-focused relationship-driven principal, school board recognized secretary, and hardworking custodian. There simply isn't enough time to share about a teddy bear-like science teacher, a college inspiring counselor, or our award winning jazz band conductor. I definitely should

GRATITUDE

have shared about the PE teacher who overcame his wife's health scare to flourish as our new athletic director, a math teacher who helped save our science teachers life with CPR, and a history teacher showing GRIT showing up to work every day as she fought and survived breast cancer, while undergoing Chemo treatments.

But here's what's truly interesting ...these teachers, educators, and support folks aren't unique to EMS. They aren't even unique to Richland School District or Washington State. While they are special and amazing people...these types of heroes aren't unique to our profession. These outstanding adults exist all around the country. Educators like this are in La Crosse, Wisconsin.....Westfield, New Jersey...and ...Chicago, Illinois. In fact, they exist outside of our country as well. There are dedicated educational leaders in every city, country, and community around the globe. They might have different names, faces or personalities but I'd be willing to bet that you recognize some of the character traits in these heroes that you have in your own buildings. Schools around the world are filled with incredible Edu Superstars that make a difference in kids' lives. They bring out the best in their peers and push education to new heights.

One outstanding principal from Texas is using his platform to share how *Every Story Matters*, when it comes to these educators. In addition to being the principal at Webb Elementary school, **Todd Nesloney** is a speaker, author and champion of sharing his teachers inspiring stories. Nesloney knows that recognition fuels gratitude.

Isn't it funny that an educator will stay committed to this profession for life with the occasional student success story as the catalyst to continue on this path? Despite all the challenging students, through the years, these successes keep us moving forward. But that same educator is willing to walk away from their "life's work" because of the "adults" even though so many of our peers are doing such outstanding work.

> **Perhaps, we need a way to recall the amazingness from our profession. Something we can refer back to and use as a beacon of hope to help keep us on track during times of collaborative frustration.**

But, wait ...I can already hear the outcry. Those folks saying 'Hans, you got the wrong adult ...it's not about our peers'. The adults that are driving us out of education are the PARENTS! I get it. In 19 years in education, I've run into my fair share of difficult parents. I've received more than enough anger, frustration and rage. Although, most educators will tell you the parents that keep us up late at night ...are the ones who don't seem to care. You contact them regarding their suicidal child, and they don't get it. Or you report a badly assaulted victim to Child Protective Services and nothing changes. These absent, neglectful unknowing parents are incredibly deflating.

But the truth is...this is only a small fraction of the parents out there. In the same way that I might detail amazing teachers at EMS, I could do the same thing for parents. If we had time, I'd share about a mom who drives her child 90 minutes one way EVERY DAY to attend EMS. Or the dad who takes off his migrant field work to come speak with his kids' teachers. I'd tell you how humbling it is to see a dad donate money to our school for every 3 point shot the basketball team makes. You'd probably love to hear about the mom who whips up an elaborate luncheon for staff appreciation week. I'll bet you'd be inspired by the mom who supports her son's quest for equality in schools. I'd certainly be tempted to show you an email from a mom/dad thanking a history teacher for both loving their daughter and holding her accountable. We all can identify amazing parents who understand the value of education, deeply love their child, and would do ANYTHING to ensure success. These parents exist in every school and in every community. And their partnership is invaluable!

So, why do we hold on so tightly to a few challenging adults?

> **The key to creating an Award Winning Culture is to assume the best in both students AND ADULTS!**

Choosing Love is usually easier with students than adults, but it's no less important. Sure, from time to time ...we'll be let down. But perhaps the key to persevering through these challenging adult relationships is an intentional focus on all the amazingness around us. What if, rather than leaving our "life calling" behind, we instead intentionally and regularly demonstrated gratitude for the incredible people in our lives. Perhaps, this positive mindset would allow us to reset more quickly when dealing with that difficult adult and create increased joy in our profession. Brené Brown, author, speaker, and researcher believes in the connection between joy and gratitude. "Practicing gratitude invites joy into our lives," says Brown.

On the other hand, assuming the BEST in others doesn't mean we should simply be a doormat. We still have to hold others accountable, speak our truth, and advocate for students at the highest of levels. I don't think assuming good in adults opts us out of difficult conversations or challenging paths. What it does, however, is keep us aware of gratitude.

> **Gratitude keeps us grounded to the mission and confident in our own ability to stay committed in the face of adversity.**

Because students are worth it. You're worth it. I'm worth it!

My challenge to our profession is to seek out and celebrate the adults around us. Create files, lists, pictures, videos that document all the magic you witness. Your co-workers, colleagues, and parents are doing unbelievable things for education. Recognize them. Appreciate them. Remember them.

What ways are you currently expressing gratitude for the people you work with?

CHAPTER 27
WELCOME BACK

As a kid, I struggled with asthma while growing up in an environment filled with sage brush, dust and pollen. The Tri-cities were indeed a hotbed of allergies for me. Despite being a competitive athlete, I routinely found myself dealing with some yearly sickness during the winter months. And while I eventually outgrow asthma, it created a lot of personal challenges to overcome.

Without question, my 10th grade year proved to be my toughest in terms of health and wellness. In late December of 1991, I came down with a full-blown case of Pneumonia; which in turn, landed me in the hospital. During my time away from high school, our head varsity coach had also been fired. Additionally, I had missed numerous assignments, projects, and tests. Furthermore, this health ordeal coincided with my 16th birthday as I literally was hospitalized 2 days after receiving my driver's license (FYI: I was born on Christmas Eve...so for those reading closely, you probably guessed that my Christmas looked a little different than most).

As you can imagine, losing 15 lbs, missing multiple basketball games, and over three straight weeks of school might prove to be extremely anxiety provoking.

How would I get caught up? Did I lose my spot on the team? Will I be interrogated about my excessive absences? Do I remember how to drive my car? Will my friends care that I'm gone?

Luckily for me, I had numerous teachers, coaches, and educators who prescribed to an Award Winning Culture mindset. These Character focused educators intentionally visited me in the hospital, brought me cards, assignments, and encouragement. Then, as I recovered at home, folks were lined up to wish me well, check-in on me, call me on the phone, and generally facilitate my transition back to LIFE at school. They even continued this wellness watch as I returned in mid-January by greeting me with smiles, "Welcome Back Hans," and helping me prioritize and strategize how to tackle the MOUND of schoolwork.

Nearly 27 years removed from this health scare, I occasionally find myself wondering what might have happened if I wasn't treated with such positivity, dignity, and respect.

During my time as an educator, I've witnessed and taken part in all forms of response to student absence. Some comments seem to do real damage:

- *"Check the box for missing work."*

- *"It's not my job to keep track of your assignments."*

- *"Looks like you finally decided to show up."*

- *"I don't have time to help you get caught up right now, I've got to teach."*

- *"Nice of you to show up!" [With sarcastic undertone]*

- *"Where the heck have you been?"*

- *"It's hard to learn, if you're never here!"*

- *"You gotta start coming to school."*

WELCOME BACK

- *"It's STUDENTS' responsibility to seek me out for missing assignments, when their absent...it's not my job"*

- *"Two days for every day you missed, NO EXCEPTIONS!"*

- *"If you were here more often, you'd know what to do."*

- *"Why haven't you completed all the work I sent home?"*

- *"It's about time you're here!"*

> **Award Winning Culture establishes conditions of positivity and warmth, to support students through absences.**

Educators recognize that excessive absence comes with elevated anxiety and decreased educational self-efficacy. By intentionally reaching out during and after attendance struggles, educators provide students with HOPE.

I recognize that educators have numerous students in their classrooms, caseloads, teams, and schools to keep track of. But as a kid who struggled through an extended health related absence, I want to assure you that your time, energy, and compassion matter.

It mattered to the kid who had to stay home with a younger sibling. It mattered to the kid who came down with mono. It mattered to the kid who had school-based anxiety. It mattered to the kid who struggled with a learning disability. It mattered to the kid who returned home from Disneyland. It mattered to the kid who returned to school with a broken hand. It mattered to the kid who failed to set his alarm because his parents left at 5am. It mattered to the kid who was kept home, as a discipline punishment. It mattered to the kid who wouldn't show up because he had no clean clothes.

And.....IT MATTERED TO ME!

Now, don't get me wrong. We all know that consistent attendance matters to student learning. Creating systems that inspire and encourage exceptional attendance is crucial to building educational momentum that exudes student empowerment. However, we run the risk of damaging student and/or parent relationships with obtuse responses. Furthermore, our unenlightened or nonexistent feedback might have the unintended consequence of perpetuating student absence.

My challenge to educators is to examine your own behaviors, words, and feelings toward students who are absent.

How might you "WELCOME BACK" your students TODAY?

CHAPTER 28
BUDGETING

One of the most frequent questions building leaders ask me is,

How did you pay for that? How did you fund that assembly speaker? Who paid for those t-shirts? What budget code are you using for that training or those events?

The truth is, we don't have some magic pot of money. Nor are we printing play money. We haven't uncovered some sort of secret hack to getting all of our things paid for. We're just a regular building in a regular district, in a regular old town.

The real secret to our budgeting success is that our school leadership along with our unified staff, students, and parents believe that building money should impact our school culture. Period. And as you learned earlier most everything that happens at school, impacts school culture. Therefore, we work from a lens of how this money can impact culture the most. Thus, the counselor budget isn't used to buy counselors new iPad and fun new toys. We use the money to purchase school supplies, food for students in poverty, or fund SEL curriculum. Our students use ASB funds to deliver high impact to our entire school. They might carve out funds to bring in a speaker to an assembly or put in brand new drinking fountains. The same is true of all our money. We take a community view on money and see it as fuel for our Award Winning Culture fire we're building. Individual budgets are not selfishly spent on frivolous items. We attempt to maximize impact on every purchase. Our PTSA is the same way. Rather than funding silly unused teacher appreciation gifts that are quickly forgotten we ask that our parent leaders spend their money in ways that truly impact school culture: t-shirts, flexible seating furniture in classrooms, guest speakers, community-wide events, etc. Every school stakeholder has a choice, and they can opt to make their money count in a big way!

Additionally, we pursue many grant and fundraising opportunities. For instance, our leadership teachers do a t-shirt, socks, and Wildcat Nation swag fundraiser each fall. That money directly supports all our PBIS/Wildcat Cash Shop events throughout the year. Simple and effective.

Even fundraising provides a source of intentionality with culture building. We believe that fundraisers should directly tie back to our school brand and house rules. If no connection to our school's why exists, then we move on to other fundraising opportunities. For example, one of our top yearly fundraisers is a Fun Run. Essentially, students raise money to get released out of 6th period to run around the track. We offer games, prizes, and treats, which are all donated by local businesses. Some years we turn it into a Color Run, allowing students to run through paint or colored smoke bombs. But the event is always in conjunction with Halloween. One of our Halloween expectations is that you can only wear a Halloween costume to school if you are participating in the fun run. We have a variety of built in opportunities for students to have their participation fee waived or covered to level the playing field for all students to participate. And as you might anticipate, the entire event which features parent volunteers, local businesses and first responders and most of our school students and staff establishes community building.

Another fundraising source, just this past year was Raise Craze. Raise Craze is a unique fundraising option that gives back by focusing on kindness. The organization has created an online platform to enable students, staff, and families to set up secure, custom websites where they request donations while students pay it forward by completing acts of kindness for others. It's geared toward SERVICE not selling stuff!

Fundraising, just like all other school choices should be intentionally thought out to directly support the school mission and overtly communicate your work with Character, Excellence, and Community. I'd highly suggest re-examining uninspired fundraising plans like candy sales, garbage bags, or wrapping paper.

The point of this section isn't to offer some master class on how to cheat the ASB laws or share some creative accounting techniques. It's to remind educators to spend and raise money with intentionality.

> **Award Winning Culture uses intentionality with any and all school purchases to reap maximum school benefit.**

How might you re-pool building, classroom, or department level monies to more effectively enhance culture and climate.

What are your current fundraising choices saying about your school's brand?

CHAPTER 29
BE PRESENT

In the spring of 2001, I was hired as a long-term counseling sub to replace a beloved counselor who had moved away at spring break. The gig was for the remainder of the school year (about three months) and had the potential to result in a long-term position.

Near the end of my first week, I found myself in a situation that I'd come to replay many times in my head. It was after school and I was helping a student with a schedule change and a parent stopped in looking for a teacher. She had a few questions and was interested in locating the teacher's room. I sprang from my chair and quickly escorted her down to the teachers classroom, before turning around to finish up with the student waiting in my office.

Approximately 30 minutes later, as I was getting ready to leave, the math teacher bolted through my door and laid into me. Apparently, the parent was very upset, and the teacher was essentially verbally attacked. Our teacher felt unsupported by me as I dropped the parent off and disappeared.

To make matters worse, I got defensive and didn't handle the teacher's feedback well. Naturally, my reaction was not winning me any relationship points. Not very award winning on that day!

In my preoccupation with returning to my office to complete a student's schedule change, I was oblivious to the signs of frustration that the parent was demonstrating. In the teachers' eyes, I abandoned her, in the moment she most needed me. Not a great first impression! Valuable Lesson:

Preoccupation is a PATH toward DISCONNECTION!

As I reflected on this encounter over the weekend, that's when I truly realized my role as a counselor. Prior to that moment, I thought I was a counselor for STUDENTS. As I continued to ruminate on my screw up, I came to a new understanding. I'm the SCHOOL counselor. Which means, I have to be there for teachers, for my principal, for parents, or other staff members...and of course the STUDENTS. However, learning to prioritize what's most salient took on a new meaning with my reworked perception of my role.

- Never put teachers in a situation where they're meeting with parents by themselves.

- Find out concerns and as much as possible give teachers a heads up on challenging situations.

- Talk with parents first...gone and got the teacher and then coached them up on the walk down to my office.

Ironically, fast forward three months, this same teacher was on the interview team, as she literally sat in between me and a long term counseling position. Truth be told, I'd later find out, she did NOT want me to get the job, as she was still angry at me for failing to support her. Luckily, I had made a positive impression on the rest of the folks on the interview team and was able to spend the next 10 years intentionally improving my relationship with that math teacher.

During the interview, the team asked me if there's anything I would've done differently during my three months of the long-term counseling sub. Naturally, I brought up this moment of being preoccupied and my failure with the math teacher and parent. It was a strong example of demonstrating humility while learning from my mistakes. Since then, I've never put a teacher in a room with a parent without myself or an administrator present.

Being present is critical to creating an Award Winning Culture in my office and beyond. We have to pick up the warning signs when people truly need support. It's not ok to be stuck in our own head.

One of my most frequently shared advice for parents is to be willing to drop EVERYTHING to visit with a teen son or daughter who expresses interest or desire in talking with you. Many children can become more closed off during teen years, as they push boundaries and work to establish their own individual identity. Adults can miss opportunities to connect with teens if they are preoccupied with other things and fail to capitalize on these parenting olive branches.

This same advice goes for educators. When a learner reaches out to you by staying after class, signing up to see you, or actively seeks you out... they need something. Put the e-mail, content, or other work aside for a moment and OPEN UP, LISTEN, AND CONNECT. And if you aren't in a position to drop everything in the moment, either schedule a time to meet up or connect them to someone who can talk.

How will you be more mindful to others needing your support?

Are there people in your life personally or professionally that have been seeking your attention?

In what ways might you better support this person(s)?

CHAPTER 30
VULNERABILITY

One day, in our school's staff meeting, someone was brave enough to share that some teachers are afraid of saying the wrong thing, when met with a student who's struggling. I think many teachers feel this way...

Which got me thinking about some recent conversations I've had with folks who are afraid to be innovative in their classrooms, afraid to contact parents, afraid to be vulnerable with students, or even afraid to challenge colleagues. I think FEAR really permeates our profession.

But having spent most of my career talking with people who are struggling, I want you all to know, most people aren't actually looking for you to solve their problems, give them inspiring advice or put together the most eloquent words. Most people are just looking for connections. Students want us to demonstrate:

I SEE YOU.

I HEAR YOU.

I LOVE YOU.

I've witnessed educators at Wildcat Nation having meaningful connection through their words and actions all over the school:

- One person took all the sting out of a difficult conversation with a simple heartfelt apology.

- One person connected online through a check-in and got the student help.

- One person moved mountains to ensure a student's home life was safe.

- One person is reimagining their workspace to create a safe landing place for struggling kids.

- One person gave up their prep period to check in on a student they DON'T EVEN HAVE IN CLASS.

- One person removed their own ego to ensure a student's needs were being met.

- One person demonstrated empathy for a family by helping them access a district program by eliminating systemic barriers.

Believe me, people notice. Relationships matter.

I even had a colleague reach out to me a while back and express concern that I wasn't acting like myself. The truth is, that person didn't have all the perfect words and in the right order, but their effort and love meant the world to me. And, in the end, they were able to help me see something I wasn't ready or able to see. And now our connection is stronger than ever!

VULNERABILITY

It really comes down to getting out of our own heads and leading with the HEART. I encourage you to side-step fear of saying or doing the wrong thing and just go all in on CONNECTION...

> "Connection is the energy that exists between people when they feel seen, heard, and valued; when they can give and receive without judgment; and when they derive sustenance and strength from the relationship."
>
> ~ Brené Brown

Just like connection, empathy, kindness, and service can be demonstrations of real vulnerability. For instance, opening ourselves to authentic relationships through acts of character defining kindness can invite opportunities to be hurt. When a student says hi to an unknown student in the hallway, invites a peer who's outside of their social group to sit with them at lunch, or compliments a classmate they are essentially risking rejection, hurt, or embarrassment. Teaching and preparing students for these moments of vulnerability are helpful to their continued willingness to pursue discomfort in order to seek connection.

There are risks each day for educators or parents as they reach out to one another to better serve learners. Or to coordinate support for students. Leadership is owning all the risk when things go bad and sharing all the success when things go well. Parents, educators, and students are all co-leaders in learning. When we empower each other to move past fear of relationship failure, we have the potential to generate cultures rich in relationships. We must teach students and staff that this uncomfortable or scary vulnerability is worth creating safe, welcoming, and relationship-focused schools.

How has fear kept you from establishing a relationship with a parent, colleague, or student?

What might your classroom, office, or school look and feel like if you granted yourself permission to lead with vulnerability?

CHAPTER 31
SIGNS OF SUCCESS

"The secret of change is to focus all of your energy, not on fighting the old, but on building the new."

-Socrates

Will I really have to wait 3-5 years to see an Award Winning Culture blossom in my school? How will I know that this intentional focus on Character, Excellence, and Community is actually working?

School Culture might feel like an abstract concept to measure. And beyond the usual suspects of measurement such as: GPA, attendance, discipline rates we might get a clearer picture of success with surveys that measure things like connection, purpose, joy, and stakeholder perception. Leaders might also examine student transfer requests, teacher retention, and graduation rates. But before you narrowly set your sights exclusively on hard data, I'd encourage you to take note of the small anecdotal examples of your culture being elevated to a new level. These enlightening reminders might be a school's first signs of success and provide the necessary inspiration to keep pushing your school culture forward on the hard days. Here's a few of our first signs of cultural success:

AWARD WINNING CULTURE

- A special education student posts on social media how proud she is for being recognized for a character award for commitment because it's "the first time a teacher believes in me."

- An honored veteran calls the principal, in tears, from our school parking lot, to thank our students for honoring him and others during our Veterans Day Assembly. According to this older gentleman, it was the FIRST TIME he's been recognized publically for his service since coming home from war.

- A handful of educators and parents, from neighboring schools, reported to me being ticked off after our community strong event. Apparently, they were mad because their schools aren't the same way. "We should be doing these kinds of things in OUR school!"

- A high needs student awkwardly dances for an uncomfortably long period of time during a lunch time talent show while 300 students give him an emphatic standing ovation.

- A disconnected teacher finds and shares with our staff motivational videos on character.

- Students, Staff, and Parents write me handwritten notes of praise for making character a focus at our school.

- A quiet introverted staff member visits leadership classes to publicly thank them for giving him the Wildcat award.

- Our lunch ladies nominate students to receive character awards for patience.

- The custodian throws a root beer float party for a couple lucky classes because she's moved by our student's efforts to take care of their school. All the food for the parties was fully funded out of her own pocket.

This isn't meant to be a complete list of early signs of success. It's meant to be an eclectic cross mix of what we started experiencing in the beginning. I hope reading these signs will help you recognize them in your own classrooms, buildings, and districts...and more importantly start sharing and highlighting them for all your stakeholders to appreciate.

What are some signs of cultural positivity that you've noticed recently?

How might you bring attention to these examples of positive culture for others to enjoy?

CHAPTER 32
CULTURE VS. CLIMATE

School Culture experts might be quick to point out that feelings are in large part connected to climate. Whereas, culture refers to how people actually behave. I wrestled with this difference for years as most all school culture literature focused on creating positive behaviors and explaining that it takes 3-5 years of habits to create culture. The underlying implication that culture is more valuable or a more noble pursuit than climate. Afterall, climate is just a temporary feeling.

Approximately a couple months into our Wildcat Nation morning greeting, the weather was beginning to change for the cold. A colleague, who had been regularly greeting with me and others each morning pulled me aside and asked: "so at what point do we NOT have to stand at the front of the school and greet alongside the students? When does this become part of our student culture, where they no longer need the adults standing out here also?" His question was filled with fatigue but genuine curiosity.

I pondered this for what must have seemed like an eternity before responding: NEVER. We ALWAYS have to make this a priority. Character is winning the daily battles over doing what we want to do vs. doing the right thing.

We always have to model Character, Excellence, and Community. Human Connection isn't just a good idea, it's essential to building the atmosphere for learning, thriving, and living.

While many organization experts believe that Culture and Climate are two very different things. Perhaps, the difference isn't as important as previous literature postulates. In an interview with Kelly Croy, on the *Wired Educator Podcast*, Todd Whitaker, author of countless books on culture and climate, including *School Culture Rewired*, connected some powerful dots for me. Todd said:

"If today we decide to treat every student with respect and dignity, and we did it for one day that changes the climate. Did you know if we never stop doing it, we change the culture? And what day it switched from Climate to Culture is irrelevant."

Whitaker's view perfectly aligned with my belief that it doesn't really matter when your efforts shifted from positive feeling (climate) to positive actions (culture) as long as the actions never stop. And our thoughts or mindset can play a large role in fueling our own behaviors.

Drew Dudley, speaker, consultant, and creator of the viral TED Talk: *The Lollipop Moment*, argues a similar point in his book "*This is Day One: A Practical Guide to Leadership that Matters*. Dudley explains that the passion, focus, and intensity leaders bring to Day One on the job is amazing. He explains,

"Day One is when you discover, define, and start to consistently deliver on your foundational leadership values."

Dudley believes that when leaders continue to attack each and every day, as if it's Day One, an exceptional atmosphere is evolved. Many of us have had that Day One experience at Disneyland. Their first-rate customer service elevates all the shows, rides, attractions, and experiences throughout the park. Would patrons have a good experience, even without the exceptional culture they've built? Probably the answer is yes. However, Disneyland's not shooting for good...they're shooting for award winning. Treating families like it's their first day on the job ensures that employees bring all the positive energy and intentionality that lifts the Disneyland experience out of the normal amusement park realm.

Similarly, kids can learn in schools with poor culture. Want to know how I know this? Because kids can learn without schools at all. They can watch YouTube videos, search google, read books, and pick up all kinds of impactful learning, outside of school. But schools offer experiences and feelings that students can't have while learning on their own. A school offers a level of human connection and sense of community that has the ability to inspire, support, and deliver futuristic hope. These elements of school provide a path to real joy. And cultural minded educators are the tour guides to discovering and developing these adventure rides of joy.

Think about day #1 as the start of the school year. Educators are filled with hope, energy, and a reconnection to their why. Obviously, if schools were as positive, welcoming, loving, and connecting as the first day of school, every day would feel amazing.

What is one action you can commit to each week to make others FEEL incredible?

CHAPTER 33
NOW WHAT?

You have the tools, ideas, and inspiration to begin crafting an Award Winning Culture. So, where do you begin? Do educators really have to delve into student-led podcasting or create a Wildcat Cafe to reach beyond special school culture? No. Of course not. The examples in this book are just that...they're examples from our culture. They may not fit your community, school, or vision for what you're striving for. Instead, take the elements of intentionality that turned hot chocolate into the Wildcat Cafe and apply those to your own school. Imagine if you applied that level of intentionality to your hiring process, Donuts with Dudes event, or your next writing assignment in US history. Take some of the elements of Character, Excellence, and Community and infuse those into actions, in YOUR sphere of influence.

By now, you've also noticed many of the examples I shared in the book might fall into multiple categories. For instance, is our Wildcat Nation Morning greeting really just a tool to SHAPE our community through personal outreach? There's obviously elements of Character and Excellence embedded into it as well. As you begin enhancing your eye for intentionality, you'll probably notice that the most dynamic culture building ideas, programs, lessons, events, people, and systems actually impact all three overarching elements at once.

The best way to get started is to begin picking apart one thing that you do. Maybe it's a lesson or a morning procedure or maybe you're on a committee tasked with an upcoming event. How might you begin to reimagine one aspect of your work in a more intentional way?

Oftentimes a great place to begin with intentionality is with something you're already struggling with. Maybe you're a principal who hopes to get into classrooms more frequently and thus finding creative ways to hold yourself accountable, share on social media, and infusing the elements of EPIC to celebrate teachers you visit might all prove to be productive ways to elevate classroom visits. You might need to invest in portable furniture, find an accountability buddy, or create a visual reminder such as postcards or a coin with every teacher's name on it, to push yourself to get out of the office to observe in a classroom. Maybe you'll need to publicly lay out your intentions and ask students to physically come bring you to their room. The point is to be as creative as necessary and as intentional as possible.

Perhaps, you are a paraprofessional leading a safety patrol club and struggling to consistently have members show up on time, while keeping students safe in the mornings. Do students need reinforcement or reward for their service? How might local police and/or firefighters support your efforts? Are there community businesses that might fund hot chocolate or hand warmers for standing out in the cold? Do you need to restructure your schedule? Offer safety club reminders to ensure punctuality? Would a screening or application process change students' commitment to their work? How might student voice be utilized to solve the attendance struggles? Would safety patrol members benefit from some type of character training and/or teambuilding? Intentional educators pick over all aspects of a problem through the Award Winning Culture framework.

Maybe you struggle with parent teacher conferences that take on a negative spin and you want to find a more intentional way to connect positively with parents, prior to the conference. Are there ways that you can celebrate awesome parents throughout the year? How might you invite, greet, and give parents the VIP treatment either in real life or virtually? Is there a common language that your content area lends itself to? Maybe there are updates or reminders that could feature upcoming lessons or ideas that will be coming from your classroom. Stop viewing challenges as barriers and start seeing challenges as OPPORTUNITIES to practice intentionality.

Do you have poor turnout at the school dance? How might intentionality with personal outreach and empowerment play a huge role in students showing up to evening activities? How could you ensure that you're connecting all groups within the school community to the dance? Would personal invitations from influential students and/or staff make a difference? Are there equity barriers that are preventing students from attending an expensive evening? Are school dances created exclusively by popular leadership students or are you including all student voices in decision making and stylistic choice? From personal experience, we noticed a dramatic increase in attendance at dances, when we put all school clubs in charge of designing, building, and running our dances. Being an intentional educator means you're not stuck doing things the way they've always been done. Get innovative with your work regarding the elements of Character, Excellence, and Community.

Starting small can help educators build momentum towards creating a tipping effect that leads to big culture and climate changes. But what happens when things get hard? Because they will. There will be failures and challenges that you can't predict and that leave others questioning the idealistic pursuit of an Award Winning Culture. Build your network of positive, intentional people who believe what you believe. And don't just limit yourself to peers. If we've learned anything from educational cross-training it's that educators are more alike in their WHY than we often think. Surround yourself with exceptional culture builders regardless of title or position.

Additionally, think outside of adult educators when forming your professional network. This might be student champions, parents or community leaders. I often tell people that a group of talented 6th grade students really fueled my passion for school culture in the early tough days. They're energy and enthusiasm helped refocus me to the greater mission anytime I felt worn down or overwhelmed. You can't do it alone but the good news is, if you share your vision for creating a special learning space, invite others into building it, and view all behavior through an intentional lens of Character, Excellence, and Community your team will slowly work towards an Award Winning Culture.

What is one school wide or class problem that an intentional approach to Character, Excellence, and Community might impact?

How might you team with others (students, staff, parents, and/or community) to infuse some positivity and action into your school environment?

How will you recognize signs of culture and climate improvement?

CHAPTER 34
CONCLUSION

On Wednesday, May 10, 2006, I had the privilege of crossing off one of Jen's ultimate bucket list items as I purchased tickets for us to go see *Lives & Experiences* with Dr. Maya Angelou at the Paramount Theatre in Seattle. Surprising my wife with tickets to one of her childhood idols filled me with more joy than I can put into words.

Ironically, the show landed on Mother's day. As we entered the theater, which was filled with a 99% female audience, I swear I could hear my wife's heart beating through her chest. As an avid reader, Jen had poured over Angelou's stories, poetry, and wisdom. Making our way to the front section of the theater was one of those cool husband moments where you simply know, you're forever changing your loved one's life, for the better.

Make no mistake, Jen, has helped me cross off many of my own bucket list items: Watching David Copperfield fly in person, experiencing Packers at Bears in the NFC Championship Game, watching Kobe drop 50 on the Bulls at Staples Center, and my first visit to the Magic Castle in Hollywood California. But this was her day! And it was absolutely otherworldly!

Ironically, most people's bucket list items involve experiences shared with people they're connected with. The nearly 2 hours were filled with so much inspiration that I'm sure everyone present felt empowered to live their best life. Indeed, there were humanistic bits of wisdom throughout her performance. Although my wife could probably recite word for word everything Angelou shared that evening, one line really stood out to me:

"People will forget what you said, people will forget what you did, but people will never forget how you made them feel."

-Dr. Maya Angelou

The above quote is one of the most frequently overused passages because it cuts right to the quick of relationships. And while I'd heard it or read it many times over the years, there was something extraordinary about hearing the words come directly from their originator. They're words that I've attempted to put into practice throughout my own life both professionally and personally. Basically...leave them feeling better than when you found them. While I understood the power of cultivating schools seeped in positive behaving culture, I could not shake Angleou's poetic observation that feeling is what's most remembered.

A few months ago, this fact was once again brought to my awareness. A student, who I had not heard from in a few years reached out to me. As one of my favorite students, I really saw greatness in her from the first time I met her in 6th grade. She was an articulate, fireball of passion and energy who seemed destined to positively change the world. I made her an office aide, steered her toward leadership classes, took her on elementary visits, and empowered her voice in projects throughout middle school. In 8th grade, she stepped in as my Teacher's Assistant (TA) in the counseling center to work with younger students who needed help navigating 6th grade.

CONCLUSION

While I and a band of several other educators loved her, there were others who didn't see what we saw. I will never forget an educator's words upon seeing her show up on our elementary feeder school visit as a leadership student:

"WOW! I can't believe you even brought her."

I hate even typing those words out. But, that's how some educators saw her.

I was thrilled to hear, she wanted to come see me! She popped in after school one day. Upon seeing her big smile at my door, I greeted her with a huge hug. We had a great rapport, when she was in middle school and I subsequently stayed in contact with her and her family throughout her time in high school. While we caught up for a few moments, part of me wondered what brought her in that afternoon. As the conversation waned for a minute, and she began shifting in her chair, I could tell she was overcome with emotion.

She explained to me that I had no idea just how much I meant to her in middle school. As I nodded and assured her that I knew we had a great relationship and that she was always one of my favorite students, she cut me off abruptly,

"No. You really don't know Mr. Appel. I wouldn't even be ALIVE, if it weren't for you!"

This statement cut right through me. For the next few moments she disclosed how much anxiety and depression she had battled and how she somehow knew it'd be alright because "Mr. Appel was there." She spoke of our connection and the purpose that she felt by being viewed by me as a leader in the school.

"You gave me meaning. You gave me hope. And now I'm going to school to become a school counselor.

Because YOU inspired me."

As her poignant words pinged off my heart like an expert pianist playing Sonata in D Major, I couldn't help but wonder if the most important Award Winning Culture I'd ever fostered was located right there in my own office. We laughed and shared plans to stay in touch before she eventually departed, while peacefully shutting the door behind her.

This is what it's all about...Angelou had it all right. Human connection. I believe that education at its highest level is about inspiring others to discover and develop their joy. Creating learning environments where others can understand their own unique strengths and passions and align those to some deeper meaning. Empowering them to live out their why with a sense of purpose.

> **When we take the time to intentionally craft an Award Winning Culture, we provide students with the OPPORTUNITY to pursue JOY!**

The truth is, I sat in silence in the relatively empty space of the office for another 15 minutes after she left that day...thinking, reflecting, and rejoicing this gift of being made aware of my impact before letting out a few tears!

Now it's YOUR turn! You can accomplish something extraordinary by turning your focus, energy, and passion into building intentionality and action around those three pillars: Character, Excellence, and Community. The time is NOW! Gather your student and staff cultural advocates and

CONCLUSION

begin infusing a couple principles TODAY! And in turn, your sphere of influence will be unimaginably impacted in life-altering ways.

Who knows...maybe you'll even uncover a few of your own tears of joy!

#AwardWinningCulture

REFERENCES

Achor, S. (2018). *The happiness advantage: how a positive brain fuels success in work and life*. New York: Currency.

Apsey, A. (2018). *The path to serendipity: discover the gifts along life's journey*. San Diego, CA: Dave Burgess Consulting, Incorporated.

Apsey, A. (2020) *The Serendipity Journal*. Livingston, TX: Gypsey Heart Press.

Apsey, A. (2019). *Through the lens of serendipity: helping others discover the best in themselves even if life has shown them its worst*. San Diego, CA: Dave Burgess Consulting, Incorporated.

AWARD WINNING CULTURE. (n.d.). Retrieved from http://www.awardwinningculture.com/

Billy, J. (2018). *Lead with culture: what really matters in our schools*. San Diego, CA: Dave Burgess Consulting, Incorporated.

Borba, M. (2017). *Unselfie: why empathetic kids succeed in our all-about-me world*. New York: Touchstone.

REFERENCES

Bostwick, E. (2019). *Take the L.E.A.P.: ignite a culture of innovation*. Place of publication not identified: IMPress.

Boyte, P., & Steckler, J. (2015). *School culture by design: building & sustaining positive school culture*. Auburn, CA: Learning for living.

Bray, B. (2020). *Define Your Why: Own your story so you can live and learn on purpose*. Alexandria, VA: Edumatch Publishing.

Brooks, D. (2016). *The road to character*. New York: Random House.

Brown Brené. (2017). *Braving the wilderness: the quest for true belonging and the courage to stand alone*. New York: Random House.

Brown Brené. (2018). *Dare to lead: brave work, tough conversations, whole hearts*. New York: Random House.

Burgess, S., & Houf, B. (2017). *Lead like a pirate: make school amazing for your students and staff*. San Diego, CA: Dave Burgess Consulting, Inc.

Cabeen, J., Johnson, J., & Johnson, S. (2018). *Balance like a pirate: going beyond worklife balance to ignite passion and thrive as an educator*. San Diego, CA: Dave Burgess Consulting, Incorporated.

Cain, S. (2013). *Quiet: the power of introverts in a world that can't stop talking*. New York: Broadway Books, an imprint of the Crown Publishing Group, a division of Random House.

Casa-Todd, J. (2017). *Social LEADia: moving students from digital citizenship to digital leadership*. San Diego, CA: Dave Burgess Consulting.

Casas, J. (2017). *Culturize: every student, every day, whatever it takes*. San Diego, CA: Dave Burgess Consulting, Incorporated.

Casas, J. (2020). *Live Your Excellence: Bring your best self to school everyday*. San Diego, CA: Dave Burgess Consulting, Incorporated.

Casas, J., & Zoul, J. (2018). *Stop. Right. Now.: the 39 stops to making schools better*. San Diego, CA: Dave Burgess Consulting, Incorporated.

CASEL. (n.d.). Retrieved from https://casel.org/

Chapman, G. D. (2015). *The 5 love languages the secret to love that lasts*. Chicago: Northfield Publishing.

CharacterStrong. (n.d.). Retrieved from https://www.characterstrong.com/

Coda, R., & Jetter, R. (2018). *Let them speak: how student voice can transform your school*. San Diego, CA: Dave Burgess Consulting, Incorporated.

Cook, C. (2017, December 5). *EDTalks: nurturing and responsive environments that promote social and emotional well being*. Retrieved from https://www.youtube.com/watch?v=okwl3ZoTKUk&feature=share

Couros, G. (2015). *The innovator's mindset: empower learning, unleash talent, and lead a culture of creativity*. San Diego, CA: Dave Burgess Consulting, Inc.

Couros, G., & Novak, K. (2019). *Innovate inside the box: empowering learners through Udl and the Innovator's Mindset*. Place of publication not identified: published by IMpress, a division of Dave Burgess Consulting, Inc.

Dudley, D. (2018). *This is day one: a practical guide to leadership that matters*. New York: Hachette Books.

Ellis, M., Houf, B., & Burgess, S. (2018). *Lead with literacy: a pirate leaders guide to developing a culture of readers*. San Diego, CA: Dave Burgess Consulting, Incorporated.

Ellwein, D. & McCoy, D. (2019). The Revolution: It's time to empower change in our schools. San Diego, CA: Dave Burgess Consulting, Inc.

REFERENCES

Fast, A. (2016). *Its the mission, not the mandates: defining the purpose of public education*. Lanham, MD: Rowman & Littlefield.

Felicello, K. & Armida, G. (2019). *The Teacher & The Admin: Making Schools Better for Kids*. EduGladiators Publishing LLC

Free Press. (2003). *Diffusion of innovations: 5th ed*. New York.

Gaillard, S. (2018). *The pepper effect: tap into the magic of creativity, collaboration and innovation*. San Diego, CA: Dave Burgess Consulting, Incorporated.

Geurin, D. G. (2017). *Future driven: will your students thrive in an unpredictable world?* Bolivar, MO: David G. Geurin.

Giordano, K. (2020, March 21). Teach Better Blog. *Maintaining Positive Culture Even When Apart*. https://www.teachbetter.com/blog/maintaining-positive-culture-even-when-apart/

Gruenert, S. & Whitaker, T. (2015). *School Culture Rewired: How to define, assess, and transform it*. Alexandria, VA: ASCD.

Heath, C & Heath, D. (2017). *The Power of Moments: Why certain experiences have extraordinary impact*. New York, NY: Simon & Schuster, Inc.

HIVESUMMIT.ORG. (n.d.). Retrieved from https://www.hivesummit.org/

Hughart, R. (2018). *Teach Further: Development Resource Workbook*. Progressive Mastery Learning, LLC.

Hunter, J. C. (2012). *The servant: a simple story about the true essence of leadership*. New York: Crown Business.

Hunter, J. C. (2015). *The world's most powerful leadership principle: how to become a servant leader*. CO Springs, CO: WaterBrook Press.

Hunter, J. C. (2017). *The culture: creating excellence with those you lead by growing leaders and building community*. Grosse Ile, MI: JDH Publishing.

Kerr, J. (2013). *Legacy: what the All Blacks can teach us about the business of life*. London, U.K.: Constable.

Letter, T. (2019). *A passion for kindness: making the world a better place to lead, love, and learn*. San Diego, CA: Dave Burgess Consulting, Inc.

LaFleur, H. (2015). *Hop on the Clue Bus: A Common Sense Guide to Leadership*. Des Plaines, IL: Heidy LaFleur.

Martin, T. (2018). *Be Real: educate from the heart*. San Diego, CA: Dave Burgess Consulting, Incorporated.

Martin, T. M. (2018, June 20). *"All the Feels: lead with culture"*. Retrieved from https://www.tarammartin.com/2018/06/

Maynard, N., & Weinstein, B. (2019). *Hacking school discipline: 9 ways to create a culture of empathy & responsibility using restorative justice*. Highland Heights, OH: Times 10 Publications.

Moore, G. (2014). *Crossing The Chasm: Marketing and selling disruptive products to mainstream customers*. Harper Business.

Nan, K. & Maslyk, J. (2019). *All In: Taking a Gamble in Education*. Alexandria, VA: Edumatch Publishing.

Ostrowski, C (2015). *The Grid Method: Mastery Learning System Development Resource Workbook*. Progressive Mastery Learning, LLC.

Ostrowski, C., Ott, T., Hughart, R., & Gargas, J. (2019). *Teach better*. San Diego: Dave Burgess Consulting.

PBIS Rewards. (n.d.). Retrieved from https://www.pbisrewards.com/

Pink, D. H. (2018). *Drive: the surprising truth about what motivates us*. Edinburgh: Canongate Books.

Raise Craze. (n.d.). Retrieved from https://raisecraze.com/

REFERENCES

Sanfelippo, J., & Sinanis, T. (2016). *Hacking leadership: 10 ways great leaders create schools that teachers, students, and parents love*. Cleveland, OH: X10 Publications.

Sinek, S. (2019). *Start with why: how great leaders inspire everyone to take action*. London: Portfolio Penguin.

Sinek, S. (2020). *Infinite Game*. S.l.: Portfolio, Penguin.

Sokatch, A. (2014, December 4). *Teaching Character: the other half of the picture*. Retrieved from https://www.youtube.com/watch?v=sxHGSTV3LF0&feature=share.

Souers, K., & Hall, P. A. (2016). *Fostering resilient learners: strategies for creating a trauma-sensitive classroom*. Alexandria, VA: ASCD.

Souers, K., & Hall, P. A. (2019). *Relationship, responsibility, and regulation: trauma-invested practices for fostering resilient learners*. Alexandria, VA: ASCD.

Steele, D., & Whitaker, T. (2019). *Essential truths for principals*. New York, NY: Routledge.

Stressed Out Ebook. (n.d.). Retrieved from https://growingleaders.com/free-resources/stressed-out-ebook/

Susman, W. (2003). *Culture as history: the transformation of American society in the twentieth century*. Washington, D.C.: Smithsonian Institution Press.

Teacher Success Summit. (n.d.). Retrieved from https://teachersuccesssummit.com/

Treu, J. (2017). *Social wealth: how to build extraordinary relationships by transforming the way we live, love, lead and network*. Lieu de publication inconnu: by Be extraordinary.

Tricarico, D. (2015). *Zen teacher: creating focus, simplicity and tranquility in the classroom*. San Diego, CA.: Dave Burgess Consulting, Inc.

Whitaker, T., & Croy, K. (2015, October 15). Retrieved from https://www.stitcher.com/podcast/kelly-croy/the-wired-educator-podcast/e/51825415?autoplay=true

ACKNOWLEDGEMENTS

It feels strange to get to the end of writing my first book and only have my name listed as the author. The truth is so many people have helped me create this work. And while space won't allow me to acknowledge them all, I want to list a few...

To my awesome wife Jennifer for showing me patience, love and support, while I pursued this crazy dream. And to Maya for snuggling next to me at 2 a.m. every day, for the past two years, to watch me write.

To mom for teaching me to BELIEVE in magic. To dad for teaching me to live my excellence.

To Paul and Jan for being my biggest supporters throughout my adult life and for helping put me back together after I lost my mom.

To all my friends and family: Thanks for all the love and support!

Marlena Gross Taylor and the team at EduGladiators Publishing: Thank you for seeing the vision from day one and for believing in an unknown aspiring author determined to disrupt education.

Julie Woodard: I'm grateful for your artistic talents! The incredible illustrations you created were better than I could have even imagined.

Jeff Gargas, Rae Hughart, Chad Ostrowski, and all the Teach Better Team: Thank-you for your guidance, friendship, and for believing in all things Award Winning Culture.

Barbara Bray: Thank-you for your unwavering support and for encouraging me to live my WHY.

John Norlin, Houston Kraft, and James C Hunter: Thank-you for teaching me how servant leadership can change lives, including my own!

To all the educators who filled me with HOPE! Special shoutout to Mr. Dann, Mrs. Nussbaum, Mr. Faddis, Mr. Norstein, Dr. Robbins, Dr. Lonborg, and Dr. Collins.

PLN: There are too many to name, but I'll give a few shoutouts to some WRITERS and THOUGHT LEADERS who really pushed me to dig deeper, in my own work: David Geurin, Jay Billy, Elisabeth Bostwick, Jimmy Casas, Todd Whitaker, Kristen Nan, Kris Felicello, Jeff Kubiak, Evan Robb, Danny Steele, George Couros, Jennifer Casa-Todd, Rick Jetter, Rebecca Coda, Allyson Apsey, Dr. Jeffrey Zoul, Darren Ellwein, Melissa Chouinard-Jahant, Chuck Poole, Pete Hall, Kristin Sourers, Sean Gaillard, Rita Wirtz, Beth Houf, Shelley Burgess, Dave Burgess, Jonathan Alsheimer, Gary Armida, Mariah Rackley, Beth Hill, Dr. Jessica Stephens, Jennifer Hogan, Chris Quinn, Roman Nowak, Morgane Michael, Dr. Brad Hubbard, Janelle McLaughlin, Tamara Letter, Barbara Gruener, Wendy Hankins, Josh Stamper, Dr. Neil Gupta, Dr. Jacie Maslyk, Taylor Armstrong, Jon Harper, and Dr. Amy Fast.

To my office DREAM TEAM and the rest of Wildcat Nation staff: Thank-you for your continued pursuit of an Award Winning Culture for our students, staff, and community. You're the reason that EMS feels like a FAMILY!

And finally, thank-you to all the past, current, and future students who continue to INSPIRE, AMAZE, and ELEVATE ME!

ABOUT THE AUTHOR

Hans Appel has worked as a counselor in the **Richland School District** for the past 19 years and at **Enterprise Middle School** since it opened. He's passionate about school culture, servant leadership, and kindness. In 2018, EMS was awarded the **ASCD Whole Child Award for the State of Washington** and the Global "**Class Act Award**" for creating a culture of excellence through kindness, service, and empathy. Additionally, they were selected as a finalist in the 2019 **PBIS Film Festival** and took top prize in the Community, Parents, and Staff category.

In 2018, Hans launched his own **blog about School Culture** and rolled out a student-led leadership podcast called **Award Winning Culture**, which can be subscribed, listened or reviewed on **iTunes Apple Podcasts**, **Stitcher**, **Google Play**, **Spotify**, **PodBean**, and **Libsyn**.

Hans' blogs have appeared on **DisruptED TV magazine**, **CharacterStrong**, **Teach Better**, and **PBIS Rewards**. He's written social-emotional lessons for **CharacterStrong**. Furthermore, he has been featured on numerous educational podcasts speaking his brand of school culture into existence.

He's been a contributing writer on three educational books: " Define Your WHY," "Reflective Impact Journal," and "ALL IN: Taking a Gamble in Education."

Hans is the **Director of Culture** for the **Teach Better Team** and a member of the coveted **Teach Better Speakers Network**. He presents at conferences, schools, and districts all over the country. Topics include: Creating an Award Winning Culture, Amplifying Student Voice, Student-Led Podcasting, Infusing SEL into Project-Based Learning, and Supporting PBIS through servant leadership.

He's a member of the Washington School Counselors Association and the American School Counselor Association.

Hans is happily married to his high school sweetheart, Jennifer, and they are proud dog parents to a wonderful Sheltie named Maya. He's active on Twitter @HansNAppel and can be reached through **hansappel094@gmail.com** or his website: **awardwinningculture.com**

MORE FROM EDUGLADIATORS

Available everywhere books are sold.

My Pencil Made Me Do It: A Guide to Sketchnoting
By Carrie Baughcum (@HeckAwesome)

The pencil is a single tool that has the power to reset mindsets, enhance thinking, improve retention, recall, and comprehension, calm us and make us smile...all this from a pencil. My Pencil Made Me Do It is a unique, hands-on, create-to-connect and doodle-to-learn book that will have readers discovering powerful moments, learning the power behind visual thinking, and doodling to learn. Through honest perspective and creative insight, Carrie opens educators and students to visualize their thinking and their learning. While enabling them to experience how they can bring visual thinking into our world.

The Teacher & The Admin

By Kris Kris Felicello (@KFelicello) & Gary Armida (@GaryArmida)

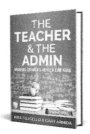

Today's kids are simply amazing. They are succeeding despite a myriad of challenges faced every day. Schools are racing to not only meet their needs, but to evolve to give kids what they truly deserve: a more meaningful education. The only way the education system can transform is to work together. The only way the education system can transform is to work together. Teachers and Administrators must work in a partnership to make lasting changes to a system that has historically been slow to evolve. The Teacher (Gary Armida) and the Admin (Dr. Kris Felicello) give the blueprint to this partnership to make schools better for kids.

Champ For Kids

by Kelly Hoggard (@champforkids)

This book is for every teacher, no matter their level of experience. For seasoned veterans confidently navigating around the ring, find inspiration to continue to push on into the next round. For educators that feel as though every time they get on their feet, they are bruised and battered by another jab, make connections to this book to help develop a solid foundation towards becoming a champion. Finally, to preservice educators standing outside the ring unsure if they have what it takes when the day comes to be tagged in, find the guidance and essentials needed to head into the ring. Champ For Kids inspires advocacy, going to the ropes for students, coaching them through mistakes so they land the TKO!

Principals in Action: Redefining The Role
By: Mark French (@PrincipalFrench), Jay Posick (@posickj) & Ryan Sheehy (@sheehyrw)

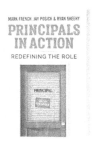

The role of the principal is constantly changing. As our students change, leaders must also evolve to remain effective, instructional leaders. Even though the role of the principal is changing, there are some who see the principal as the stereotypical disciplinarian who sits in an office, waits for problems, and talks to students who make poor choices. Dive into real-life stories from these three principals as they recount their personal journeys as an administrator and the strategies of being a visible leader - out of the office and in classrooms. This book will provide practical ideas motivating all school administrators to get out of their office and become a real part of their school.

The Future Is Now: Looking Back to Move Ahead
By Rachelle Dene Poth (@Rdene915)

If we are dedicated to facilitating the best futures for our students, we must be fully invested in lifelong learning and our personal and professional growth. In this book, the reader will hear from different educators, each sharing anecdotes and wisdom about becoming more connected, taking risks, and using failures and past experiences to help prepare for the future. Inspirational quotes appear through-out, prompting introspection and a call to action. A student also lends her perspective in a chapter, offering reflection from the other side of the classroom. When we strengthen ourselves as educators, we in turn empower others to do the same. Stronger together, we face whatever the future of learning will bring.

Bold Humility: Growing Students by Empowering Teachers

By David M. Schmittou (@daveschmittou)

It may seem like an oxymoron, but it is anything but that. BOLD humility is that secret "it" factor that we look for when trying to discover great- ness. It is the balance of confidence and grace. It is wisdom coupled with vulnerability. It is the ability to bravely embrace what you know while being willing to seek support where you need it the most. In this book, Dave takes a look at how educators can embrace BOLD humility to help tap into the greatness inside all of us. By sharing his own struggles coupled with his own successes, Dave paves a path that allows us all to walk away feeling empowered and ready to tackle the challenges that await us all.

R.E.S.U.L.T.S.: Promoting Positive Behavior and Responsibility for Learning

by Krista Venza (@kristavenza) & Jon Treese (@jt2510)

R.E.S.U.L.T.S. is a book that provides applicable strategies for teaching students to make positive choices, take necessary action and promote growth. This book is an enjoyable mixture of inspiring stories and a framework that promotes positive behavior and responsibility for learning. From R.E.S.U.L.T.S., educators will feel empowered to make a difference in the lives of their students.

CPSIA information can be obtained
at www.ICGtesting.com
Printed in the USA
LVHW010803300520
657008LV00003B/293